UNDAUNTED

A Memoir by
Van B. Choat

Undaunted

A Memoir by
Van B. Choat

Orphan Petals

All rights reserved. No part of this book may be reproduced or transmitted in any form or by any means, electronic or mechanical, including information storage and retrieval system without written permission from the author, except by a reviewer who may quote brief passages in a review.

ISBN: 978-0-578-78498-4

Copyright © 2020 Van B. Choat. All Rights Reserved.

Credits: Covers/Inside layout by Julieanne Benson
Illustrations by Phong Van
Van B. Choat's protrait by Guy Viau

Disclaimer:

This book is designed to provide information about the subject matter covered. The opinions and information expressed in this book are those of the author. Every effort has been made to make this book as complete and as accurate as possible. However, there may be mistakes both typographical and in content. Therefore, this text should be used only as a general guide and not as the ultimate source of information. The author of this book shall have neither liability nor responsibility to any person or entity with respect to any loss or damage caused or alleged to be caused directly or indirectly by the information contained in this book.

Printed in the United States of America

Dedication

To the happy memory of my parents and my grandparents.

§

To every Orphan around the world:
May you find peace and strength within yourself and
be determined to fulfill your dreams.

For those who hold the hands of the Orphans,
may you be blessed for your kindness and compassion.

§

To all my friends and family, especially my sons,
Eric and Jon,
who share with me life's journey...

Undaunted

adjective: not intimidated or discouraged by difficulty, danger, or disappointment.

synonyms: unafraid, undismayed, unflinching, unshrinking, unabashed, fearless, dauntless, intrepid, bold, valiant, brave, courageous, plucky, indomitable, gritty, confident, audacious, daring.

antonym: fearful

Table of Contents

Map of Vietnam	8
Family Tree of Van B. Choat	9
Preface	11
Prologue: Out of the North — What Was Ours, Once Upon a Time	13
The Road —1964	23
Fork in the Road—1964	37
Leaf House—1965	47
Stucco House—1967	69
Tsunami—1968	81
Flotsam and Jetsam—1968	87
Chasing the Moon—1968	93
Into the Dragon's Den—1969	107
Fish Farm—1971	119
Mouth of the Dragon—1974	145
Escaping the Dragon—1975	175
Home of the Brave—1975	187
Over the Rainbow—1979 – 1987	215
Epilogue: A Sense of Purpose	227
Acknowledgments	243
About the Author	245

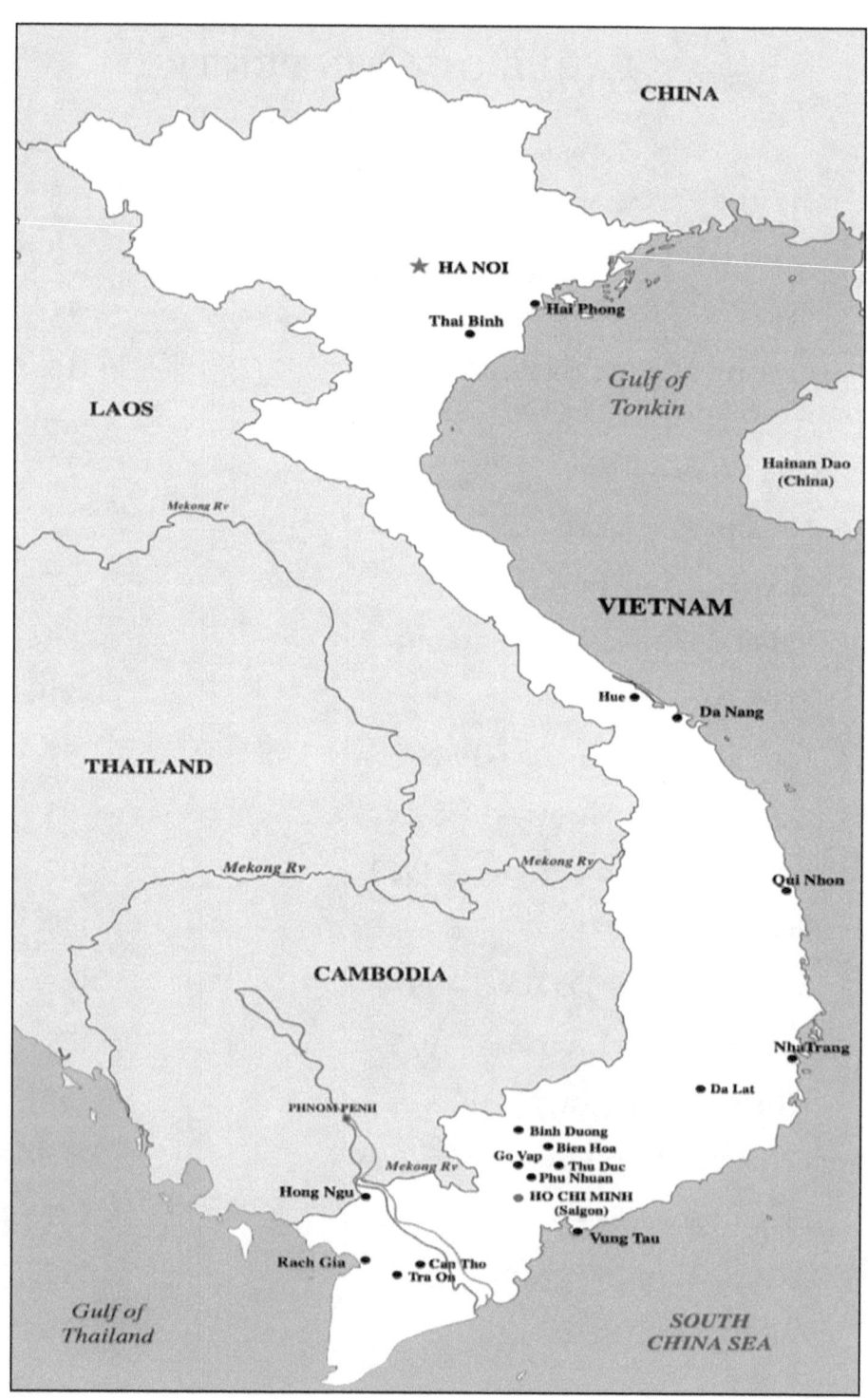

Family Tree of Van B. Choat

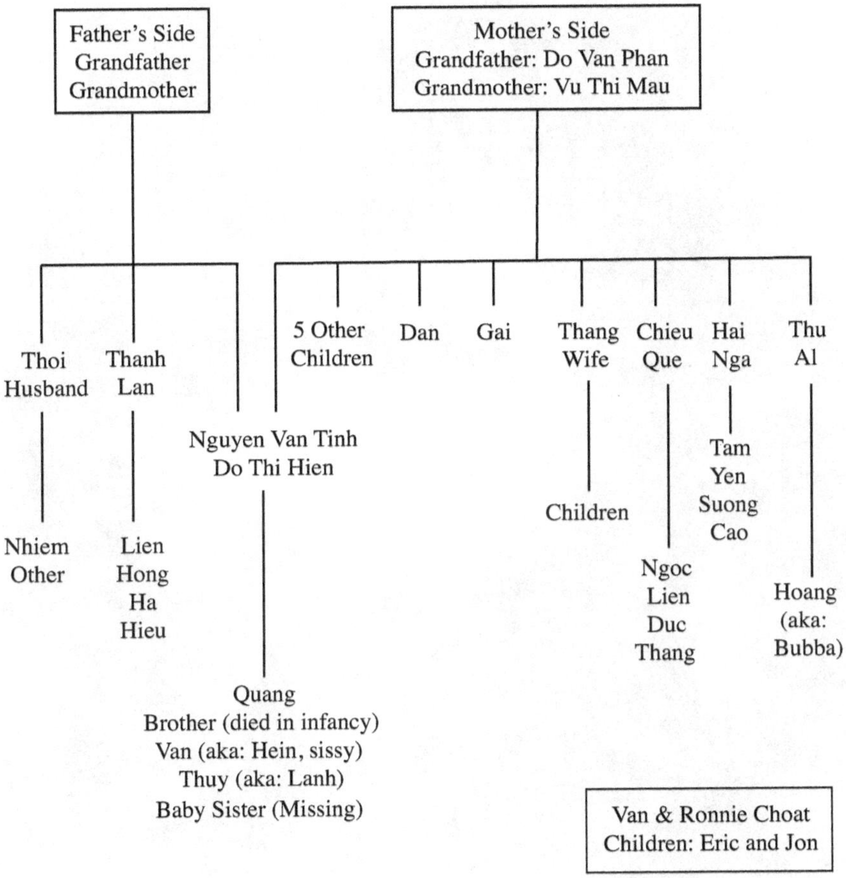

Father's Side
Grandfather
Grandmother

Mother's Side
Grandfather: Do Van Phan
Grandmother: Vu Thi Mau

- Thoi Husband
- Thanh Lan
- 5 Other Children
- Dan
- Gai
- Thang Wife
- Chieu Que
- Hai Nga
- Thu Al

Nguyen Van Tinh
Do Thi Hien

- Nhiem Other
- Lien Hong Ha Hieu
- Children
- Tam Yen Suong Cao
- Ngoc Lien Duc Thang
- Hoang (aka: Bubba)

Quang
Brother (died in infancy)
Van (aka: Hein, sissy)
Thuy (aka: Lanh)
Baby Sister (Missing)

Van & Ronnie Choat
Children: Eric and Jon

Van (aka: Hien, Sissy), 1965

PREFACE

Life eventually makes orphans of us all. Some of us get an early start.

I should begin this story when I was born, but I don't know exactly when that was, and those who could tell me are long gone, as is the world we once shared. It probably doesn't matter. Ours is an old story begun afresh each day in war zones around the world. Orphans create one big family who seldom get together. We know only those who hold our hands, and we have only two of those. This book is about the two kinds of "sisters" who held mine.

The first are the little girls, strong women, weak women, kind women, cruel women, and old ladies who, being real or spiritual sisters, guided me from ignorance and despair to some kind of peace and understanding in my life. That took a really long time, and I'm afraid I wore some of them out. But as long as I'm alive, they will be, too, if no place else but in my heart.

The second are the angels who watch over us from eons before our births to what, sooner or later, will become the end of time. The Earth—whether the Land of the Viet or the Home of the Brave—gives birth to everything, so I figure she must be female. Real women come and go, but some sort of heavenly mother always watches over us. It is not presumptuous for me to call her *sister* because she, too, has led me by the hand through an extraordinary life.

When I arrived on Earth sometime in 1960, it was into the arms of two loving parents and an older brother who would become my lifelong friend. I had caring grandparents, too (one of whom would hold my hand the longest and during some of the worst times of my life, and an assortment of aunts and uncles who, depending on their own situations, put wind in my sails or held me back like rusty anchors. Even the best roads can be bumpy, and, for my first fifteen years of life, mine was seeded with bullets and bombs.

That brings us back to war and orphans and for me, a vanished world that still passes in a blur until I make myself stop, take a deep breath, and look before I leap—always a good idea when you grow up in a place where family members and strangers can help or hurt you—and you don't know which until it happens. To survive such perilous passes, it helps to have a guide. This book honors those sisters who showed me the way, who gave me the courage to continue to persevere along my road, and the nerve to look back at the long and sometimes awful road we traveled together.

§

People may accuse me of many things in my first half-century of life, but ingratitude isn't among them.

I am grateful, first and foremost, to my mother, Hien, and my father, Tinh, who gave me life, and to "Ba," Mau, my maternal grandmother, who gave me love when that precious commodity was in short supply. I am grateful, too, for the Heavenly Father who sent my younger sister Thuy and older brother Quang to accompany me on my journey. They are brave survivors who, through these pages, I hope you learn to love as much as I do. I would have remembered only half as much, only half as well, without their help. And because life's sea is both turbulent and calm, I give thanks to my Uncles Chieu and Hai who, in different ways, helped me steer a course through treacherous waters; and to Aunt Thu, who deserves more happiness than she got—except, perhaps, through the blessing of her son, Hoang, who we called Bubba, the best little brother a "sister" like me ever had!

§

Okay, it's time to go. The one blessing of starting out lost is that any road may take you home.

Prologue

Out of the North—
What Was Ours,
Once Upon A Time

Wiser people than me have observed that "north" is more than a direction. In many places around the world, it represents a way of life—an outlook, a philosophy that is often so different from other regions, even in the same country, that it is truly antipodal, a pole star guiding those who should be brothers and sisters in completely opposite directions. This was never more true than in Vietnam.

My siblings and I were born in the South, but that did not make us Southerners. On the contrary, our parents were raised in the North by Northerners who for generations embodied the traits of their homeland, drawing life and strength from their families and neighbors, from their past, from the very air they breathed and the soil they tilled. With less arable land, a harsher climate, and the constant threat of Han (Chinese) invasion, Northerners became as hard as the world around them. They were seen as a serious people, even severe, although like all Vietnamese, they enjoyed life's smaller pleasures even if they did not celebrate them as grandly as those in the easier-living South. At their core was spirituality as strong as any in Confucian culture, a seed that burned like a nuclear reactor, propelling them to great accomplishments with a persistence unknown to the rest of the world. If the South was the heart and belly of my old homeland, then the North was surely its head, with eyes set on the future and teeth clenched in grim determination. This was the womb that produced my grandfather, Do Van Phan, and the woman he would later marry, my grandmother, Mau, who you will come to know in these pages.

According to Grandma Mau, Phan was born in the Northern province of Thai Binh to a high-ranking Mandarin official, a man of some influence in the Nguyen Dynasty that had ruled Vietnam for centuries. My great-grandfather died during a period of relative calm and left most of his fortune to Grandpa Phan, who used it to run a large and profitable plantation in the North. There, he built a respectable "palace" where his new wife, Mau, could live in the comfort and dignity befitting a Northern matron, in the style to which she had become accustomed as the daughter of parents wealthy in their own right. It was a joining of two eagles, and the world around them was their oyster—at least in the beginning.

Grandma Mau's father owned salt mines in the Northern province of Hai Phong, where she was born around 1890. In those days it was not customary for girls of any rank or station to go to school, so although her parents encouraged her education, they left the decision up to her. She chose to groom herself for a domestic life and although she may not have intended so, Grandma remained illiterate all her life. Instead she learned how to run a rich but frugal household, supervise servants wisely, and eventually raise a family for a worthy husband.

That worthy man appeared in the form of Grandpa Phan, and each began their marriage determined not to disappoint the other. Their mansion, its manicured grounds, and the acres of valuable rice paddies that provided much of their income employed over one hundred contented workers. From her description—and she spoke with pride—Grandma lived in luxury, like a princess, with personal servants even for her bath, and to care for her eleven children (eight sons and three daughters, only two of which survived her passing more than a century later). But she was not a tyrant. She treated all, including her personal handmaids, with great respect and honored hard labor for its own sake, no matter who performed it—another Northern trait.

In the first half of the 1950s, the Viet Minh communist insurgents were fighting and finally winning the years-long war against the French, who had colonized Vietnam for a hundred years. Grandpa and Grandma were literally caught in the middle between the warring factions. They favored neither the French nor the communists, and so were considered the enemy of both. But even in those perilous times, they were able, for a while, to maintained their plantation in Thai Binh, a town in Ha Nam Province. Then, according to Grandma, a Viet Minh organizer sent an anonymous letter to French officials claiming that Grandpa Phan had participated in a secret meeting with two dozen other Northerners to conspire against the government. This charge was totally false, as the family knew all too well the dangers of taking sides in a civil war and made their neutrality widely known. Despite these efforts, their favorite son, Dan, who had just returned to the family home from a fishing trip, was accosted by a contingent of French soldiers who were sent to punish the conspirators named in the anonymous letter. The household servants scattered as the troops approached, and Dan himself was forced to hide in a pond behind the house. The French soon discovered him though, and after dragging him behind a horse around the property, a brief, perfunctory interrogation was conducted while Dan hung upside down from a tree. He was then shot between the eyes. Although just a child at the time, Aunt Thu remembers this episode vividly, despite her older sister Gai's attempts to shield her from the sight. Gai herself was later murdered for refusing to collaborate with the French—an ironic end to the lives of a brother and sister who, after World War II, had both been educated in Paris.

As if the murders of two of their children were not enough, the world of my grandparents began to truly crumble in 1954 after the victory of the Vietnamese nationalists over the French. The peace treaty divided the former French colony into two parts, North and South, on either side of the 17th Parallel. This was only a temporary arrangement, the treaty said, to be discarded when national elections—scheduled for 1956—would unify the two Vietnams under a single government. Until then, the North was to be administered as a socialist state under Prime Minister Ho Chi Minh, a Marxist-Leninist who had learned his statecraft in Russia and communist China, while the South was entrusted to Ngo Dinh Diem, the Prime Minister appointed by Emperor Bao Dai himself, as caretaker during this interregnum. It was a transition that never came.

The reason for this rift was as old as Vietnam's traditional North-South distinction. Ho Chi Minh—or "Uncle Ho" as he was lovingly called by his followers—saw reunification as a process to be supervised by "local commissions," a code term, opponents claimed, for communist cadres who would undermine free choice in the South.

Diem, on the other hand, with the backing of the U.S. and Britain, demanded a popular election supervised by the U.N., a solution vetoed by Uncle Ho's chief sponsor, the Soviet Union. This debate became moot when Diem called his own referendum in the South to depose Emperor Bao Dai and install himself as President of a new republic. Northerners said this violated the treaty, and they broke relations with their brethren, returning the North to a wartime footing. In the South, the Viet Minh was referred to as the Viet Cong, or National Liberation Front (NLF), and the Second Indochina War—known as the "American War" in the North—was underway.

Ho Chi Minh moved quickly to secure his position in the region and at home. Elements of the North Vietnamese Army, or NVA, occupied parts of neighboring Laos in anticipation of operations in the South, and Northerners with economic, political, or cultural ties to the South were arrested or expelled. Naturally, the new Democratic Republic of Vietnam (as the North officially called itself) quickly targeted the usual "enemies" of a socialist state: the wealthy, the religious, the educated, and the more free-thinking individuals—which in this case included Grandma and Grandpa Phan.

Their final persecution began shortly after Ho took power and intensified as war drew near. They had been devastated by the murders of Dan and Gai, and when those losses were coupled with the confiscation of their land, businesses, and personal property by the expanding communist government (who claimed that Grandpa had "donated" all for the good of the people and the Party), they realized that their family was no longer welcome or secure in the land of their ancestors. They eventually made the difficult decision to flee North Vietnam. After the partitioning in 1954, Vietnamese in all parts of the country were given three hundred days to move north or south of the 17th parallel. For some, such as my grandparents, persecution in their home districts made such a move imperative. For others, it involved deciding where their family roots grew strongest: in the North, where anti-Western feelings were widespread, or in the South, which was more open to religion, free thinking, and free enterprise.

Like everything else in that turbulent time, escape was not easy. The route to the imagined sanctuary in the South was long and circuitous. Grandpa Phan took his surviving sons—my uncles—Thang, Chieu, and Hai, to the port city of Hai Phong, where they were given sanctuary by Vietnamese Catholics, themselves a target of the communist regime. Grandma Mau and her two daughters, Hien (my mother-to-be) and Thu (my aunt), stayed with friends and relatives in the nearby village of O Trinh, praying for a return to sanity in Northern affairs. Here, they worked in the rice fields like everyone else and often went hungry when communist officials demanded a bigger share of their harvest for poorer districts or to feed the NVA. On one occasion, the situation got so bad that Grandma sneaked back to the old plantation to reclaim a bushel of rice she had hidden for such emergencies. She discovered, however, that the main house was now used as a headquarters for the local communist party and was caught as she tried to escape. She was imprisoned for "theft from the People" but spared execution—the usual punishment for such things—when her many friends and former employees collected enough rice from their own reserves to "donate" to the officials and ransom her off. Unfortunately, with the location of her daughters now known, they, too, were arrested, and all were sentenced to double shifts laboring on public land. This did not sit well with my mother, who was now old enough to express her feelings. She declared to anyone who would listen that she'd "had it" with the government's crimes against her family and her people. The authorities struck back by putting her in solitary confinement and denying her food for several days. Once again local friends and relatives rescued her with bribes. She was released, but with a stern warning that future misconduct would result in harsher treatment.

Grandpa and Grandma's dire situation was finally resolved when their son Thang, who had served in the war against the French, was given permission on October 20, 1954, to relocate to the South along with his entire regiment, which was deemed untrustworthy by the NVA. Most of those soldiers—part of the mass internal migration that followed the Paris Treaty—moved their immediate and extended families. By the grace of God and the courage of Uncle Thang, my grandparents and their surviving children evaded almost certain death and headed south, beginning an odyssey that would last for two years.

§

Since the family left with only the clothes on their backs and a few provisions, the journey to their final destination was punctuated by stops at various towns and villages where they worked as common laborers long enough—sometimes for weeks, sometimes for a few months—to earn more cash and rations for the trip.

In Da Lat, for example, Grandpa Phan—who had once employed a small army in a variety of enterprises in the North—found work as a carpenter with Uncle Hai as his apprentice. Grandma Mau, my mother, Hien, and Aunt Thu also pitched in by harvesting tea leaves on a mountainside and taking other odd jobs along the way. True Northerners in the old sense, they held no scorn for honest work that put food on the table and a roof over the heads of loved ones.

Together, the family earned enough money to fund their journey. They traveled until they reached Rach Gia in the extreme south of Diem's republic—as far away from the communists, I suppose, as they could get. Grandpa Phan was quickly befriended by a Roman Catholic priest who allowed him to settle on a plot of land that belonged to the Church. Grandpa was so moved by this gesture, as well as the kindness he had received from other Catholics in the North, he and the rest of the family converted to Catholicism. (This included Thang and Chieu, although they had become separated from Grandma and Grandpa during the journey and took a little longer to make it to the South.) Shortly thereafter, Grandpa bought some additional land where he could grow enough rice and vegetables to live beyond subsistence.

My dearest Grandpa Phan and Grandma Mau

§

I was born in Rach Gia, as were my siblings, so this is an appropriate place to recall my own parents' life in the North, their courtship and marriage, and their own travails moving to the South.

My father's name was Tinh. He met my mother, his future bride, through her brother, Thang, who served with him in the nationalist army in the North. They were both enlisted men, though my father was a bit senior as a non-commissioned officer, or NCO. Both had seen action against the French and resisted the increasingly powerful and intrusive communist state. He came from a Catholic family who was also forced from the North during the great migration. His parents were killed toward the end of World War II, when all of Indochina was occupied by the Japanese. His older sister, Thoi, raised him and his younger brother, Thanh. As the matriarch of his family, Thoi arranged his marriage to Grandpa Phan's daughter, Hien, when they all settled in the South.

One term of this arranged union was a provision Grandma Mau insisted upon, using her awesome power as prospective mother-in-law—a position of great importance in traditional Vietnamese families. This provision in the marriage contract called for Tinh to join Grandpa Phan's household and "audition" as a try-out son-in-law. His job was to impress Hien's parents with his hard work and obedience, and to gain as much knowledge as he could about Grandpa Phan's way of doing business, first as a farmer-laborer, then as a plantation manager. As I have said, Northerners are persistent, and also thorough and demanding in everything they do. Arranged marriages were no exception.

After a year of this audition, Tinh "got the part" and his engagement to Hien was announced. They were married in 1957, but their honeymoon was anything but romantic. Mama began their wedding night by chasing Papa around the bedroom with a broom, threatening to brain him if he didn't leave her alone. After he escaped, she locked the door behind him and shouted that she was too young to be married, even though she was twenty-two years old. Grandpa Phan was not pleased by his daughter's reaction to her hand-picked husband, so he unlocked the door, gave his "little girl" a good spanking, and reminded her that her task now was to become a good wife. After a few days of reflection (my mother was very willful—another Northern trait), her new husband was admitted to her bed, which was good news for the spirits of Quang, me, Thuy, and Baby Sister (as well as a second son between Quang and me, who sadly did not survive infancy)—all waiting patiently for conception on some angelic cloud.

Although many arranged marriages never rise above the level of a business deal, theirs blossomed into genuine affection and, finally, a deep abiding love that permeated all aspects of their lives, including their relationship with us kids. This may have been one reason Aunt Thu harbored secret resentments against her sister. Hien enjoyed the loving husband and happy family that fate always seemed to deny Thu, but that's only a guess. For a few brief years we formed an idyllic family unit—a rare gift for people anywhere, especially in the upside-down world around us.

Mother and little Quang

Grandpa Phan died a year after I was born, so I remember little of him beyond his delight in carrying me around on his shoulders and showing me off to the villagers in Rach Gia. By now both Uncle Thang and Uncle Chieu had gotten married and moved out. Uncle Hai had joined the South Vietnamese Navy. The Northern-sponsored insurgency was gathering steam in the South, and Papa re-enlisted to defend our new country. With no males to work the rice paddies at Rach Gia, Mama (now in charge of family affairs) sold our land and moved everyone—herself, Quang, me, Thuy, Grandma Mau, and Aunt Thu—to Saigon in order to be closer to Papa, settling in the Phu Nhuan district. Before we left, though, Mama used most of the money from the sale of the land for my father's younger brother's (Uncle Thanh) wedding, and we didn't have much left for the move.

That journey from Rach Gia to Saigon was one of my earliest memories. The bus we took was old, jam-packed, and smelly. I was nauseous the whole time from the gas fumes and exhaust. The trip took five or six hours, and we were exhausted when we arrived, but we had to house-hunt right away—or we would have no place to sleep. Mama was a savvy shopper and turned down several places not because we didn't like them, but because the landlord wouldn't budge on price, something that is usually negotiable in Vietnam, even today. Finally, she met an owner who was as desperate for income as we were for housing, so after the usual bluffs and posturing, an acceptable deal was struck.

Sisters— Aunt Thu (left) and Mama (right) as young women

Our new home was about 350 square feet attached like a shed to the back of the landlord's house, with a noticeable gap for air, insects, and mice between the top of the knit-leaf wall and its corrugated tin roof. The only furniture on its well-worn concrete floor was a splintery wooden bed and an old armoire just big enough for our things. It was certainly a come-down for Grandma Mau and her daughters, and no improvement over our farm house in Rach Gia, poor as it had been, but as Mama put it, "All we need is a dry bed and a roof to keep the rain and sun off our heads until my husband can send us more money. We'll make do."

And we did.

Chapter 1

The Road—1964

On a humid morning in Hong Ngu, South Vietnam, two unaccompanied children, a sister and brother, aged 4 and 6, climb aboard a bus to Saigon in the hope of finding a way home—and to somehow stay alive...

Quang and I didn't sleep a wink. Staying awake was easy because the creaky old bus hit every pothole and its grinding gears were louder than the smoky engine. And it was crowded. When tired, sweaty adults carrying half of their worldly goods share a bench with a skinny four-year-old and her sniffling older brother, they don't care if their hips and elbows and suitcases poke you in the ribs or bump your head or their snoring keeps everyone awake except the driver. At least he knew the route between Hong Ngu and Saigon so well that he could drive it with his eyes shut, which I'm pretty sure he did.

We arrived at the Phu Nhuan bus stop late in the afternoon. It was the end of the line, so families with kids and grannies and lone travelers with impatient faces scrambled around us to get off. The driver waited like the captain of a sinking ship until everyone was gone, then lit another cigarette and glanced down the aisle toward Quang and me. His expression showed he was off duty.

The typical inter-city bus in the 1960s, very much like the one we rode between Hong Ngu and Saigon

Quang was taller and steadier than me—despite what we'd been through these last few days—so I followed him toward the exit as he fished a handwritten note from his pocket. The driver read the note, puffed smoke from his nose like a dragon, then passed it back to Quang.

"Can't help you," he said, motioning toward the exit. "I don't have time for this crap. You gotta get off of the bus—*now*."

We did. The *Out of Service* sign flipped on, and the bus pulled away into quitting-time traffic, leaving us like two fire hydrants on the sidewalk. Quang began to cry. I did, too.

When the waterworks were over, nothing had changed, so Quang wiped his eyes and looked around. I could tell from his expression that none of the street signs, shops or houses looked familiar. He opened the note and held it up to passers-by like a panhandler's sign.

"Please..." he said. "This is from a policeman! Please, mister. We need to find our grandmother! Please, miss, we..."

Everyone on the sidewalk had better things to do, and the dried blood still speckling our clothes probably didn't help. I squeezed Quang's hand until it turned white, and while that didn't help either, it made me feel a little less lost.

Quang decided we'd have better luck across the street, so he dragged me into the traffic. Halfway across a taxi screeched to a stop and honked its horn.

"Jesus, you little twerps!" the cab driver shouted, at least as scared as we were. "You trying to get killed? Where are your parents?"

Good question. For some reason, I answered first.

"Mama's hurt and Papa is lost. We need to find Grandma."

Meantime, Quang gave the driver the note, which he read despite a line of honking cars behind him. Without hesitation, the driver reached over the seat and opened the rear passenger door.

The Saigon Cab Driver who saved Quang and I from becoming homeless

"Get in," he said, and we did.

We spent the rest of the evening touring the Phu Nhuan District from the cozy bench of the cab. I had to kneel on the lumpy seat to see out the window. Since I didn't know what to look for, I slumped with the setting sun and drifted in and out of sleep. My tired little mind was plagued with insistent memories of what we had experienced the last few days that caused this journey to find our grandmother.

> *Mama never looked happier. "We're going to visit Papa at his post in Hong Ngu!" she says. "No, no, not sister Thuy. She's too little. She'll stay with Grandma. But you and Quang will come, and Baby Sister—she has to nurse—and Aunt Thu if she wants to join us. What? No, it's not far. Less than a day on the bus. We'll stay with Papa in his hut by the river. Won't that be fun?"*

The cab hit a bump and woke me up. I peeked from my window while Quang stared out the other. It was dark now, and the house lights and street lamps were on. I sank back onto the vinyl seat and dozed off.

> *"Don Ke Sach." Mama reads the sign above the gate as we get off the water taxi and an armed soldier waves us through. Papa is there to greet us—handsome in his undershirt and work pants, not in the green Army suit with all the sleeve stripes that I remember. "He's in charge, you know," Mama whispers. "That makes us special!" Other kids and mothers scamper around the outpost, playing and cooking dinner. It looks like one big happy family. Papa's panda bear arms surround me and Quang and pick us up. He smells like sweat and coffee and... well, Papa...*

"No... no... no..." Quang said politely every time the driver asked if this house or that looked familiar. Traffic in the street was getting thin, and there was nothing to see, so I sank down, drowsy again.

> *This is Papa's Army house? It looks like a hutch for really poor people back home. Bamboo frame. Leaf walls. Dirt floor. Clay pots for rice and water. A single reed-mat bed. Where are we going to sleep? "It's a palace!" Mama tells Papa, hugging and kissing him again. They obviously miss each other a lot. His Army uniform hangs in a corner like an unwelcome guest, and*

I wonder why he doesn't wear it—but then again, neither do the other soldiers in his camp. What are they afraid of? Just after dark, when I am almost asleep, I hear Papa tell Mama and Aunt Thu, "You need to go home soon. Hong Ngu really isn't safe." I look into the night beyond the door and feel creepy eyes look back. "I'm catching the bus tomorrow," Aunt Thu says with a quavering voice and means it. Mama answers in an equally determined tone, "We came to stay a week and we will."

About midnight, Quang pushed me on the arm. The cab was passing a market where Quang remembered Grandma once bought us fresh fruit, so we stopped. Instead of throwing us out at the first hint of a familiar landscape, the driver parked, shut off his lights, and got out with us. I guess he saw we were still scared so he took our hands. He turned around and a look of worry came over his face as he stared back at his taxi.

"Will your cab be okay?" I asked.

He shrugged. "Don't worry about it...although it will probably be gone by the time I get back." With both of us in tow, he took us to the nearest vendor, who was closing for the night.

"Excuse me," he said. "Do you know these kids?"

"Who remembers little kids?" The vendor didn't even look at us.

"Well, how about their grandmother? The boy says she does a lot of shopping here. She wears a big North-style *khan dong* hair-wrap and smokes a pipe. Or maybe you remember their mother. Kid says she's real pretty."

"Nope."

The other vendors were no help either, and soon all the stalls and carts were closed. The driver pulled us back to the main street where pedestrians nervously skittered by, anxious to get home, few pausing to hear his pitch. I didn't know much at my age, but I knew it wasn't smart to be out after dark.

Papa stares beyond the camp's barbed-wire fence into the tall grass. The air is still, but in a few places, the wild grass shakes and shudders. He looks worried, so I worry, too. Quang cleans up after dinner while Mama nurses Baby Sister. We've had fun all week—Papa teaching Quang how to swim and trying to teach me too, though I learned mostly how to sink. Now he puts his foot down. "Take tomorrow's bus and go back to Saigon," he commands. "No discussion." Mama tells us kids, "Don't worry. The family will be together again soon..."

The driver was now knocking on the door of every house we came to, dragging us behind him on noodle legs. Finding Grandma had turned into a quest, but our knight-errant wasn't about to quit.

An hour into our long march, an old woman with a kerosene lamp opened her door. Strangely, she not only listened to the driver's story, she read Quang's tattered note and lowered her lamp to look at our faces.

She said, "Sure, I know these kids. They're Mau's grandchildren. She lives a few doors down. Come on, I'll show you."

The night was getting chilly, so she paused to put on a frayed sweater, then led us down the street with her honest lamp. Another door, another knock, and there was Grandma. Just the sight of her shocked face put starch back in our legs.

"What on earth are you children doing here? You're supposed to be in Hong Ngu!"

She scooped us into her arms. The comforting fragrance of her tobacco-scented clothes made me dizzy. She asked the driver, "Where is their mother?" And just who are you?"

The driver produced Quang's note.

"You read it to me, young man." Grandma Mau, once a princess in the North, never found it necessary to learn to read and write.

The driver read aloud, which was the first time I learned what the note contained. It was written by the policeman who had helped us at Hong Ngu, so I started to feel uneasy. I didn't get most of the words—he was writing for grown-ups, not little kids—but I could tell from the look on Grandma's face that it held terrors just like those hovering on the edge of my memory, monsters waiting to catch me whenever I shut my eyes. She looked like she was going to cry, but her Northern strength held back the tears. Her other daughter, Aunt Thu—a strong and pretty woman who looked a lot like Mama and, heeding Papa's warning, had left Hong Ngu for Saigon after our first night—now joined us from the back of the house. While Grandma's face held back a rainstorm, Aunt Thu's froze just like a zombie's—a fortune-teller seeing some terrible fate in a crystal. The driver finished reading the letter and handed Aunt Thu the paper. Grandma fumbled for the kerchief where she kept her money and thanked the driver profusely. She was anxious the bill for his services would be enormous.

"Not necessary." The driver put his hands on our small shoulders and gave us a fatherly squeeze. He bent low over us. "You kids be strong and help your Granny and your Auntie, okay?" Then he left and the door closed behind him. We had only known him for one evening, but I felt I had lost an uncle.

Grandma fed us leftovers from the evening meal, then cleaned us up and put us to bed, taking care not to wake our sister, Thuy, who had slept through it all on her mat. Getting drowsy, I listened as the two women's voices tip-toed around tears, discussing the letter. I understood almost none of what they said except that we would all return to Hong Ngu the next morning, probably on the same rickety bus. It was not a trip I wanted to make again.

> *We kiss Papa good-bye and take the water taxi into town where we catch the bus to Saigon, but Mama has a tummy ache and tells the driver she can't make the five-hour drive without throwing up or worse, so he lets us off and we return to Papa's camp. I know Papa is displeased, but his face shows mostly worry. While Mama and Baby Sister rest on his bed, Quang and I play around the hut. "Don't go far," Papa commands, as if we were his soldiers. He then turns his binoculars back to the shivering grass. "They should have taken that bus," he says to nobody in particular.*

After a good night's sleep, we were up before the chickens. We slurped down a breakfast of rice soup, then dropped off sister Thuy for safekeeping at Uncle Thanh's on the way to catch the bus. My father's younger brother was a quiet, thoughtful man who had just recently joined the army, unlike my father who had already enlisted—twice. The first time Papa resigned because the war with the French was over. Now trouble had started with Northerners and their friends in the South, and he thought it was his duty to serve again. This seemed very strange since both Mama's and Papa's parents came from the North and Grandma's family, in particular, had been quite well-to-do with lots of servants to pamper them. They favored neither side in the French War but were penalized by both. Maybe that's why Uncle Thanh's level gaze always reminded me of a wise old owl. He knew when to keep his mouth shut and when to give a hoot. The one thing everybody in both families knew, though, was to stay away from trouble.

The bus ride from Saigon to Hong Ngu seemed shorter this time, but more unsettling. We got off in a familiar-looking neighborhood, although being a poor fishing village hard against the Mekong River, it was more of a slum than a city. At least Saigon had pretty parks and broad streets and big buildings where cat-eyed Europeans walked around in fancy clothes.

Apparently Grandma and Aunt Thu disliked the place, too, because they cried almost constantly from the moment we arrived and kept on crying as we went street to street looking for the house mentioned in the policeman's letter. Finally, Aunt Thu stopped at a peasant hut just a little bigger than Papa's.

" This is it," she said, as if warding off a curse.

A slim man in civilian clothes like Papa's answered the door. He looked familiar, even kindly, and although he nodded to Quang and me, he paid attention mostly to the women. An infant wailed behind him. I recognized it as the hungry-call of my three-month-old baby sister. Since I was used to seeing her glued to my mother's breast or nestled in one arm, her distant voice now seemed strange and scary. Baby Sister without Mama was the moon without the earth.

"I am mother to Do Thi Hien," Grandma said solemnly, not a very friendly greeting. She pointed to Aunt Thu, then to Quang and me. "This is her sister and these are her kids. I hear her baby inside your house—"

"Yes, I remember them." The policeman gave us a sad glance. "I'm glad they made it home. And the baby girl is fine. My mother is looking after her."

"Good. Well, then, we would like to see my daughter," Grandma went on. "Right now, if it is convenient."

Convenient or not, the nice man spoke quickly to his mother in the other room, then led us down a street toward the river. He spoke in low tones with Grandma and Aunt Thu. I heard little and understood less. He continued until we entered a two-room leaf house with a corrugated roof and a front door painted with a big red cross.

The inside was even more grim than the Hong Ngu bus. Like the bus, like the policeman, I'd seen this place before, and it turned my stomach. Its two rooms each held several metal-framed beds, with families—kids, moms and dads, grandfolk, people like us—ambling like mourners between them. It was crowded so Grandma plunked me onto a wooden bench in the small waiting room as they went in. A glimpse at the beds showed people with white swaddling around their heads and sometimes the stumps of a just-gone arm or leg. The once-white sheets were flecked with red and brown. Threading their way among the beds and visitors were nurses in plain clothes bearing trays of medicine and instruments. The place smelled terrible, like bad tasting medicine, blood, and the stale cheap wine Grandpa Phan used to drink from his old wine cup.

Mother and I at the Red Cross Aid Station, Hong Ngu

Eventually, they clustered around one bed and called me in. Being the shortest, I had to push my way to the front. Grandma was bending over the patient and when she stood up, I saw that it was Mama.

> *Papa and his soldiers frantically build a small bunker in front of his leaf-and-bamboo hut. It starts as a slit just long enough for three, with sticky mud piled up and around it like a dome. They finish the exterior with half-coconuts—not for decoration, but to satisfy Papa's orders: "It deflects the bullets," I hear him say. After a tense and silent dinner, the sun goes down and the fireworks begin. When the floodlights over the barbed wire go out, Papa hurries us into the coconut dome bunker—Mama first, then Baby Sister, then Quang, then me. He stares at us, clearly anguished, then his face disappears as he nails the blue dragon blanket over the entrance.*

Mama was the most beautiful woman in the world. Amazingly, she still was, even with the heavy blood-soaked gauze pinned to her left shoulder. She looked like a crucified angel.

Suddenly, I remembered where and when I had last seen her. This was exactly how Quang and I left her two days before. Sickness rose from my stomach to the back of my throat. *I don't want to be here! I don't want Mama to be here!* Only the sight of Quang's little face, strong and fixed like a marble Buddha, kept me from throwing up or bursting into tears.

As if moved by my unspoken thoughts, a nurse took me under the arms and eased me onto the bed next to my angelic mother's undamaged wing. My wet eyes widened to take her all in, but my dry throat couldn't let out a peep. She smiled at me through her pain and with her good hand brushed the hair back from my forehead.

"Little Hien," she said. "I'll get up soon and go to the market. What would you like me to bring you?"

My brain roared inside my head. All I could think of was *sticky rice* and I whispered the words.

"Okay. Sticky rice. Anything else?"

I knew exactly what I wanted, but no more words would come. My mother's eyes teared up, and she looked at the nurse.

"Please take my daughter away," she said. "I don't want her to see me like this."

The nurse picked me up and held me against her shoulder. "Can I get you anything?" she asked my mother.

"I...I can't see," my mother said.

The nurse put me down and bent low over my mother. She pulled an eyelid back and squeezed Mama's wrist and put two fingers on her neck and I don't know what else. By then Grandma had taken my hand, and my mother's bed disappeared behind a wall of grown-up backsides.

"I can't see anything." Mama's voice was weaker. "I think it's time."

Another nurse pushed by with half a lemon and squeezed juice in my mother's eye, but Mama didn't blink. The whole scene disappeared again behind all the shirts and trousers.

"She is going," somebody said. I think it was Grandma Mau.

"We could've saved her with whole blood," the nurse commented, "but that's only for the soldiers."

At that point, the wiry policeman scooped me up and carried me like a sandbag out of that horrible place. I expected my mother and family to follow because something was obviously terribly wrong—but they didn't. Looking back over his shoulder, I saw some gawkers drift near my mother's bed and the pace of the nurses quickened. I was outside in the river air when the policeman set me down. Oddly, he said nothing and just held my clammy hand. He looked past the gloomy waiting room and moved us back and forth when people went in or out.

After a few minutes, Grandma, Aunt Thu, and Quang came out with bleach-white faces, followed by two orderlies bearing a rolled reed mat. By itself, this was not unusual; that was how we often moved our sleep-mats to clean under them or make room for indoor activities. But this time the mat hung heavy from a bamboo pole, swaying from side to side. As they passed, the policeman released my hand, so I peeked through the doorway one last time to see if my mother was still in bed. She wasn't. I told myself right then and in no uncertain terms that she had most certainly gone to market to get my sticky rice, as she had promised.

Then policeman's big hand gently turned my shoulder, and we joined the sad procession.

The walk to the Mekong River was short—just a few steps across the dirt road to its mud-slick banks where some flat-bottomed taxi boats were tied to a bamboo pole. Without much talk, a pair of ferrymen jumped into the knee-deep water, pushed two boats toward shore, and hauled them up. Like a line of ants, our little procession filed aboard one while the orderlies with their long pole and lumpy mat climbed aboard the other, along with the policeman. Without a word, the silent ferrymen shoved off, swishing

The ferrymen take us across the Mekong River to the Isle of the Dead

their oars back and forth at the stern until we reached a long, low island in the center of the river. It was a pretty place, with a grassy tree-lined field in the middle—at least it seemed that way until we got close enough to see the vine-covered Buddhist headstones and Catholic crosses tilted in the loamy soil. We landed, and, inexplicably, the river breeze stopped, leaving the island air close and fishy.

The orderlies began excavating a short trench in the wet dirt near the shore. When they were finished, they laid the reed mat into it, drew out the bamboo pole, filled it in with the dirt they'd displaced, and returned to the boat. While they'd worked, Grandma stared at the trees with her arm around Aunt Thu, calling out to Quang once or twice for wandering too far. I stood at the edge of the graveyard and watched the two men labor, wondering silently when Mama would return from the market.

When the trench was filled and tamped down, Grandma Mau and Aunt Thu knelt beside it, tears streaming down their cheeks. Suddenly, Grandma looked around as if confused, then ordered Quang and me to gather sticks from the graveyard, which we were glad to do. We found only two twigs that seemed to meet with Grandma's approval ("I guess that's the best you could do," she muttered). Like a fisherman repairing a net, she pulled some reeds from the riverbank and tied the sticks into the shape of a rough cross and pushed it gently into the earth at the head of the trench. Despite everyone's somber mood, I was proud of my contribution.

"Mama should see this," I said, still expecting her to arrive in a river taxi with an armload of groceries and treats. My words brought more tears to everyone's eyes, so I started crying, too, although I wasn't sure why. I knew Grandma and Aunt Thu must be sad over Mama missing the ceremony, but I was disappointed, too, that I would have to wait longer to enjoy my sticky rice.

We took the flat boats back across the river and returned to the policeman's house, still sniffling like babies. We weren't exactly guests, so the policeman asked us to wait by the door until his sour-faced mother produced Baby Sister, handing her to Grandma like a stinky overripe yam. Grandma sniffed her to make sure she didn't need changing, then refolded her ratty swaddling.

"She seems to be in good health," Grandma announced, nodding politely to the imperious old lady who looked happy to see us go. We all turned except Quang. Instead, he held out his palm toward the woman.

"Mama's rings," he said in a tough voice. The words struck me like lightning.

Mama is terrified. I've never seen her like this! Quang and I cover her with a dirty blanket, scooping a space for Baby Sister, who is howling like a Banshee. Mama seems to relax. Beneath the blanket she rips off the tail of her bloody blouse, then twists two rings from her swollen finger. One is her own wedding band. The other is the ring that belongs to our father. She passes the strip of cloth through the rings and knots the end, anchoring the circle of cloth tightly around Quang's shoulder at the armpit, causing him to squeak "Ow!" before she loosens it. "Keep it hidden under your shirt. Sell the rings if you need money for yourselves or Baby Sister." "Okay, Mama," Quang says. "I'll take care of them."

Then I remembered. Shortly after our arrival, the policeman's mother confiscated Quang's ring-cloth when she removed his shirt to clean him up—though why we were with the policeman and why we hadn't used the rings for bus fare was still a fuzzy blur. She must have kept the rings as a deposit, maybe to ensure that we would come back for Baby Sister. Now Quang wanted his heirlooms back.

After a long pause, the old lady went to the back of the house and returned with the knotted cloth, which she dropped into Quang's little hand. He inspected it the way Grandma had inspected Baby Sister, wrinkling his nose.

"One is different," he said angrily.

"What are you talking about?" the old lady demanded.

"Look—this ring is smaller than the other one. This was Mama's ring. Papa's was bigger. Both fit on her finger. This one is too small. Where is Papa's ring?"

"Stop complaining, you little snot!" the old lady snapped. "Just be glad you're getting anything back at all."

Quang raised the ring-loop like a mace, preparing to smack her, but Grandma grabbed his arm.

"Quang! Behave yourself!" she said. "It doesn't matter. This nice lady took care of Baby Sister. She fed you and Hien and her son gave you money for the bus and took time to write a letter. He even took us to see your mother in the hospital. Now say you're sorry and we'll go home."

Quang did no such thing, but we left anyway after Grandma and Aunt Thu bowed again and thanked the policeman profusely.

The bus ride to Saigon was bumpy and bitter, made worse by nobody talking. Except for me, everyone was preoccupied by silent worries that only made a bad day worse. It was evening when we got home, and although everyone was exhausted, nobody but me seemed happy to see our house. As soon we turned onto our block, I ran ahead, shouting, "Mama! Mama! We're back! What did you get for us at the market?"

There was no answer, and when I pushed the front door open, the house was dark. I would have to wait awhile longer for Mama.

Chapter 2

Fork in the Road — 1964

Our first night back in Saigon, I slept with Grandma instead of Quang or Aunt Thu. I guess Grandma wanted company while Thu took charge of Baby Sister. Grandma's crying woke me several times in the night. I was not yet sure what had made her so sad, but I would roll over and silently touch her back, letting her know that I was there and to offer her comfort. The next morning, Quang was still fuming over the rings, and although he never stayed mad for long, he was very quiet at breakfast. This didn't leave much for me to do but listen as Thu and Grandma talked.

"We should take them to Thanh's," Grandma said. "He is their father's only brother and now the head of that family. It is his responsibility to decide what is to be done with his brother's children."

"You're right." Aunt Thu cradled Baby Sister and looked me and my brother up and down, like fish in a market. "He'll know what to do."

The words felt cold, but I didn't think much about it. After all, my younger sister Thuy was already at Uncle Thanh's, and we would eventually have to retrieve her. Mama wouldn't be gone forever, and when she came back from the market, she would want to see all of her kids in one place. So would Papa when his tour of duty ended.

We took a cab to the big Army compound on the road to Tan Son

Nhut airport where Uncle Thanh and his family lived in the enlisted family quarters. He had married a woman I knew as Auntie Lan, but I didn't see her often and so didn't know her as well as Aunt Thu, my mother's sister. Lan was very pretty and had a reputation in the family as a sort-of princess—and an expensive one at that. Grandma once complained how Mama had wasted most of the money from the sale of Grandpa's farm in Rach Gia to buy expensive, traditional wedding gifts for Lan when she married Thanh. If this was a bad idea, I wondered why Papa didn't object, but by then, he had re-joined the Army. Mama handled our finances, even when Grandma and Aunt Thu lived with us. If she thought our proud family needed to throw a lavish wedding for Papa's brother, that was how it would be.

The taxi dropped us at the compound's main entrance—only military vehicles could go farther. A sentry phoned Uncle Thanh's post, and he appeared minutes later behind the wheel of an American-made jeep. I had no idea what soldiers did, including my father, except that it had something to do with guns (usually in clothes that looked alike) and putting the edge of your hand above your eye when you passed another soldier. Uncle Thanh's Army job apparently made him happy. He was assigned to drive a jeep for somebody called "Top Brass" which—along with his starched uniform, yellow scarf, and well-shined boots—told me he was someone important. When he showed up at the gate, everyone was very businesslike and a lot of papers changed hands. After the sentry was satisfied, he opened the pedestrian gate and we filed in like timid mice. Thanh drove us to the enlisted men's quarters, and, because of all the noise around the base, I couldn't really hear what he said to Grandma and Aunt Thu, but all of them looked glum.

Sister Thuy was playing with Uncle Thanh's three girls in front of their house when we arrived. His kids were mirror images of Quang, Thuy, and me—about the same ages with personalities to match. The eldest girl was good-humored and protective like Quang. The middle one was quiet and inquisitive like me. The youngest was shy and retiring, the way Thuy clung to Grandma's leg whenever strangers came to the house. I had always enjoyed our visits and was sorry they weren't more often.

"The war," Grandma answered when I asked why we saw them so rarely. "Your father and his brother are soldiers. Nobody chooses what happens."

Lan came out to meet us, her normally sunny face as sad as a cloudy day. The children stopped playing as soon as they saw the gloomy adults.

"Tell Lan what happened," Uncle Thanh said to Aunt Thu. She explained in words that didn't make sense, but as she spoke, sister Thuy's little hand found mine.

By and by we went into the house, and we kids quietly busied ourselves on the floor.

The adults continued their solemn conversation. *What happened to Tinh? What about the children? We'll have to make some changes. How can we collect survivor benefits if neither parent around?*

This last part puzzled me. I didn't know what "survivor benefits" were, but surely Mama would. Since I expected Mama to be home from market any time, and Papa always returned from the field after a few months. It didn't make sense. At that moment a big Army vehicle roared past, making more noise than the Hong Ngu bus, and I almost jumped out of my skin.

> *Fireworks go off in my ears, inside my brain. PopPopPop. Whoomp. Men shout in the dark. Men scream. Why doesn't Papa come for us? The blanket he nailed to our door brushes against my face, and I feel hot wind. Mama moans and pulls Baby Sister tight. They both may be crying, but who can hear? Stones and mud sprinkle down from our bunker dome each time the black air explodes. Smoke fills my nose. I want to get out, but Quang's hand holds me down like an iron band.*

I clutched one of my girl-cousin's shiny toys to my chest and glanced at Quang across the floor. He flinched, too, but gave me a "that's okay" Big Brother look. The adults at the table still talked.

"I'm thirsty!" I suddenly said to Grandma.

She looked back at me with sad eyes.

Lan said, "Okay. I'll make tea."

After a tense, nearly silent round of *tra* (tea), a dry-eyed Grandma took Quang, Thuy, and me outside and sat us down in the shade of a tamarind tree.

"Okay," she said. "Your Uncle Thanh is now head of the family. He has decided."

"Decided what, Grandma?" I asked.

"Who goes where," she replied. "First, Quang and Baby Sister will stay here with Uncle Thanh and Auntie Lan. You and Thuy will live with me. But we can't afford your parents' house anymore. We're going to move out of Saigon. I am sure your mother's brother, Uncle Chieu, and his wife, Aunt Que, will take us in. They live on a big plantation in Binh Duong north of the city."

"Uncle Chieu has a plantation?" Quang gasped, not wanting to miss out on a deal like that.

Grandma's fingertips popped him gently on the forehead. "No, you silly beetle. He and Aunt Que are caretakers. He's the butler, and she's the maid. They live in the servants' house that was built to hold lots of workers. There will be plenty of room for us."

It finally sunk in that *us*, of course, did not include Quang and Baby Sister. I was still unsure why Mama and Papa would be detained so long that the family needed to split up, but the sting of losing my big brother was soothed by a guarantee that sister Thuy and Grandma would be close at hand. Anyway, we had moved before, and one roof seemed as good as another—first from Rach Gia to Saigon, where Mama and Aunt Thu bargained for a room with holes in the wall and mice that nibbled on our toes; then to Go Vap where Baby Sister was born and I discovered the luxury of tiles on the floor and indoor plumbing. My parents would be back soon, and everything would be fine. I at least was sure of that. And remembering the stories Grandma told about the North, living in a big house like the one Grandpa Phan used to own, sounded like fun so it was hard for me to work up tears when we said good-bye to Quang and Baby Sister. After all, they got to stay with the uncle who looked like Papa, and they would have a queenly caretaker who could go on pretending to be a princess for all I cared, because I would soon be living like a princess myself.

§

Uncle Chieu and Aunt Que's family was the reverse of Uncle Thanh's. Instead of three girls, they had three boys, the eldest of which, cousin Ngoc, was one year older than me. They also had a daughter, exactly one year my junior, but with shy sister Thuy demanding most of my attention, I had little time for my cousin—although I think she was happy to finally have a couple of girls in the house to balance her bouncing brothers.

Chieu and Que were employed by a wealthy French couple who looked like they belonged on a glossy magazine cover. They spoke their native language, which was not uncommon in the South, so Chieu and Que spoke it, too. However, we newcomers did not, and the language barrier was another complication to overcome. Chieu was well-entrenched as the household's major domo, just as Que was Queen Bee of the cupboards, brooms, and bedclothes. Initially, we humble hangers-on were

Family day at Saigon Zoo—Grandmother (back row center), with Aunt Que, and her cousin. Thuy and Van (front row, second and third from left) with Aunt Que's children (Ngoc, Lien, Duc, Thang)

given duties around the side-house, such as keeping the servants' quarters clean and cooking for both families so that Aunt Que wouldn't have to do it. Grandma later started a flourishing business trading with the Muong tribes people who came down from the mountains to swap fresh corn, sweet potatoes, and yucca roots for things they couldn't get at home, like newspapers (which they used to plug holes in their crude houses), and metal pots and pans that wouldn't break like the clay vessels they made themselves. Both Muong men and women were muscular, dark-skinned, and humorless. Frankly, my sister and I couldn't tell them apart. It was another sign that there was a big world all around us, filled with lots of things we couldn't imagine. Only my mother's voice, speaking softly to me in the dark after one of my nightmares, assured me that such a world contained not only mysteries, but love.

One day while her mistress was out, Aunt Que took me to the mansion to have a peek. I have never seen anything so beautiful, like a fairytale. The interior was even more grand than its columned front, with shiny tiles and parquet floors below crystal chandeliers and vaulted ceilings. The draperies alone would have made fine roofs for a block of houses in our old neighborhood. Aunt Que was so concerned that I might smudge the glass or scratch the woodwork that I had to float behind her duster like one of the cherubs on the mantel. It was all pure magic until the mistress came home unexpectedly, pivoted on her stiletto heels, and peered over her designer sunglasses at us two deer frozen in her headlights.

"*Et qui est cette jeune femme?*" she asked, cocking her exquisitely coiffed blond head.

My heart pounded. I had no idea what she said, but her tone sounded a little suspicious.

"*C'est ma nièce. Elle reste avec nous dans la petite maison. Son nom est Hien Nguyen.*" Aunt Que lowered her eyes deferentially, and so did I. Then I peeked.

"*Ah!*" Our mistress's face brightened. She crossed the room and held out her hand for me to shake. Wide-eyed now, I accepted her hand. It was red-nailed, soft as butter, and bore enough rings and bracelets to fill a jewelry shop. "*Bonjour, Hien Nguyen. Vous etes serez toujours le bienvenue ici!*"

She smiled and winked at me, then threw her slim handbag over her shoulder and went upstairs.

"What did she say?" I asked Aunt Que. "Are we in trouble?"

"No. And you can thank your guardian angel! She just asked who you were, and I told her you were my niece. She said it was all right for you to be here. Thank goodness you're wearing a clean shirt! Now get back to Grandma Mau and try to stay out of trouble!"

My clean shirt must have made more than a good impression. Later that evening as we cleared away our dinner dishes, the mistress came to the door of the servant's quarters and asked Aunt Que to call me. When I appeared, she gave me a box containing several beautiful children's dresses, all cut in the European style. I was stunned. The dresses were for me? She patted me on the head, pinched my cheek, and said something else in her hypnotic, melodic voice, before returning to the main house. When she was gone, I displayed each dress for everyone to admire, unable to believe that they were truly mine.

"What did she say?" I asked Aunt Que.

Aunt Que arched an eyebrow and fingered the fabric as if checking for moth-holes. "Oh, nothing. She just said these used to be her daughter's and thought you might like to have them."

I felt honored and surprised that such a grand lady would think those nice dresses belonged on a pipsqueak like me. It was only later, when Grandma took me aside, that I learned Aunt Que was less than thrilled because she, too, had a small daughter but had never been favored with such a gift, despite her years of service. It was an object lesson—a slap in the face, Grandma said—that some women never forget.

§

Our three or four months at the plantation were a relatively settled, happy time. I still had no understanding of death, and Grandma would cry when I asked her when Mama would be home from the market. She would say, "you poor child," but she would not try to explain what had happened. There were no schools nearby, and no war—not yet, anyway—so when my chores were done, I played with my sister and cousins in and around the servants' house or ventured into a forest of rubber trees where the curved dirt road split in two. One fork of the road circled back to the plantation, a roundabout route that dimly reminded me of the times Grandpa Phan used to carry me around our Rach Gia garden on his shoulders.

The other fork led to a rusty old water tower that leaned precariously over the trail. My cousins were used to it so they just scampered through its shadow and continued on their way. Not me. I started calling it *The Monster* because it looked spooky even from a distance—a big mechanical fist that could crash down without warning and squash me, leaving me in pieces on the road with no mother's voice to put me back together. I usually turned tail and ran, but the awful image—and others—came back in dreams.

A rooster crows outside our bunker. It's dawn, and nobody is screaming. No explosions, no PopPopPop. "Go out and find your father," Mama tells me and Quang. "Tell him I need him." I'm nearest the Army blanket that covers our door, so Quang gives me a push. "Go on," he says. "You're closest!" I struggle but something pins the blanket at the bottom and it won't budge. Quang adds his weight, and the whole thing collapses, the blanket and me with Quang on top. He rolls back and pushes me out with his legs. "Go! Find Papa!" The sun still isn't up, and in the grey air, the ground looks lumpy. I take one step, then another. It's hard to keep my balance— like walking on a mattress. My toes feel wet and sticky. I look down. I'm standing on somebody's chest, but it's not Papa. I bend closer to check the face. No face. No head! Just a collar wrapping a neck like butcher's paper. I look a few feet away, and a head stares back at me with dull eyes, sand half-covering the hair and cheeks. "Quang! QUANG!!!"

I told my cousins a couple of times about this dream, but they thought I was nuts. Grandma, however, listened intently and told me that some people see things that others can't. She said that's why good Buddhists and good Catholics pray. I remembered one time a year or so before, when Mama was in the kitchen, sister Thuy called me to "Come quick!" I ran outside just in time to see Mother Maria in a long blue and white dress flying over our house, accompanied by two angels in cream-colored gowns with golden belts. They made a grand, hollow noise, as if blowing trumpets, then disappeared. That didn't make much sense either, but, like my dream, it seemed all too real—and I couldn't ignore it. Either the world was telling me something important or it wasn't. Maybe I was crazy after all.

Nonetheless, the memory of the dream always faded, but The Monster was still there. It became my nemesis. After the other kids left me behind once too often, I got tired of missing out on their games and decided to do something about it.

Plantation's leaning water tower, "The Monster"

One day, after my nap and another sweat-soaked dream about the headless man, I took a small loaf of French bread from Aunt Que's basket and went to the fork in the road, scared but determined to deal with, once and for all, The Monster. I wasn't particularly hungry, and Grandma always told me to ask Aunt Que before I took any food, but I needed help. Somehow, taking the bread felt like the right thing to do—as if that little loaf contained all the strength of my family. I took a bite and began to talk to The Monster. "Please don't fall on me." I watched it for a moment, but it seemed indifferent to my presence. *Okay, maybe it's asleep.* I inched closer, then looked behind me, hoping to see my sister or cousins coming to my rescue, but I was definitely alone. I listened for my mother's voice, but all I heard was the wind in the trees.

Then I got an idea. If I closed my eyes, I couldn't see The Monster, so maybe it couldn't see me. After all, I had gotten quite good at closing my eyes on a lot of things: holes in my clothes, bugs in my rice, mice in the corner, and the noises outside my window at night. So I fixed my eye on a tree just beyond the shade of The Monster and calculated the number of steps it would take to reach it. Taking another bite of bread to ingest more courage, I closed my eyes and started running. Somewhere along the way I lost count of my steps, but it didn't matter. I kept running, fearing a crushing blow at my moments, until I felt tall grass against my knees and stopped just short of the tree. I opened my eyes and looked back. The Monster, huge and indifferent, now looked serene—a companion I need never again try to outrun. I jumped up and down and yelled with triumph, though no one had witnessed my courageous act. I was no longer a prisoner on the side of the road. In crossing under the leaning water tower, I learned how to act alone, calculate risk, be brave, and start running.

I munched more bread and walked...*walked*...back toward the plantation, this time taking the circular route. I was in no hurry. It was nice to be alone, and I had a lot of new stories to tell Mama.

Chapter 3

Leaf House—1965

A few months later we left the plantation with war snapping at our heels. The Central Highlands were heating up. Distant explosions rocked the night and the mountainsides flashed orange. Binh Duong, Grandma said, was no longer safe even for natives, since "the enemy"—the Viet Cong as adults called them—were locals who had sided with the North to make trouble in the South. I thought about my father and how this bad news might delay his return; and how his brother, Uncle Thanh, might lose his nice job driving a jeep and be forced to carry a rifle into the bush, where more Monsters had to be tamed—and not just by shutting one's eyes.

I remembered one time in our Go Vap house when Uncle Thanh brought a letter from Papa saying he would soon be home on leave. Mama got very excited and gave me a cute short haircut to match Cousin Lien's—I'd been begging for it for weeks—and bought me a new dress. We went to the market to get fixings for Papa's favorite meal: *Ga Kho Gung*—caramelized ginger chicken—for a homecoming dinner. Papa arrived with a small duffle bag and a manila envelope he said contained papers he had to deliver at once, the reason for his trip. He only stayed one night, and when he left to deliver the envelope, I asked if I could come. He hesitated, then said, "Yes, but only if you promise to be quiet!" So I buttoned my lips.

The Army driver who arrived to pick up Papa was surprised to see me, but Papa outranked him so I tagged along. We stopped in the middle of the countryside—a beautiful place like the land around Plantation House—and Papa gave his mysterious envelope to another soldier, barely saying two words. On the way home to drop me off, I asked Papa if we could buy some coconut juice from a vendor by the highway, but the driver said, "No! It's too dangerous to stop!" Papa again pulled rank and I got my juice, but we didn't stay long. The driver stood on the gas as soon as we got back in and made tracks toward the city. That was the first time I realized something really bad, like one of my nightmares, was going on around the country.

§

So Uncle Chieu and Aunt Que quit their plantation jobs and used their savings to buy a house in the Phu Nhuan District outside of Saigon. It was really a step down. After the marble columns and crystal chandeliers of the mansion and the nice servants' quarters, our one-room house looked like a refugee's shack. With a dirt floor, outdoor plumbing, a worn-out wood-frame bed that also served as our dinner table, and bamboo poles supporting flimsy walls of knitted coconut leaves, the slightest breeze made the whole place quiver. Grandma wondered how it would ever withstand the next monsoon. Even the bamboo-framed windows needed sticks to hold the shutters open, but Thuy and I pretended it was like living in a doll's house. We laughed while Grandma fretted, and I called the place our "Leaf House" because it felt like we lived in a tree.

Uncle Chieu joined the National Police force, and Aunt Que got a job at an American installation—one of many now sprouting up everywhere. They didn't spend much time at home so Grandma took charge of the household and the kids. She put a saw-horse table at the back of the room to hold our charcoal stove and put our modest collection of dishes, pots, and pans on a small shelf left by the previous owner. She organized us kids into a squad of workers with specific duties. My job was to help Grandma haul water from the neighborhood's communal well. She balanced two buckets on the ends of a bamboo pole she carried on her shoulders. I had my own small bucket, which I dutifully filled and carried home, although I stumbled often and spilled a lot. The other kids swept the floor and cleaned the dishes, so between the work and the heat (the close-in city air was warmer than in the open space around the plantation) we tumbled onto our shared bed exhausted every night. Our tired brains had further trouble making sense of Grandma's strange bedtime behavior. Although she worked harder than anyone, she almost never slept. After she put us kids down, she sat at the foot of our bed under the mosquito net praying in a low voice that sounded like Mama's. Later, she sat up in the middle of the night and muttered in a voice that sounded like Grandpa's, "It's my fault. It's my fault." to nobody in particular, occasionally slapping herself on the chest. This was pretty scary. Thuy and I spent many hours wide-eyed in the dark, simply watching and waiting to see what happened next, but we eventually returned to sleep.

Once, when her chest-slaps became a real beating, I slipped next to her, touched her arm, and said, "Grandma—wake up, wake up!" Without giving me a look, she lay back like a skeleton and stared at the ceiling. When I returned to my place, Thuy was rolled into a ball, sobbing and clutching her blanket. Without Grandma to cling to—her usual hugging post—I was second best, so she rolled next to me like a sweaty coconut as I held her until we finally fell asleep.

The next morning, things got even stranger. While Grandma was making breakfast, I saw that she was bruised underneath her shirt. I asked what had happened, assuming she'd tell me about the night before, but she just stirred the pan and said, "Grandpa Phan is punishing me."

"For what, Grandma?"

"For not going to church and praying for our children. They may not get into heaven."

Maybe our cousins heard this, too, and told their parents. Then Uncle Chieu and Aunt Que must have said something to Grandma, because a few weeks later she started saying her rosary and taking us to Mass at the Catholic church a few blocks away. Grandma stopped beating herself, and the praying in a lower voice stopped, too. I kind of missed the praying because it had been strangely comforting when I heard my mother speak through Grandma's mouth. At least for those few moments, I could stop worrying about why Mama was taking so long to return from the market.

§

The wartime buildup put a strain on Grandma and us kids, but it was especially hard on Chieu and Que. They kept odd hours, and even when they came home for dinner, they often left right away in different directions. Neither took much interest in their kids, which was odd for Que because Mama always said that taking care of one's children—loving and nourishing them—was a Vietnamese woman's highest duty. Maybe that was one reason she and Chieu started arguing, not caring who listened, which was never smart on a street where neighbors live shoulder-to-shoulder.

I don't know if I heard it from Grandma, or a neighbor, or a neighbor's kid, but Uncle Chieu accused Aunt Que of cheating on him with an American and threw her out. Maybe she simply left on her own to live in the American's nice apartment. That left Grandma to take care of six kids, none old enough to be much help. Money for food, clothes, medicine, and any extras came mostly from Uncle Chieu, but as a rookie policeman, he didn't make much and spent many nights in a barracks near his station or at the apartment he got when Que moved out. On those nights when he did come home, he always looked like an old man and often fell asleep in his uniform still wearing his boots and gun holster.

Aunt Que dropped by occasionally, when she knew Chieu wouldn't be there and left a little cash for food. She made it clear by her absence that we children, including her own four, were now Grandma's responsibility—repayment for the "free" room and board she and Chieu had provided at the Plantation. What they never realized—or chose to ignore—was the fact that we were always hungry.

I felt especially bad for Ngoc, their oldest son. Thuy and I had parents who were away for important reasons and *couldn't* be there or help us. But Ngoc's parents weren't there to help out because they simply didn't want to be, and I know that hurt his heart. He reminded me a bit of Quang, whom I had seen only a couple of times since the family split up. The first time Quang showed up, unannounced, at our door, was a few months after we arrived at Leaf House. This was peculiar, because he came alone and looked like he had run the whole way from Uncle Thanh's Army post. He was beside himself with grief and rage.

"What's wrong?" Grandma asked him, blotting his sweaty, teary face with her shirt tail.

"Something's happened to Baby Sister," Quang wailed. "I came back from school yesterday and she was gone. I couldn't find her anywhere. Something has happened to her!" He was inconsolable and hyperventilating.

At this, Grandma shooed me and the other kids away, guided Quang to sit on the sofa, gave him some water, then sat beside him and just held him for a minute. "I'm sure there's an explanation," she said calmly, smoothing the hair from his face.

Quang mumbled, "Uncle Thanh said that Baby Sister was given up for adoption to a wealthy family…"

Grandma said with her gentle voice, "You poor child, don't worry. We'll ask Uncle Thanh about Baby Sister." Now tell me what happened."

Quang began his sad story...

"I came home from school yesterday and Baby Sister was not there, so I asked Uncle Thanh where she was. He told me that she had been adopted by a wealthy family and was in good hands. I know that Aunt Lan does not like me or Baby Sister. They just had another baby, a little girl, and she sure doesn't want to take care of two babies. I kept asking questions because I didn't believe them, and Uncle Thanh and Aunt Lan stopped talking to me. I left and went to ask some neighbors if they knew anything about Baby Sister. One neighbor told me that there was much yelling and screaming earlier, that both babies were crying, but that was some time ago. Another neighbor said that Aunt Lan sold the baby for money. I didn't think so...little girls are always harder to sell than boys, and there are lots of orphans around now, no reason to buy one. Then, some of my friends tell me that they heard Aunt Lan screaming at one baby or the other to "stop crying, you little brat!" Then, crashing noises from the house, then silence. No more crying. I asked their mother what she knew, but she refused to answer, looked at the ground, and shook her head. So today, I am confused, frightened, and sad because Baby Sister is gone. I dressed for school just like every other day, but instead of school I came to you Grandma. I didn't know what else to do."

Grandma decided right away that she had to see Uncle Thanh and Aunt Lan and find out more about this. She sent a message to Aunt Thu at her work and asked her to come home. The next morning, all of us—Grandma, Aunt Thu, Quang, sister Thuy, and me—went to see what we could learn about the fate of Baby Sister.

When we arrived, Uncle Thanh sent all of the children outside to play, including his four, saying the adults had business to discuss. But Thuy refused to budge and clung to Grandma's leg in her usual manner. She was allowed to stay. Quang and I were also reluctant to be dismissed so we did not venture far from the front door. I felt a sense of immense sadness, heaviness, and unease in the air, tension and underlying hostility, especially around Aunt Lan.

The discussion regarding Baby Sister began. Grandma raised her voice, which she rarely did, demanding to know why she was not consulted before whatever was done was done. Uncle Thanh did not directly answer but said that Baby Sister was with a respectable, well-to-do family. Then Grandma asked to see the adoption papers. Uncle Thanh said no, that it was a done deal, and nothing could be done to undo it. Thuy was now sitting on Grandma's lap so I slowly inched my way to Grandma's side, sensing that the discussion was about to be over. And it was. Uncle Thanh had nothing more to say, and Aunt Lan never said anything.

Without a word, Grandma stood up with Thuy in her arms. Aunt Thu, Quang and I moved to stand beside her. We left the house silently, walking toward the gate. In Vietnam, it was an expected courtesy to escort visitors, even family, to and from your front gate, but neither Uncle Thanh nor Aunt Lan made a move to accompany us. In a low voice, Grandma told Aunt Thu that she did not believe the "adoption" story and that they should discreetly question the neighbor woman that Quang liked and knew well enough to ask about Baby Sister.

The neighbor woman repeated what Quang had already told us, then added that she had heard screaming babies, followed by a sudden silence— exactly the same story told to Quang the day before by his little friend. Grandma and Aunt Thu looked at each other, then started the walk home. Quang stayed behind, but it was not his choice. Uncle Thanh insisted, and Grandma, not having the strength to stand against the "head of the family," fragmented as it was, relented. Quang was forced to stay in that miserable, frightening environment.

After that day, I was not aware of any significant effort on the part of any of the adults—Grandma, Uncle Chieu, Uncle Hai, or Aunt Thu—to dig deeper into the mystery. They all gave up, and none ever mentioned Baby Sister again.

The second time we saw Quang was when Uncle Thanh brought him for a visit. I noticed a gauze bandage on his forehead but didn't think much about it. Boys hurt themselves all the time, and living on an army post, Uncle Thanh (as his guardian) undoubtedly had a nurse or doctor handy to patch up scratches. Anyway, Grandma knew something was wrong, though she couldn't guess what. Quang stayed a few days, then left without telling us what had happened.

After Quang went home, I realized how much I missed him. I found new excuses to talk to Ngoc, my new surrogate big brother. I asked him to repeat old stories about our family and our country's mythical heroes. Truthfully, I just liked the sound of his voice. It reminded me of Papa and made me wonder what my father was doing and where he might be stationed. He used to send us letters, parts of which Mama would read aloud, but we hadn't received one since before Hong Ngu. Because Mama was gone now, too, I guessed we would just have to wait for the war—for everything—to settle down so things could be all right again.

Almost a year would pass before my longing for my old family was satisfied, at least in part. When I was about five, Aunt Thu showed up at our leafy door. While the rest of us had gotten skinny eating Grandma's skimpy meals, Thu had managed to gain weight. "She's carrying a baby," Grandma said, although I don't know why she whispered. I barely remembered the time my mother carried Baby Sister, and that was a time of laughing and big plans. Grandma gave Aunt Thu some weak tea, and we sat on the wooden bed and got lost in family gossip. I was surprised nobody mentioned Aunt Thu's wedding—normally big news for a Vietnamese family—but later found out that was because it had never happened.

Of course, Thu had visited us before with boyfriends. A year earlier, she introduced us to a handsome Vietnamese Army officer who invited Mama and me to go with them to a Bollywood movie. Since the ticket taker had a crush on Mama and used to let us in for free, this didn't seem like a big deal until Grandma told me how unusual it was. Courting couples liked to be alone, and since Mama seldom took us kids anywhere, she must've thought I'd done something special to deserve a treat. The reason didn't matter to me, but it was the first time I realized how much trouble men and women took to get to know and impress each other before they got married. Maybe Thu and the baby's father didn't have time to go through all that. She'd been working as a live-in housekeeper for a well-to-do family downtown, but with a baby now on the way, Grandma said that would all come to an end.

So Thu looked down at me and asked, "What do you think we should call him when he is born? I just know it will be a boy!"

Nobody had ever asked my opinion about anything, let alone such an important question. I yammered and stammered and began to run through every boy's name I could think of until finally she stopped me and said, "Hoang. I think we should call him Hoang."

"That means *prince*!" I said, feeling proud I had remembered something Ngoc taught me.

"Yes, right." Thu smiled. "He will be my little prince! And I will let you help me take care of him. Would you like that?"

I said I would, and thus Hoang entered my life. Thu let me feel his little head or his foot or his butt through the tight material of her shirt and I felt I was holding the world.

§

A short time after her visit, Aunt Thu moved in with her baby—another mouth to feed, and a noisy one at that. But I didn't care. She allowed me to hold Hoang on occasion, or rock him to sleep when the women were busy or too tired. I sometimes felt like a mother myself, although I was only about six years old. I grew to love Hoang as my own younger brother. Because of her nursing infant, Thu couldn't take work outside the house, so she bought a small food cart with her savings. Her product—shaved ice covered with syrup that quickly turned into sweet slush—was a favorite in our humid, airless neighborhood. With the cart only a few feet from our house, she sold every drop she could make.

Her habits taught me a lot about industry. She got up before dawn and began simmering mung beans and red beans—necessary for taste and consistency—then mashed them into paste. At just the right time, she added basil seeds, tapioca strings (in rainbow jelly), grass jelly, coconut milk, and syrup. A block of ice wrapped in rice husks and burlap was delivered early, so by the time I washed my face, she was grinding ice for customers and dropping coins into an old tin can.

Although Aunt Thu could do all this with a baby slung across her chest, it was easier when I held Hoang, so we often worked as a team, clapping like cheerleaders whenever Thu made a sale. Before long, she knew all of her customers' preferences and added different kinds of beans, extra cooked tapioca, more or less coconut milk, and plenty of sugar syrup, as demand for her shaved ice went up. Since we had no refrigerator, she gave us kids her leftovers at the end of each day, but by then it was mostly sugared water. We didn't care. It was still a treat, and we always prayed secretly and selfishly for rain clouds to keep the customers away.

Still, Aunt Thu hesitated to call her venture a success. The ingredients weren't free, and her markup had to match the going rate for street food, which wasn't much. Bad weather meant bad business, and as much as we kids loved to guzzle leftovers, we knew we were drinking up her profits. When the monsoon finally hit and it rained for days on end, people scurried to get where they were going and sales slowed to a trickle. Aunt Thu decided to sell the cart and find a permanent job since Hoang (at three months) could get along now on powdered milk. Because housekeeping was all she knew and most maids lived with their employer, she had to move out. That meant Grandma's informal "orphanage" now blossomed to seven, all under seven years old.

The monsoon months are dark and dreary, and even Grandma became sullen and quiet, living in forced confinement with us little pests.

Chieu and Que came by less often, and Aunt Thu's new duties kept her busy day and night, so we had little money. Grandma often had to make a day's food last a week. One of her favorite tricks was to cook a handful of fresh rice in three gallons of water, serving it like soup with just a few grains in each bowl. She flavored it with salt, and when I once suggested that we just drink it from our bowls (so I wouldn't have to wash the spoons!) she said, "No—a spoon makes you eat slower and fills you up better. Besides, you don't want to miss any rice!" Occasionally we got a good portion of solid rice, flavored with fish sauce and, occasionally, weak tea, which made it easier to swallow and filled us up faster. Sister Thuy especially liked tea on rice, so I gave her part of mine when we had it. Grandma slapped my hand when I did this, but since Grandma always served herself last and ate the least, I figured I was just following her example. One of our neighbors, Mrs. Han (whose husband had a steady job), came over from time to time with leftovers that Grandma pretended we didn't need—such was the pride of a "princess" raised in the North. I got to be best friends with Mrs. Han's daughter, Truc, who was about my age. Visiting her made a nice break from the roomful of cousins, so I hung out with her as much as I could.

Truc was a bright girl, mature for her age, who didn't care much for childish games so we spent a lot of time during my visits talking like grown-ups. Her family was Buddhist, but she seemed fascinated by everything Catholic, from Grandma's rosary beads to the tiny cross on our leafy wall. She wanted to know what it all meant, so I sprinkled the few facts I knew on top of the stories I made up since at Mass, our priest did all the talking and the biggest religious duty for us kids was staying quiet and sitting still. In exchange, Truc told me all about the Buddha and his life and teachings, which made him sound more like a happy uncle than our solemn and suffering Jesus. In the end, we decided that both men were good and holy. Nobody would go wrong living the life that Jesus and Buddha exemplified.

Spirituality and the Spirit World are very real to most Vietnamese, whether Roman Catholic or Buddhist. Unhappy spirits must be placated—or there will be trouble. We had one in our neighborhood, and he inhabited his tombstone, which for some reason sat outside Truc's house instead of in a cemetery. When I asked Truc about it, her eyes widened and she whispered to me that the Spirit had recently spoken to her parents. He was unhappy with the neighborhood children peeing on his tombstone. This did on occasion occur; the little boys thought it was great fun. The Spirit did not. He said that if the tombstone was not moved to a safer, and drier, location, that it would "destroy" her family's business. The threat was taken seriously. A few days later, Truc's father moved the tombstone to their backyard, built a little altar to accommodate it, and, to make doubly sure the Spirit would be content, began to place incense and food offerings on the altar like those for their family Buddha in her home. He also placed a marble bench where the tombstone had originally been so that nothing else would ever occupy that space. The Spirit remained quiet thereafter, and all of us were relieved and much happier. As it happened, Truc's family business did indeed halt its downward spiral and began to improve dramatically. Make of that what you will.

The best thing about visiting Truc, was that if we talked or played long enough, her mother would call us to lunch, so I sometimes had at least one square meal on days when the rest of our squad was on half-rations. I resisted this at first, telling her it wasn't fair for me to eat if my sister and cousins were fasting, but Mrs. Han insisted. In fact, my objections increased her curiosity about our family. During one of those lunches, Mrs. Han asked casually about the parents of all the kids in our house. I told her what I knew, which was that Uncle Chieu was a policeman, Aunt Que worked for the Americans, and Aunt Thu was a housekeeper who lived across town. I said my own father was a soldier assigned far away, and my mother was detained at the market in another city but would rejoin us any day.

The table got very quiet at that point. When we finished, Mrs. Han cleared the dishes and Truc pointed to the little black patch above the pocket of my shirt. I had worn it for so long that I usually forgot it was there.

"What's that for?" Truc asked.

I looked down and fingered the frayed black patch, which Grandma had sewed there soon after we returned from Hong Ngu. "Um, Grandma says I'm supposed to wear this to show people how much I love and honor my parents."

Truc was quiet a moment, then said, "I bet you wear it for two more years."

That was startling. "Why?"

"Because I've seen other kids and grown-ups wear it, too. Mama says it's a sign of mourning."

"Mourning?"

"You know, like when you're sad because someone died. You know what dead is, right?"

Actually, I didn't, and since Truc's house was now getting very dark inside and things were becoming fuzzy in my head and my heart was starting to pound so loudly that I had trouble hearing her words, I could only give a little shrug.

"Dead is when a person stops breathing and gets buried in the ground," Truc said. Not meaning at all to be cruel, she added, "Your mother has been to market for a very long time, hasn't she?"

> *"Quang! I can't move! I'm standing on a dead body!" From the darkness of the narrow bunker, Quang says, "Okay. Just pretend we're playing hide-and-seek. Close your eyes and count to three, then jump and go find Papa." I do, and land on the dirt. The dawn is lighter now, and I can see past the body and severed head to other torsos and scattered arms and legs and shirts and equipment and empty boxes and shattered huts. The air is cool but smells like the inside of a stove. Quang follows me out of the bunker, and Mama hands him Baby Sister, who is covered with blood. Mama comes out next, and she is bloody, too, from her left shoulder to her hip. While I stare at her, Quang gives her the baby then retrieves a sleeping mat from Papa's hut, and drags it next to our bunker. Mama eases herself onto it and tucks Baby Sister under her good arm. At that instant, a half-dozen people—grey ghosts with blank faces—approach us, driven by three men with rifles. As they get closer, I see that half of the blank-faced, unarmed people are soldiers like Papa, and the other dazed people look like the wives and grandparents we'd seen camped around us for a week. The men with rifles look like older versions of Quang, not men at all, but boys. The unarmed ghost-soldiers are ordered to kneel and face what remains of the barbed wire. The families of the ghost-soldiers sit on their haunches outside Papa's hut. WHOOMP! A Big explosion out of nowhere. Air blows from my mouth and pushes into my ears. Everybody ducks or falls, but not everyone gets up. One man with a rifle stays down, along with a couple of family members including Quang and I. Quang grabs his own neck, then looks at his bloody hand. Squawky birds flutter away from the riverbank. The surviving men with rifles look around, their eyes wide, then run away. The camp survivors look around, too, then scuttle off in the opposite direction toward the river. Quang and Mama and Baby Sister and I are the only ones left. Baby Sister starts crying, so Mama tries to nurse her. The sun is now above the trees, and I notice a big red gash on Mama's shoulder, near her neck. Blood bubbles from it like water tricking into a paddy. Mama's voice breaks my trance. "Find Papa. Quick."*

After the battle – Massacre at Papa's Army Post in Hong Ngu (1964)

"Little Hien, are you okay?" Mrs. Han touched my shoulder and bent low over the table, peering into my face.

I looked up, my forehead beaded with sweat. I couldn't speak, couldn't blink.

"It's time for you to go home." Mrs. Han helped me to my feet and shoved a small basket filled with fruit and rice cakes into my hands. "You girls can play again tomorrow. Tell your Granny these bananas and papayas are for the kids. It's just Buddha food from our shrine, and it's getting old. No point letting it rot. I'll get more tomorrow at the market."

At the market...I got up and left, wobbling like a toddler. For the first time, I wondered if Mama was really gone to the market...*you know, like when you're sad and miss someone who died and gets buried in the ground*...

I gave the basket of Buddha food to Grandma, who looked at it askew. I was afraid she would send me back across the street into the black-hole room that made my eyes sting and my ears ring and order me to return it. But instead she sniffed the fruit for freshness and said, "Well, we can eat Buddha's food as long as we don't serve him. We can thank Mrs. Han for her Christian kindness even though she's not a Christian. Go tell your cousins we'll have a big dinner tonight."

So I went to bed with a double-full stomach but didn't sleep much. Grandma went back to her nighttime ritual and softly beat herself until she sobbed, looking like an angel of death beneath her worn mosquito net, then she lay back and closed her sunken eyes. I closed my eyes, too, trying hard to blot out *The Monster* that had returned to loom over me like a terrible loud dragon, waiting to pull off my head and push me into the earth. Finally, I heard Mama's distant voice calling me from the market, and I went to sleep.

Strangely enough, it was the neighborhood market that eventually saved us all.

§

I never knew what Mr. Han did for a living, but he must have lost his job. Mrs. Han no longer invited me to lunch, and the baskets of used Buddha food we counted on slowed to a trickle, then stopped. Even Truc had less to say and spent more time on other streets with other friends, where I guess she, too, had become a professional guest. At least our shared hunger and the example of the Hans' generosity convinced Grandma to put aside her pride and go into the world to fill our bellies. She was illiterate and thin as a stick, and with seven kids to care for, couldn't take a job even if she found one. Instead, she enlisted me as her helper, and while the other kids napped, we went to the neighborhood market and perfected a new way to shop.

First, Grandma struck up friendly conversations with the vendors while she pretended to examine their produce, occasionally buying something with one of Uncle Chieu's rare bills. After a while, she timed our visits for late afternoon, when the stalls were closing. The vendors were all anxious to go home, so they didn't mind if an old lady and her small granddaughter helped them clean out the bottom of their bins and baskets, collecting wilted greens, including tea stems that Grandma prized. If some whole piece of fruit or a vegetable remained—one obviously bruised or starting to go bad—Grandma would remark on it and lament that while she had no money at the moment, she would return later in the week to buy it. Well, most vendors knew bad produce wouldn't last, and even if it did, nobody would buy it so half the time they just told her to take what she wanted as they dropped their shade or awning. I always wondered why she needed me for this routine until one lady merchant patted me on the head and called me the "cutest little *cu gau*" she'd ever seen, then gave me free chunk of yummy brown sugar. This happened again at another stall where a kind man gave us an extra orange, and at a third where the owner let Grandma take a pinch of fresh tobacco for her pipe. Even though my formal education had been limited thus far to only a few months of pre-school, I could still put two and two together. A chatty old lady with a cute little kid could make a minimal living just by being nice. But there were limits even to Grandma's willingness to bend a pride-stiff back.

One Sunday after Mass, our parish priest announced that the American Red Cross would distribute rice to needy families through the church. This sounded great to me, but Grandma thought standing in line for church charity was different and somehow worse than cadging fruit from friendly vendors. I pointed out that while we had indeed been lucky to get some produce to stretch our meals, none of the local merchants handed out free rice, a staple throughout all Asia. To make things easier, I told her that I would go with her and stand in line with my own little pot, doubling our take from the church. Reluctantly, she agreed.

The line was long when we arrived, so we had plenty of time to hear bystanders discuss the rules: *one portion per family—two scoops only, not a grain more*. I already felt guilty for eating Mrs. Han's Buddha food. I wasn't sure it was smart to insult Jesus by double-dipping from Christian charity. On the other hand, we had more than one household under our leafy roof, with Uncle Chieu's family and Aunt Thu's baby Hoang, not to mention sister Thuy and me, so if adding my pot to Grandma's was a sin, it couldn't be a big one.

Slowly, the line moved forward. Grandma got her ration with eyes respectfully lowered, as did the next woman, then it was my turn. I held up my little pot—about half the size of the containers around me—and looked into the face of the pretty nun.

"Why, little Hien." The nun smiled. "I believe I just gave your grandmother the portion for your family. Didn't you see her? She could've saved you a wait in line."

I felt my cheeks burn, but now it was all or nothing. Jesus would understand. "I know," I said, then burnished the truth a little. "This pot is for my Uncle Chieu, who is at work and can't be here today."

She gave me a sideways glance but filled my pot anyway—it amounted to less than a scoop—then told me to "scoot," which I was happy to do. Grandma just sniffed and looked away when I told her the story (confession is supposed to be good for the soul). I prepared

Grandmother and I, in line for US Red Cross rice at Phu Hai Catholic Church

to get either a medal or a lecture when we got home, but neither happened. We did have rice soup for two months, though, topped with our marketplace treasures. If Jesus or Buddha held it against us, they never let it show.

§

The next six months passed with our hearts and bellies full, having more than before though less than we might have liked. Except for the occasional nightmares bursting like bombs in my head, it was a quiet and happy time. I enjoyed playing Auntie to little Hoang and carried him around on my hip like a mother, feeding him rice paste and coconut milk until one day Aunt Thu showed up with his father.

Hoang's papa was young, handsome, and tall for a Vietnamese. Grandma told me that he had a "white collar" job with an airline and lived with his mother like a dutiful son. And like a dutiful son, he refused to marry against her wishes, which was why Aunt Thu was a single mom.

"You see," Grandma told me after they left, "most mothers want their boys to marry up in the world, and your Aunt Thu has no education. If she had money, this wouldn't matter. But as it is, she's beneath him, and that's that."

"But Grandma," I said, "you didn't go to school and you married Grandpa Phan and lived in a big house in the North. You had servants and cooks and pretty dresses—"

"That's true." She smiled. "My father told me to choose between getting married and getting educated. I chose a family life. Why learn to read when you have a husband to run a business? And a book never changed a diaper! I thought life would go on like that forever, but of course…" She trailed off like she did when she beat her chest, but it wasn't bedtime yet—and those evil spirits never came until after dark.

"Anyway"—she patted my knee and got up to fix dinner—"Aunt Thu just wanted her man to see his son before they broke up. She's taking a job with the Americans at Quy Nhon. Hoang will stay here, of course, until she gets settled. Then, who knows? Maybe she'll find a husband."

Not long after that, we had another, less cordial family reunion. Aunt Que dropped by to give some cash and candy to her kids, who were obviously happy to see her, although she pointedly ignored her nephew, Hoang, and her nieces, Thuy and me. Turning to go, she said in a businesslike voice, "Sorry, no treats for you. If you were my kids, it might be different, but that's what parents are for. Just be glad you're not in an orphanage, and I give you food and a place to sleep. Now go help your grandmother fix the evening meal. I'm hungry and need to get home before dark."

She turned away, and Thuy looked at me, her eyes huge and bewildered like a drenched kitten's. "Why is Aunt Que so mean? Why doesn't Mama come back from the market and take care of us? When are we going to see Papa?"

I couldn't answer any of her questions. I was sad and hurt myself, and I tried very hard to not cry. I just let her hug me and squeezed little Hoang as I got set for *The Monster's* next visit.

§

Unfortunately, the dreamtime *Monster* was not my only tormentor. Whether because of the Hans' casual talk with neighbors about our situation or because it was just common knowledge, more people—kids and adults alike—began treating us like Aunt Que, calling us *Stupid girls with bad manners and no parents. Orphans bring bad luck!* I knew I wasn't stupid, and lots of kids were more noisy and rude than me. Although I had a couple of fights over name-calling, I still didn't know what they meant by *orphans*, so I put the question to Grandma.

"Don't worry about it," she said, as if it was a just a skinned knee, but I knew it bothered her, too. Once, Grandma had to drag an irate mother off my back after I got into a hair-pulling match with her daughter, who had called me a "stupid orphan with no manners." Since, according to her, I had no manners, I figured I could slug her, so I did. She went down, taking me with her by the hair. Her mother ran out of their house and grabbed me by the shoulders, which caused Grandma to respond in kind.

"Your little urchin is a monster!" the younger woman shouted. "Somebody needs to teach her a lesson!"

"Well, she won't learn manners from you!" Grandma shouted back. "Who does your little brat think she is, calling people names in the street?"

That did it. The fight was on. The woman slapped Grandma, who clocked her back, and both fell in a clench to the dirt. I jumped on the woman's back as the other girl started slapping and kicking Grandma and me. Almost at once, Truc and her parents ran out of their house and separated us.

"What are you doing?" Mrs. Han scolded the younger woman. "Beating up an old lady? And you've got the gall to talk about manners!"

"Orphans are bad luck!" the woman yelled, turning with her daughter back toward their house. "They're a curse on the whole neighborhood! Just look at your husband—out of a job! If you like them, you can have them. And you can all go to hell!"

The Hans helped me take Grandma to the Leaf House—one sleeve was torn off her blouse, and her face was bruised and cut. While I was really sorry that Grandma had been hurt defending me, I never regretted punching that mean little girl in the face. She did not bother me again. Mrs. Han cleaned Grandma's injuries with a damp cloth, but frankly, I had seen Grandma look worse after one of her self-flagellations. Sister Thuy watched in silence, dimly aware that this might become a familiar sight. After that, I put on a brave face for her every morning, the same way I put on a clean shirt and wore my black patch—a shield that protected us both.

§

A few weeks later, I discovered that Aunt Que's visit to dispense cash, candy, and ill-will had been no accident. Her fortunes had changed for the better, which meant she could now do something about us. Business was booming for anyone connected to the Americans, who appeared in ever-increasing numbers throughout the city. She had saved enough money to hire a contractor and make Leaf House more habitable for her four kids. If that benefitted Thuy and me, it was only incidental—and temporary. Que clearly thought life would be better for her children if we were out of the picture.

The job was to replace the leaf and bamboo walls with a two-story, cinderblock structure to better withstand the wind and rain. The inside would be stucco to make it cooler and look more attractive—not the plantation house, to be sure, but a lot better than before. Que was so happy with the idea that she paid us another visit and declared another dividend of candy and cash for her kids. We cousins were still left out, of course, but by now that was nothing new. What had changed was that her oldest daughter, Lien—about Thuy's age and now starting to notice what went on in the family—came to me while Que was in the kitchen and whispered, "Don't worry, I'll share my stuff with you." A lump came to my throat as my eyes began to water. I really didn't care about candy, and although we could always use money, cash was no substitute for caring. I had no idea why Aunt Que had suddenly turned against us, but fate seemed to compensate me a little by providing another sister.

Unfortunately, my good luck ended that same day.

While the cousins and Grandma took little Hoang out to play, Aunt Que came from the kitchen with two ropes. They were coarse and tough, like the kind of rope used to join the bamboo poles that supported our roof, so I never thought much about them—until now. Aunt Que carried them like whips.

"What are those for?" I asked cautiously.

"Nothing," Que said. "Just some old rope I need to test. It's for the remodeling. This will just take a minute. It won't hurt much."

Won't hurt much?

She told Thuy and me to stand on Grandma's bed just under the beam that supported the roof. She quickly tied the end of each rope around our wrists, then ran it up to our head. She looped each end a couple of times around our necks and tossed the rope over the beam. She then tugged the ends sharply, hoisting us off our feet.

We tried to scream, but the rope cut off our air. With workmanlike precision, Que tied the long end of the ropes to the legs of the bed, then stood back to admire her work. We twisted like gutted fish, silent tears streaming down our cheeks, but she just stared. She let out a grunt, or maybe a giggle, then untied the ends from the bed legs, and

Thuy and Van hanging from the rafter

we plopped onto the sleeping mat.

"Okay, not too bad, eh? Let's try something else—"

She freed our necks and our hands, then tied the rope to our ankles. We were too young or scared or stupid or trusting to kick or scream or punch when we had the chance. Before we knew it, the rope went tight again—and we were hung upside down like chickens for sale at the market.

"What have we done to make you so angry?" I asked through quivering lips. "Why...why...do you want to hurt us?"

"Oh, shush," she said flatly. "You're not going to die. Just be quiet. I'll be back."

With that, she left the house. Somehow, being alone without an adult—even a tormentor—scared Thuy worse than the ropes, so she started to wail. But crying kids were no novelty in our neighborhood. Between our cousins and kids screeching and playing outside and the sounds of traffic in the street, nobody heard us. I tried to pull myself up to untie my ankles, but didn't have the strength, so I flopped back. The more Thuy screamed, the more determined I was not to cry. I twisted until I glimpsed the front door, but Que had closed it behind her. Helplessly I twisted back. Inside, my terror turned to rage. For the first time, my six-year-old heart experienced hate, and I swore that Aunt Que would never again make me cry. Aloud I said, "When we grow up, no one will bully us. Don't cry anymore, sister…"

> *Quang grabs my hand, and we run as fast as we can around the outpost, hopping over bodies and debris calling, "Papa! Papa!" but there is no response. We return to Mama and Baby Sister on their mat, and she tells us to fetch the charcoal stove and a pot from Papa's hut. Following her instructions, I scoop up rice that's been scattered in the dirt as Quang fetches water from the river. We start a fire, and the pot begins to boil. "Put some rice-water in a bowl for me to drink," Mama says. "I need liquid to make milk for Baby Sister." Her shoulder is still oozing, and she's beginning to look like an old banana—dried out, discolored, bruised. Quang spoon-feeds her rice water when two baby-faced soldiers in black pajamas, straw hats, and thick rubber sandals appear at our little camp. These boy soldiers, though, have big knives on the end of their rifles. One kicks Quang away and tears open Mama's blouse. They expose one breast and then the other, laughing until they see the wound on her shoulder. "She's not going to make it," one says, then turns and pats my head. "Don't worry, little sister. Someone will find you." They disappear. Quang makes little fists and starts to throw the spoon at them, but Mama yells, "Stop."*

After hanging for what seemed like a long time—an hour? longer?—Grandma came through the door with Hoang. She saw us and froze. "Merciful God!" she cried, put Hoang down, and ran to the bed. She untied my ankles first, dropping me to her mat. "What's all this about? Who did this to you?" Thuy fell in a heap beside me. We rubbed our welted ankles as Grandma drew the ropes from the rafter. Before either of us could answer, Aunt Que came through the door.

Grandma glared at her angrily. "Did you do this?"

Que gave us a disgusted look and said nothing.

"Well," Grandma snapped, "God may forgive you for this, but I won't! This is just too much! Too much!"

Que retrieved her purse from our small shelf and headed back to the door. "Oh, calm down, old woman," she said as she passed. "They're not going to die." She left the house and called sweetly to her kids, "Good-bye! Be good for Grandma!"

Thuy finally stopped crying as Grandma inspected our wrists and necks. "Why did she do this?" she asked, incredulous as we were. "Did you make her angry?"

"We didn't do anything," I said woodenly. "She just doesn't like us." A pause. My new-found determination welled up in me and I blurted out, "And we don't like her."

"No, I don't guess you would," Grandma said, surprising me with her understanding. I half-expected a scold for talking disrespectfully about an adult.

If Aunt Que didn't like us—hated us enough to torture us—then she must have a reason. If she wanted to kill us, there were quicker, surer ways to do it, the way adults killed chickens and pigs. If she wanted to make us feel bad, she already knew how to do that, too—preferring her own kids over us to the point of humiliation. No. She had something else in mind. She wanted us to go. She wanted to terrorize us into running away or scare Grandma so badly that she found us another home or put us in an orphanage. That was the only explanation.

I looked at my sister and helped Grandma massage Thuy's white feet. Her breath came out in wet sobs. I resolved right then that while Grandma was a potent protector, the only person I could really count on was me.

Chapter 4

Stucco House—1967

If Grandma confronted Aunt Que or Uncle Chieu about our rope torture, we never heard about it. All Thuy and I knew was that Que stayed away from us (an easy thing to do since we avoided her like the plague). It eventually became another dark family secret that faded into nightmares.

Meanwhile, work to convert the Leaf House into cement and stucco began that summer, when I was about seven. The first story went up fast, but I guess Chieu and Que ran out of money. The second floor was raised only a few feet above the old roof line, then covered with corrugated tin. Uncle Chieu finished the tile floor himself, working under lamplight each night after his shift with the police. Eventually, we would have electricity, but no "juice" until the remodel was complete. Because it was new and better insulated, Chieu and Que decided that their kids would live and play on the second story while Grandma, Hoang, Thuy, and I slept and worked on the first floor, which now had a better kitchen. Chieu and Que must have reconciled, since they occasionally spent the night together in the upper loft, sending their kids down to the first floor to sleep with us. Although it was clear that the second floor was off limits to Thuy and me, we sometimes crept up the ladder to nap and chat with Lien and Ngoc, the two secret allies we now had in the "enemy's camp."

I must admit, the remodeled house was a big improvement. The stucco walls made the inside bearable even on the hottest days, and the blue-edged ceramic tiles were much cooler than dirt under our bare feet. The kitchen now had a big water tank we could tap from a faucet, although a tradesman still had to refill it using a siphon from the community well. All we lacked was an indoor toilet, so we still had to trudge a few blocks to the communal lavatory built out over the Saigon River.

The addition of electricity radically changed the way we spent our evenings, at least initially. As a reward for raising Hoang, Aunt Thu gave Grandma a small black-and-white TV. I had seen these miracle boxes a few times at other kids' houses and in store windows, but never dreamed we'd have one. Now we did, and it quickly became our family shrine, although its luster didn't last long. Even with wires in place, electric service to our house was spotty, and broadcasts were unreliable. Local programs like news, Chinese opera, and game shows made no sense to me, but all of us kids loved American television, especially *The Wild Wild West*, which caused Lien and me to fall instantly in love with Robert Conrad. On the evenings it worked, and if the antenna was arranged just so, our neighbors would gather at our windows and watch the glowing tube. This made Grandma feel like a princess again so she didn't mind the crowd, but occasionally *shushed* them if comments got too loud. We kids felt like local celebrities, and everything was fine until Grandma got her first electric bill at the end of the month. From then on, the TV stayed off unless Thu or other guests visited. But it was still a handy flat surface, another thing we had to dust.

After the time that our Leaf House was transformed into Stucco House, Grandma became ill with a flu virus. She was bedridden and wanting a bowl of pho (noodle soup), hoping it would restore her strength. I asked if I could go to the market and buy the soup for her, and at first she hesitated. Finally I convinced her that I could successfully carry out this very important task. She retrieved her handkerchief that held our household funds and gave me some coins. I got a large bowl from our kitchen and ran to the market. I stood in line at the local noodle shop for the soup, feeling very grown up to be permitted to carry out this mission for Grandma. Of course, I was hoping I might get a little, too. The broth for this traditional soup is kept boiling in a very large cooking pot all day long so it is always hot for customers. My turn came, I paid for the soup, my bowl was filled, and I turned around to leave the noodle shop.

Pho Accident

    I stepped out to the sidewalk, and a boy about my age struggling to ride an adult bicycle hit me and flipped the entire bowl of soup on my face. I screamed with pain and at the boy, all at the same time. The shop owner came outside, not to see to my injury, but to yell at me for my clumsiness. As for another bowl, of course not…"Bad luck, go home," said the woman, and I was shooed away from her door. I ran home to Grandma with the empty bowl in my hand and told her through my tears what had happened. Seeing me in such pain made her instantly well, and she jumped from her bed to see what could be done to help me. By now I was crying loudly and in a lot of pain. Of course, we had no medicine and a real doctor was out of the question, so Grandma went searching out neighbors for help. Soon she returned with ladies in tow, all with suggestions. No one had medicine, but someone suggested putting a cold knife blade on the affected areas to prevent blistering and scarring. And another woman suggested pouring fish sauce on my face. Grandma tried both of these remedies, but with little apparent success. Then the next morning, another neighbor came over to suggest that we burn some bamboo leaves and cover my face with the ashes. I have no idea where those home remedies came from, but none of them worked. On the third day after the incident, Truc's mother brought over an ointment from America. She said she borrowed the medicine from a lady she knew at the market. "American medicine is very good, should cure the pain," she said. Whether through God's grace, a combination of the treatments, or both, I cannot say but I suffered no permanent scarring, except for a small place on my cheek. I remember that my forehead, cheeks, and lips hurt badly, and I had bad blistering that took many days to abate.

§

That fall, Grandma enrolled cousin Ngoc and me in the local Catholic school in Phu Hai Parish. This was not my first adventure in education. At our Tile House in Go Vap, Mama had enrolled Quang in first grade at a nearby parochial school. Since I tagged along, the Mother Superior noticed me and said my age qualified me for pre-kindergarten. I was stunned, too stunned to speak. Until then, I thought only big girls went to school. Beside myself with joy, I grabbed Mama's hands and vigorously nodded. I was going to school! Quang saw things differently. He knew Mama would make us walk to and from school together, and that put him in charge of my behavior—not a job he relished.

Mama would poke us out of bed, then pour breakfast down our throats, usually hot bread dipped in condensed milk, but sometimes, on special occasions, sticky rice garnished with sugar, coconut, and toasted sesame seeds. She helped us into our uniforms which were white shirt and blue shorts for Quang, white blouse and blue pleated skirt for me. She then combed out my long black hair and tied it into one or two pony tails, depending on her mood. "My daughter has such silky black hair!" She cooed the words like a song and gently kissed the top of my head.

One time we'd just left our house when Quang stopped, saying we should ask Mama for snack money, which most other kids had but we seldom got.

"Mama will get mad," I protested, going by her reaction to past requests.

"Not if *you* ask her," Quang said. "She always gives you what you want. You do it!"

"What if she says no?"

"Then throw a tantrum. Roll on the floor. Tell her if she doesn't give us some money, we won't go to school. Go on. What can she do about it?"

We found out.

Mama turned beet red and grabbed the bamboo switch she usually reserved for Quang after one of his pranks. I barely beat her out the door.

Quang saw instantly what had happened and began putting distance between himself and Mama's switch. I poured on the coals, but Mama was closer to me than to Quang and caught me with the tip. It stung, and I started to cry for real, but she kept after Quang and swatted him at least once before we reached the school gate. She wasn't about to take on Jesus, though, so she stopped.

When Quang and I met outside the gate at mid-day to walk home, he apologized for getting us in trouble. I told him to get lost. He then reminded me that if we didn't go home together, as Mama instructed, we'd get in even more trouble, and I had to agree. So Quang walked, and I sulked a few feet behind him, kicking up dirt. When we got home, Mama had lunch on the table and was humming a little tune as if nothing had happened. I guessed we weren't such bad kids after all. Even Quang was sorry when the school year ended, with or without our snacks.

Now, I was seven and Ngoc, eight. I started off in first grade and he in second. Although I knew I wasn't stupid, my aptitude for schoolwork surprised even our neighbors, and the daily hazing about *stupid orphans* began to slow, especially the following year when I entered second grade and little kid songs, crafts, naps, and playtime gave way to reading, writing, and arithmetic. I was determined to prove my worth to others in spite of my "orphan" status, and my little successes in school began to be noticed by my peers.

Although Phu Hai was a poor parish, Catholic schools got funding from both the church and private donations. As a result, we had perks unavailable to students at government schools. First, we got to wear uniforms that set us apart from public school kids. Textbooks were rare, but at least we had a few, although these were for classroom use only. Each school day was pretty much the same: half the students went to class in the morning, the other half after lunch. We arranged ourselves on benches behind long tables and copied lessons written on the board by our teacher. We learned by rote and repetition, and by competing in recitations before the class, winning applause and small prizes as if we were verbal gladiators. We'd learned from infancy to revere education and respect anyone who could master facts and figures. Those of us who took school seriously began to see our lives in a different light.

One of the good things about going to school with Ngoc was spending afternoons in the upstairs loft reading Vietnamese comic books the "big kids" circulated among themselves. His favorites were detective and ghost stories, so I cut my teeth on those. I was pretty good at sounding out words and getting the story from the drawings, but it never occurred to me that the two of them went together. One day, when Ngoc laughed uproariously over a cartoon I'd never seen, I asked what was so funny.

"Here, String Bean." He passed the folded-back page to me. "Read it out loud, one sentence at a time, and pretend the guy in the picture is saying it."

I did, then burst out laughing. I got it! Words could mean something besides themselves, and that knowledge took my breath away. After that, I gobbled up every comic Ngoc brought home as if it were holiday candy. A new, imaginary world had opened up for me—and it was one that did not have *Monsters*.

§

Near the end of second grade, one day, Grandma met me with a solemn expression at the Stucco House door. This was unusual, since she was typically making lunch when I got home and the pre-school cousins were either bouncing off the walls or clinging to her legs, like Thuy. Something important was happening.

Without saying a word, she knelt and removed the small black patch above the pocket of my blouse. Looking down at me, she announced, "It's been three years. That's long enough. You don't need this anymore. Do you know what that means?"

"That Mama is home from market?"

She continued to stare down at me, saying nothing. I felt heat rise to my cheeks. My eyes began to water, but I did not cry. The time for crying was over. I closed my eyes tightly, squeezing them as if to test my resolve.

"That Mama is not coming home from market?"

"What else?"

My mind raced through blurry nightmares and daytime terrors, and although I knew the words she wanted to hear, I was afraid to say them.

"What else?" Grandma persisted.

"That Papa...that Papa..." I could not bear to say it, but her face was unyielding and expectant. "That Papa is not coming home either?" New images danced in the darkness.

Quietly, she took me in her arms, pushed my head to her shoulder, and cried. I cried in my heart. I had known for a long time, and Grandma had never realized it. I learned it in school when other children made fun of me and called me a stupid orphan. I learned it from Truc, when she confronted me about the black patch and told me what it was for. I learned it—I knew it—when I remembered Hong Ngu.

> *...the sandy bunker covered with half-coconuts; Papa's smiling face when he greeted Mama, Baby Sister, Quang and me at the gate to his doomed outpost; his sweaty, anxious face as he and his soldiers dug the final trenches that became their graves; the awful black night of bombs and bullets and Mama's bloody shoulder; the gray dawn when I stumbled onto a dead man's chest with the severed head grinning back at me; the Viet Cong boys rounding up survivors and "making trouble"—shaming and degrading our mother; the wiry policeman with his pad who discovered Quang and me cowering by Mama's blood-soaked mat, still suckling Baby Sister; going with the policeman to the Red Cross aid station, then to the policeman's house where we spend the night and his mother took Quang's loop of rings; our lonely bus trip to Saigon and return with Grandma and Aunt Thu to tell Mama good-bye and ride with her to the Isle of the Dead in our flat-bottomed boats; the lumpy reed mat eased into a shallow grave over which Grandma, Aunt Thu, and Quang cried; the scrawny cross Quang and I made to mark our mother's resting place...*

I do not know how long I knew it for a certainty, but saying it that day to Grandma was the first time I said the sad words aloud.

Yes, Grandma, I know it has been long enough.

§

Without my black patch of mourning, such visions melted into a new way of life. A few days later, the postman delivered a letter addressed to Vu Mau—Grandma's name outside the family. Of course, she couldn't read it, so, to her great surprise, I volunteered. Her surprise surprised me. What did she think I learned at school?

At her request, I tore open the envelope and announced, "It's from Uncle Hai!" which excited me even more because as a Navy man, I suspected Hai kept track of Uncle Thanh and his whereabouts with the Army, which meant we might finally have more news of Quang and Baby Sister.

"Uncle Hai says that after a year at sea, his ship will dock in Saigon at Bach Dang pier at the end of the month. He wants to come for a visit, and since he knows I'm a big girl now, he wants to see me in a big girl's dress and take me shopping at Ben Thanh market. He says if I don't have money for a new dress, to ask Aunt Thu since he says she's made lots of money working for the Americans. Oh, please, Grandma. May I write to Aunt Thu and ask her for a new dress?"

We already knew Aunt Thu was doing well because she sent money for Hoang more often. Grandma hesitated to ask her for more, especially for something so frivolous as a new dress, but considering all that I'd been through in the last few years, I guess she thought fate owed me a favor.

Whatever the reason, Grandma gave me permission to write a short letter, which I did that very day. Within a week Thu wired some money—not a lot but enough for some new clothes. Instead of a dress, though, Grandma bought me a new school uniform, which I sorely needed, and made sure it was one size too big so that I could grow into it and postpone needing another. With the remains of Aunt Thu's gift, she also bought me a small pair of earrings to commemorate my first communion—solid gold with dangly blue stones that I picked out myself! I put them on at the market and vowed to never take them off. I didn't say it aloud, but I knew my mother would've been proud.

At the end of the month, Uncle Hai pulled up to Stucco House on a new blue Vespa wearing his sparkling white sailor suit, complete with black-visor service cap, epaulettes, red shoulder rope, and a line of ribbons on his chest. Because we didn't know exactly when he was coming, I was still in my play clothes when I ran to hug him, but he held up a hand like a policeman.

"Whoa! Not so fast!" He grinned. "You'll get my uniform dirty!"

I stopped, bounced up and down giggling, then ran back inside to put on my new blouse and skirt while Grandma talked to her son. When I came out, he started the scooter, and I stood on the floor-board in front of him as we buzzed off toward Ben Thanh market.

To be honest, I never really knew why Uncle Hai was so keen to take me shopping. After all, I wasn't his kid, and he was a handsome bachelor—why did he need a little pipsqueak like me to cramp his style? When we got to the market, though, I found out. His good looks and sharp uniform were enough of a lady magnet by themselves, but with me in tow, all cleaned up and dressed up, he looked like every woman's dream: a man with a job who liked kids. Female customers and shop girls struck up conversations with him about his "beautiful little girl," which gave him

*The reason why Uncle Hai's uniform is so white is because
I was not allowed to touch it*

an opening to say, "Yes, she's my daughter" if the lady didn't interest him, or "Oh, she's just my niece" if the woman looked cute and available. It was for good reasons that Grandma always thought Uncle Hai was the sharpest businessman in the family!

But our family's "Navy man" had another boon to bestow. Grandma had enrolled me in grade school under my father's name, so I was registered as Nguyen Thi Hien. However, all records of my birth had been lost after Hong Ngu, I had no way to prove when and where and to whom I'd been born, and that could one day prove a problem—and the same was true for Thuy. So Uncle Hai decided we needed new birth certificates, and since they would be blank slates, we could fill them out any way we wished. Hai came up with new names which I must admit sounded better than the old. I became "Do Thi Bich Van," or "Bich Van" for short, which meant *Jade Cloud*. My sister kept most of her old name but became "Do Thi Bich Thuy, or *Jade Ocean*, perhaps to honor our uncle's love of the sea. At any rate, we girls now had "city names" befitting two future Saigon heartbreakers and were no longer saddled by names that tagged us as dreary Northerners, a Saigon synonym for "country bumpkins." I loved my new name and started using it immediately.

Of course, all this attention—new clothes, new jewelry, new name, and the kindly attention of a worldly man like Uncle Hai—made me feel very grown-up, even though I was only about seven. When Aunt Thu came to show Hoang to her new boyfriend, a tall American soldier a little older than she was, I noticed how handsome he was—the first time such things registered in my life. She told me his name, but it was so hard to pronounce that I instantly forgot it, preferring instead to simply call him "GI" or "Mr. GI" like the other neighborhood kids. This American, like his brothers-in-arms who came to our street, was kind and generous and had bottomless pockets filled with candy or small coins that he dispensed liberally to us kids, creating an instant posse.

However, due to my attentiveness to Hoang, he apparently viewed me as something of a "little sister" to Aunt Thu and was therefore entitled to a special treat. After distributing sweets to everyone else, he gave me a big bag of M&Ms chocolate-covered peanuts. These were great because in addition to the rarity of chocolate (especially the kind that didn't melt in tropical heat!) each candy contained a luscious peanut—a real delicacy in Asian cooking. I took it reverentially and thanked him in the broken English I was slowly learning. When the other kids ran out to play and Thu and her GI said good-bye to Hoang and Grandma, I was left on the bed with my treasure. I tore off a small corner and tapped some candies onto my palm. I popped one into my mouth, but I just couldn't bring myself to empty the bag the way the other kids had emptied theirs. Instead, I began to think like Uncle Hai.

What do I need more than a bag of candy? If I gobble it down right away, I will just have a stomach ache and be back where I started. No. There must be a better way to use my nest egg.

I went to our kitchen and got a wooden bowl and two stools. I then went into the street in front of our house and set up shop: me on one stool, the bowl—now filled with the entire package of M&Ms—on the other.

Naturally, every kid on the block swarmed around me, asking for handouts. I gave my cousins, sister, and, of course, my best friend Truc, free samples but told everyone else they would have to pay one *dong* for each piece. This shut them up for a minute, but their eyes were as big as the

The M & M Merchant

candy bowl. Those kids, who did not have ready cash, went home to get some—and my store was open. One boy in Ngoc's class asked if he could buy two M&Ms for the "same price". I said, "Sure, you can have two M&Ms for two dong!" He thought for a few seconds, then forked over the coins. The dish was cleaned out in an hour. I took my profit to Grandma and asked her to keep it safe, as she was in charge of family finances. I really had no place to put money except in the pocket of my blouse, which didn't seem like a good idea.

Grandma praised me for being "a sharp cookie" and put my cash in a screw-top jar high on our kitchen shelf. I felt more than happy. I felt rich, and I didn't touch a single coin for what seemed like forever. At seven, I was now a successful business woman as well as a nanny for Hoang, a scholar in second grade, and a part-time chick magnet for Uncle Hai. I knew I would have to behave responsibly. A week later, though, I helped myself to a few bills and bought a folding paper fan for Grandma and a few rice cookies for us kids as an after-dinner treat. I can't say which thrilled me more: the clever way I earned the cash or the happiness I gave my family when I spent it, but I do know that I never looked at money in quite the same way again.

§

By late 1967, other changes were in the wind. Aunt Thu brought another American boyfriend to visit, only this time a much older man—not a G.I. but a civilian contractor. "Alvin Strauss" was how Thu introduced him, and he seemed like a nice person. This turned out to be important since Aunt Thu announced in her next breath that they were engaged.

Now, as a good student and successful entrepreneur, I thought I knew something about people. Although Uncle Hai sometimes used me as conversation-starter when trolling for dates, I knew other types of people didn't take kindly to kids who were not their own. Aunt Que was an example of that. I had seen the look of quiet desperation that crossed the faces of other men when Aunt Thu introduced them to her fatherless son—and the curse of *stupid orphan* still rang in my ears. Still, this cagey-eyed, wiry older man with his thinning hair and pencil moustache didn't seem fazed by little Hoang or the other kids that hovered around him. He took a particular shine to me and sister Thuy, maybe because of the special kindness Aunt Thu had shown us. You'd also think that a little smarty pants like me would know that nothing good can last forever.

CHAPTER 5

TSUNAMI—1968

The year 1968 started with a bang. Tet, the lunar New Year, was upon us—Vietnam's biggest national holiday. It was a time of fireworks, big meals, and family visits. Grandma had hopes, as all mothers do, of seeing her surviving children all at one time, all in one place, and all having been around for at least another year.

We kids had a special reason to love Tet, especially this one, because we had not had the means to appropriately celebrate the holiday for several years. On the first day, we got new clothes and a traditional "Red Envelope" bearing cash—always in short supply. When received this way, it came with special permission for a little wasteful spending, perhaps on candy, toys, or jewelry. This was an especially good year, too, because of Aunt Thu's marriage to the American contractor, Al, and promotions for Uncle Hai in the Navy, Uncle Thanh in the Army, and our long-suffering Uncle Chieu with the police. The only thing I needed for a perfect holiday was the reunion of Thuy and me with our brother Quang and Baby Sister. After all, it was Tet. Miracles were possible.

Unfortunately, what happened next was anything but miraculous.

About three in the morning of the night we got our Red Envelopes, everyone in the Stucco House was awakened by the sound of distant fireworks. This was a breach of etiquette, since fireworks usually ended in the afternoon or right after dinner so that extended families could visit and get a good sleep after their big meal and get ready for the next day's parties. Not tonight.

Thuy and I awoke with big eyes. The distant crackle was now very close thunder, and we felt the house shudder and shake. Dust rained down from the ceiling as pots and dishes tumbled from the shelves. Grandma was out from her mosquito net—bigger things were about to eat us!—and gathered all the kids into the center of the room away from the walls. Lightning flashed orange outside the windows.

After what seemed like forever, black night gave way to dawn, but the storm outside got louder. By the time the sun came up, the fighting was on our street, with heavy explosions. Men running, shouting, shooting. Dying men only yards away. Rattling gunfire came closer still while the explosions banged our shutters open and closed. Big vehicles we'd never heard before raced up and down the street beyond our neighborhood alleys with roaring engines and grinding gears. Thick smoke, acrid and burning, filled the air and seeped into our little house.

Grandma could do nothing but press us closer to the tiles and squeeze us tighter under her bed, but I was seized by a desire to look out. I had defeated *The Monster* that chased me after Hong Ngu; maybe I could also defeat this one. I only knew that I could not bear to see Grandma like Mama, with a hole in her shoulder, or see Thuy or Lien or Ngoc emerge from our shelter carrying little Hoang, his body slick with blood like Baby Sister. This was one Monster I had to meet with open eyes.

I skittered across the floor and punched the front door open. Sunrise blanketed the neighboring houses across the street while dark shapes ran to and from More staccato bursts. More concussion. Cracking wood and raining dirt. Groans and screams. Orders and curses. Then silence. Acrid smoke billowed through our door, and I dropped low until it passed.

I had no idea of what to do other than to yell at both sides that there was no enemy in this house. *The war you want is someplace else!* But my little mouth was speechless.

The ominous silence got deeper. I heard Grandma and the other kids sobbing and probably I was, too, but instead of crawling under the bed, I crawled outside when Grandma's back was briefly turned. I saw soldiers in green uniforms and soldiers in black pajamas disappear down alleys and into the smoke. I could see no "papa-man" in charge, and I doubted if even God Himself directed anyone but me. Some of the soldiers passed; some paused and crouched; some looked around with terrified faces. Certainly

Tet Offensive, fought at our front door (1968)

there was more purpose in the action than the chaos I was witnessing. But in my own brief observations of a real battle, I could not have known that this was exactly what the battle for Saigon was all about...back and forth, street after street, house to house, until the Viet Cong and the North Vietnamese soldiers retreated from the city.

More explosions on other blocks. More thunder and running feet. I pressed back against the house.

Now, a few yards away, two soldiers confronted each other, as if in one of our school plays about mythic warriors. They slammed together like wrestlers, and I had no idea if the gunshots and flashes of steel were theirs or more bits of metal stinging the walls. They grunted and punched and rolled on the ground, then found their feet. For some reason, they both looked at me, and I stared back. I was not afraid. I had no feeling regarding the possibility of death. With the scene of the soldiers playing out in front of me, I was curious and merely wanted to understand what their battle was all about. What would happen if one of them actually got shot or stabbed? I was beginning to make a connection between what I was witnessing here and what I had seen at Hong Ngu when I first saw dead bodies. I had even stepped on one. Back then, after we got out of the bunker, Quang and I became prisoners. Three VC stood as our guards.

There were several surviving South Vietnamese soldiers down on their knees against the barbwire fence and some families in a separate group against the wall of our Father's hut. A crying woman sat next to me cradling a baby that was quiet and whose head was rolling about. She kept trying to shake the baby awake, but there was no response. She stood up, and in a hysterical, crazed manner, she kept running back and forth between the two groups. The Viet Cong soldiers screamed at her to get down on her knees. But she ignored them. Then, she was pushed toward other survivors along the fence. She collapsed and then tripped over the severed head that I saw earlier. I remember seeing her fall to the ground, and then, a very large explosion. She must have fell upon and set off some kind of unexploded ordnance, perhaps a grenade or land mine. The explosion killed everyone in that far group by the fence including one of the three VC guards and knocked me and everyone else over. Shrapnel flew everywhere, and one piece of metal struck Quang's throat, leaving a scar that is with him today. I had seen live bodies become dead ones, although I lacked the understanding to "connect the dots." Now, as I watched the two soldiers, I was beginning to understand what had gone on during that long awful night of fighting at Hong Ngu...

I heard Grandma call my name from inside the house. I ignored her, knowing that if she found me outside I would be in big trouble. But then one of my cousins ratted me out. The next thing I knew, a hand grabbed the back of my shirt and I was flying through the air into the house. I landed hard on the polished tile floor and slid across the living area, crashing in a little pile against the far wall. The door slammed shut, and the war disappeared. Grandma loomed over me with a face just like the soldiers'— terrified and determined.

"You stupid baby! Are you *trying* to get killed?" She pointed. "Get back under the bed and do it now!"

Grandma had never raised a hand to me before, and her throwing me across the room frightened me more than the battle. Bullets and steel fragments continued to slam into our house—now thankfully cement— leaving only a few holes. Still, the tsunami raged outside our door.

The cousins and sister Thuy made room for me under the bed. Little Hoang screeched like a monkey for his mama, then quieted down when he saw me, but my mouth was open, frozen in a silent scream.

Gradually, the raining steel and boiling smoke moved on, turned to distant thunder, and then was gone. After a long wait to make sure the coast was clear, we crawled out from under the bed. Everything was covered in dust. Half the beautiful floor tiles were broken and mysterious chunks and gouges had appeared in our walls and ceiling. Broken dishes covered the floor. Like groggy hosts of a too-long party, we started to clean up.

After an hour, our neighbors began to creep outdoors, and so did we. I went first since I knew what mangled bodies looked like and wouldn't be upset like Thuy and Lien would be. Grandma seemed to respect my veteran status so she let me reconnoiter on my own. The biggest surprise was the two dead soldiers lying by our front door. They were not there when Grandma yanked me inside. I had no idea where they came from unless they were the two soldiers I saw fighting their private battle. Their faces were bloody but oddly at peace. Their mothers would have recognized them. Many other bodies lay strewn across the street, their blood splattered everywhere on the sidewalks and walls, pooling like rusty rainwater in the street. Their weapons lay either next to them or a short distance away. The scene was horrific, but frankly, the butcher's yard at Hong Ngu had been worse. Although it was mid-morning, the thick haze that hung in the air made it seem like twilight. The ascending sun was a flat red disk. Along with the acrid smoke, I smelled—what? I'd been around slaughtered pigs and chickens and ducks many times, but this smelled nothing like that. I guessed it was how people smelled when you turned them inside out and mixed in gunpowder, sweat, and fear. I realized it was the smell of Death. I went back inside just as Grandma ventured out.

"Stay inside now," she said to me the way Papa used to command his men. "Keep *them* inside, too."

I had no idea how I would stop cousin Ngoc if he decided to leave, perhaps to find his parents, but Grandma seemed to think I had that control. I followed her orders, and while the cousins cleaned up the house, I watched from the window as Grandma helped the neighbors clear the street of weapons and bodies. Nobody seemed to know or care which soldier was which, who was a troublemaker from the North or who was a freedom-fighter from the South. They all wore the same red uniform, and none of them complained.

Chapter 6

Flotsam and Jetsam—1968

L ike a typhoon, the Tet Offensive left eerie quiet in its wake.

From bits and pieces I heard from Grandma, Aunt Thu, Uncle Chieu, and neighbors, the Viet Cong and North Vietnamese Army regulars had hurled themselves at a hundred targets throughout our country in one massive effort to win the war. They beat themselves bloody against our bulwarks, succeeded in taking a few towns and villages, but they were forced out in the days and weeks that followed—especially once the Americans cranked up their awesome war machines. While our soldiers and politicians counted the battle of Tet as a great Southern victory, especially devastating to the VC, "Uncle Al" (as we now called him) wasn't so sure. Americans in Vietnam were surprised by the scope and ferocity of an attack by an enemy they thought they had on the ropes. While our government issued proclamations of joy and declared holidays to honor our brave soldiers, Western journalists published harrowing accounts of close-quarter fighting and warned their respective nations that while the South may not have lost as Hanoi predicted, the outcome of the war was now far from certain.

Still, like people after any catastrophe, our neighbors in the Phu Nhuan

Parish did their best to get everything back to normal. One of these signs of normalcy was Quang returning to live with Thuy and me, though it happened in an abnormal way.

It was no secret that Quang didn't like his guardians, and nobody had seen Baby Sister for a very, very long time. Grandma never spoke of it. Quang was tight-lipped, too, but he finally had a big falling out with Uncle Thanh and "princess" Lan over something horrible and came again to our house. This time, when Uncle Thanh arrived in his jeep to retrieve him, Quang climbed on to our tin roof and vowed to jump if Thanh came near him. He had obviously confided in Ngoc because our favorite cousin climbed up with him and warned the adults to keep away. This was astonishing. Not only was it unheard of for kids to defy their elders, but the Quang I knew seldom lost his temper about anything—and when he did, got over it quickly. Not this time. Thanh called up threats and Grandma begged, but neither boy gave in. Finally, Uncle Thanh threw up his hands and drove away. Quang never went back, and Thanh never again tried to fetch him.

Quang and cousin Ngoc, Quang's mutiny on the roof of Stucco House

However terrible this breakup had been for Quang, it was a godsend for Thuy and me—and, I think, for Grandma and Ngoc as well. We made a special meal to welcome Quang to the Stucco House, crowned by an unexpected announcement by Aunt Thu that she and Uncle Al had legally adopted us into their family. This was good news for many reasons.

First, it meant that Quang, Thuy, and I were no longer classified as *orphans* and so were spared the curses and dirty looks we occasionally got in the streets.

Second, it meant that we would eventually move out of the Stucco House, giving Grandma and our cousins extra room to live and to grow. I would miss daily contact with Grandma, who had taught me so much about life and living. I would always respect her as the one person who was willing to sacrifice her own life to nurture mine. But my new residence would be a modern apartment in a neighboring town, and while not as grand as the plantation mansion, was a palace compared to a Saigon slum. I could be nothing but grateful for that.

Finally, and maybe best of all, Al and Thu were adopting Hoang, Aunt Thu's fatherless son. He was now an energetic, curious toddler and the cutest, funniest little kid on the block who was finally getting the full-time mom he deserved. Now that I knew I would continue to share my roof with my honorary "younger brother," I considered our extended family complete. Except for our missing Baby Sister, we were as reunited as any wartime family had a right to expect.

§

Not long after these big doings, Aunt Thu revealed the reason for them. Al loved Vietnam and, like most Americans, was shocked and saddened by the Tet Offensive. He worked closely with military and civilian officials and had reluctantly concluded that conditions in the country would get worse before they got better. As a result, he decided to move his household to the Philippines as soon as he finished his contract in Vietnam. The only fly in the ointment was just who that household would contain, at least at first. Al and Thu and Hoang were the core of the new family, but Quang was a question mark because of his problems with Uncle Thanh—who wanted a "problem" child? That left me and Thuy. Since Hoang already regarded me as a big sister and I had spent way more time caring for him than his natural mother, I was an obvious choice to continue on as nanny. Quang and Thuy, though officially Al's dependents, would remain with Grandma until he could make other arrangements. This plan was disappointing, but as Aunt Thu said, a banquet isn't cooked in an hour, so we accepted it. Actually, I think Thu was worried that once little Hoang left familiar faces and places, he would reject his new parents and cry inconsolably. I was Aunt Thu's safety net, and we would begin testing her theory with my move to their apartment in Quy Nhon.

To cement this new bond between Al and his "instant" family, the head of our new household gave Hoang and me new names.

Al informally christened Hoang "Bubba"—a term of endearment, he claimed, from the United States that meant "little brother" or "good guy"—terms that fit Hoang perfectly as far as I was concerned.

For me he came up with the nickname "Sissy," which was short for "Sister" and long for "Sis." I was not quite as thrilled with my new name as with Hoang's because I liked Van, the name Uncle Hai had given me. Still, I was now part of Al's family, and a parent can name a child anything he wants. I could think of a lot worse things to be called than *sister*, and "orphan" was at the top of the list!

Sissy it would be.

§

While I prepared to depart for Quy Nhon where Al had to finish his contract, I spent as much time as I could with Quang, trying to recapture in a few weeks that sense of brother and sister that had been thinned by our separation.

"You remember that time you came to Leaf House all worried about Baby Sister?" I asked. "And we all went to Uncle Thanh's house the next day?"

Quang put on a guarded face. "What about it?"

"Grandma never told me *why* Baby Sister was given up for adoption to a wealthy family. Do you know why?"

"Because Aunt Lan just had her own baby girl. She didn't want to take care of another girl who belonged to her dead brother-in-law—"

"That's not true!" I snapped. "Nobody knows if Papa is dead! We just couldn't find him, that's all!"

Quang shook his head. "It doesn't matter. Dead. A VC prisoner. Aunt Lan didn't care. She hated us, always threatened to send us to an orphanage. And Uncle Thanh couldn't do anything about it."

"That still doesn't mean Baby Sister wasn't adopted," I said stubbornly.

Quang just stared at me, his eyes blank.

A horrible thought came to my mind. "So you think Baby Sister...was killed?" I could hardly speak the words.

"I don't know. I just think that if Baby Sister had been adopted, Uncle Thanh would've shown Grandma the papers." Quang swept aside the lock of black hair that perpetually covered his forehead. "See this scar? Do you remember when Uncle Thanh brought me to Leaf House with that bandage?"

I squinted to get a closer look. "Yes."

"You won't believe how I got it. Uncle Thanh's family keeps chickens behind their house. One day Aunt Lan noticed that some were missing. She blamed me for stealing them or leaving the coop open. I tried to tell her it

Shoe heel to the forehead—Quang's punishment for missing chickens

wasn't my fault—some of the posts and wires were loose—but she wouldn't listen. She yelled at me, 'You little thief! You're a waste of space!' I started to argue, and she got so mad she pulled off one of her high-heeled shoes and hit me on the forehead with the spike, just like a hammer. Then her face got real white, and she stepped back. It hurt a lot, and I knew something was wrong and ran screaming to my sleep mat just as Uncle Thanh got home. He saw me and gasped. The heel of the shoe was still stuck in my forehead! There was blood all over my face! He bawled out Lan, but she just got madder. She said, 'Let him die! He's useless! He causes trouble and costs money!'"

I was horrified. "So what did Uncle Thanh do?"

"He pulled out the shoe and drove me to the clinic. The nurse asked me what happened while she put on a bandage, but Uncle Thanh said something like, 'Oh, you know kids!' That's when I had to leave. I was afraid to go back until Aunt Lan cooled off."

"Okay, so if they killed Baby Sister," I asked, "why didn't they kill you?"

Quang shrugged. "I don't know. I guess because I'm a boy."

Beyond his painful encounter with Aunt Lan's shoe, Quang spoke little about his time away from us. He said that for extra money, he did chores for a neighbor family, and that they always fed him when they could because they could tell that Aunt Lan was not feeding him properly. All of the household chores were his responsibility, along with the chickens. After school and mandatory chores, he and his friends went door to door to purchase glass bottles, paper and scrap metal for extra money. Sometimes they dug through trash piles and dumpsters for junk proper for recycling, items that Aunt Lan would re-sell to scrap vendors. He knew not to come home with empty hands from his foraging expeditions or he would be beaten and cursed for being "lazy and irresponsible." Quang was lucky that his junking was in the city. Many young Vietnamese children were doing the same thing in the countryside. Many times the "metal" they found turned out to be unexploded shells, or even mines, and the consequences for these children was often tragic.

Quang's terrible abuse at the hands of Aunt Lan reminded me of how Aunt Que had hung Thuy and me up by our ankles. Other children may have called us names, but our greatest tormentors had been "family." I was glad Quang was free of Aunt Lan now. These all too common experiences as orphans gave Quang, Thuy, and me a bond that went beyond being brother and sisters.

Chapter 7

Chasing the Moon—1968

Aunt Thu ran into trouble getting us adoption papers. She had already obtained new birth certificates for Thuy and me reflecting our city-girl "Jade names." The magistrate at the Special Court in Saigon set up for such matters thought that things should end there. He referred her to the court's clerk, who was more understanding, especially when he found out that Thu, like Grandma, was functionally illiterate. She had no idea of what to do with all the bureaucratic red tape.

"Why don't you just declare yourself the natural mother of all the children you want to adopt?" he asked reasonably. "The three older kids have no parents and the toddler is half yours. Pick some birthdays that seem close to their ages, and you'll be on your way."

This was a good suggestion. One by one the proper documents got produced, filled out, and signed—although this involved another name change, the third I had experienced so far in my young life. Discovering I was a better reader than Aunt Thu, I examined the certificates when she brought them to Quy Nhon. The document affirmed my parents were now "Mr. Alvin Ambrose Strauss and Mrs. Do Thi Hien Hue," which was part of the plan. My name appeared as "Thi Bich Van Strauss" which made me sound like a European composer, but at least I kept part of my city-girl name. Hoang became "Van-Hoang Strauss" so everybody on the team still recognized everyone else. Al continued to call us Sissy and Bubba. For some reason, although Aunt Thu was now officially our mother, Al's name was left off Thuy's and Quang's certificate. Don't ask me why.

My adopted parents Uncle Al, my mother's sister, Aunt Thu, and her son little Bubba and me

§

Quy Nhon was a nice suburb on the edge of the big American air base where Al worked. We lived in a small apartment attached to the front of a home owned by a well-off Vietnamese family. Though small, it gave each person more space than we'd had in the Stucco House and was furnished in Western fashion, with indoor plumbing, sturdy furniture, and a well-stocked kitchen. Aunt Thu wasted no time introducing me to my main duty which was taking care of Hoang. It meant I would have to quit school, which was disheartening and a little surprising. You'd think that after all the trouble Thu and Grandma had due to a lack of education, she'd make sure the next generation of our "sisterhood" got a better break, but that was not the way she reasoned. Now she had a husband—and a well-off American husband to boot (all Americans were "well-off" as far as we were concerned)—so for her it was back to traditional ways. Those traditional ways included being a good mother and the official reason she gave for quitting her job. But time soon showed that the part about being a good mother had been dropped from her script. In reality, except for the part about missing school, I didn't mind. I already thought of Hoang as my little brother, and if I was going to be his primary caretaker, I at least had a better place to do it.

Bubba was a chubby, pleasant-natured little boy for the most part, but he had his annoying little quirks. My most vivid and unpleasant memory was Bubba's terrible "habit" of going to the bathroom right at mealtime, and he would not leave the dining area in order to do so. He insisted on staying right where he was, next to the table, until his potty business was finished.

As awful as it sounds, Aunt Thu and Al tolerated this, even thought it was cute and endearing. After Bubba finished his mealtime ritual in a chamber bucket provided for his convenience, the cleanup was my duty. It is amazing what one can get used to. Since Aunt Thu and Al were very good to me and treated me well, I didn't complain. My duties were light, I had a few more clothes to wear. I wasn't hungry all the time, and no one was shooting at me, but I was lonely. However, I knew that I was much better off than most of the ever-growing population of Vietnamese orphans.

Bubba on potty

Over the next few months, we entertained a variety of visitors from the base, and I learned a lot about Al. He was an Area Engineer and Maintenance Supervisor for the local American and Vietnamese forces, an important, well-paying job that required him to travel a lot. He always had cars and helicopters at his disposal, and he once took us up in a Chinook (a big U.S. Army helicopter with two engines). That gave me my first look at my homeland from the air, a sight I couldn't believe! I also learned that he was a *lot* older than Aunt Thu—by over twenty years. He had adult children from a prior marriage back in the States, including a son named Eddie, who was Aunt Thu's age. I learned about all this when Eddie's wife sent us a parcel filled with American stuff, including new clothes for us kids. When it came, I was the only one at home who could read the note.

Although I dearly missed my family from the Stucco House, I became good friends with our landlord's daughter, a pretty girl slightly older than me. I called her "Chi," or "Older Sister." We went to market together, worked hard at ignoring the boys (at least when they were looking at us), and did all kinds of "girl things," like brushing each other's hair and trading clothes. Most of all, my new friend was a schoolgirl who enjoyed her classes and shared her passion for books with me.

One of her greatest loves was the famous Vietnamese poet, Han Mac Tu, who had died of leprosy before he was thirty. His work emerged in Vietnamese poetry during the 1920s and '30s, the broken-hearted voice of a young man doomed by his incurable disease, and whose nearby tomb we once visited. His too-short life, like mine, had been punctuated by bitter loss. In his case a young woman he loved but whom he would not live long enough to marry. He hoped instead to encounter her again in another life, and a lot of his poems dealt with that—fate and hope filled with unfulfillable longing. I was captivated by his work, by the beauty of his words, which spoke to my own heartache, to my own grief and terrible losses, to my very soul. His verses poured over me like water on a wilting flower. Chi and I read many of them aloud, words that held more meaning than any song we heard on the radio.

One of my favorites started like this:

> *Who can buy the moon? The moon is for sale.*
> *The moon lies quiet on the willows, waiting, waiting.*
> *Who wants to buy the moon? My moon is for sale.*
> *But my love is not. It has no price.*

These lines and others echoed the heartaches in my own life, the sense of loneliness I felt even in the middle of big cities and big families, where people worried about everything but me. The things that mattered most to me were usually gone before I knew it.

Aunt Thu, Sissy (Van) and Bubba (Hoang)

By mid-summer, 1968, Al had tied up the loose ends on his job and put our move to the Philippines on the front burner. Our destination was San Pedro Cutud, a small village whose old Catholic church and annual re-enactment of the Passion of the Christ were local tourist attractions. It was near a larger town, San Fernando, about sixty miles northwest of Manila, which was itself adjacent to Clark Air Force Base, one of America's biggest military installations in the Pacific. While I understood Al's desire to find a safer place to live, I couldn't see why he'd trade one jungle for another, especially since all of Aunt Thu's friends and relatives lived in Vietnam, where he was guaranteed a good job and a big paycheck for the foreseeable future. But my new "father figure" was pursuing a long-held dream. Decades before, when he served in the U.S. Navy, Al worked as a ship's cook, progressing to Master Chef. He knew good food and how to supervise workers, and could be very cordial to strangers—an important skill for anyone in the hospitality business. He planned to operate an upscale restaurant and make a fortune.

So off we went—Mr. and Mrs. Strauss and their two kids, Sissy and Bubba.

Although it was my first time away from Vietnam, the Philippines held few surprises. The people still looked Asian enough for me to feel at home (although their language was confusing), and the terrain was mountainous and verdant, like much of Vietnam. Cities and villages clustered where rivers came together, leading to flat plains indistinguishable from our Southern paddies. What did surprise me (besides the general cleanliness of the cities, at least when compared to Saigon) was the opulence of Al's rented house. Rambling over thousands of square feet, its style was a Spanish version of the French plantation at Binh Duong, with grand balconies, a broad terrace, elegantly furnished rooms for sleeping, dining, and entertaining, and a kitchen worthy of a big hotel. We had barely unpacked when Aunt Thu introduced us to the full-time live-in butler and housekeeper Al had hired. Apparently it was important to him to keep Thu's feet and hands un-calloused. It was as if we had changed places with the French planter and his gorgeous wife, and these poor Filipino servants had become our very own Chieu and Que. Unbelievable! And from there, things got even better.

Despite Aunt Thu's indifference to my education, Al insisted I enroll in school, which was fine by me. He mainly wanted me to learn English because his Vietnamese was almost non-existent and even his wife communicated with him mostly through pidgin phrases and a variety of looks and gestures. He spent a lot of time at his new business, a nice but unprofitable restaurant he bought as a going concern, probably for a bargain price. He renamed it "Albert's," which had a nice continental touch, and began almost at once serving American, Chinese, and Filipino cuisine—food reflecting the nationalities of his staff and the preferences of the clientele he hoped to draw from as far away as the Capital.

On my first day of school, Aunt Thu—technically, now, my "mother"—put a U.S. dollar in my pocket.

"I don't know how much this is worth in Philippine pesos," she said, "but it should be enough to buy lunch and a snack."

As it turned out, my American dollar was not only "enough," it made me immensely popular with students and teachers alike, who were happy to make change in the local currency. I brought a few unspent pesos back to Aunt Thu, who was thrilled that I had not lost any of the business acumen I had shown in Vietnam. I continued to please her as her pile of pesos grew, until her first trip to the market introduced her to the concept of exchange rates. Still, every morning she gave me a new dollar, and every day I made new friends, buying candy and ice cream from playground vendors and pointing up the hill to my big new house and promising that I would, one day, invite them all up for lunch served by my personal maid and butler. If the "Northerners" hated capitalists in my old country, I was hard-pressed to see why. Money didn't make life perfect, but it sure made the bad parts better.

Off the playground, things didn't turn out as well. English had never been easy, and every rule seemed to have an exception. Tagalog wasn't much better (a language spoken in the Philippines), but at least I could practice it on the cooks and waiters at the restaurant where Aunt Thu and Bubba, now almost three, spent most of their time. Secretly, I envied them. *Vietnam* was a dirty word to a lot of people outside of my country, and nobody—teachers, classmates, administrators, or town folk—made the slightest effort to help me or even sympathize with my problems as an immigrant. Overnight, it seemed, I had gone from being the whiz-kid of my parish grade school to "that foreign kid" who didn't know a toaster from a tortilla. Only my steady allowance of Yankee dollars kept me from becoming a total pariah. I could see now why Grandma and Aunt Thu prized good husbands over the hidden pleasures of books. What good were words and pictures when their meaning was cloaked in the history and culture of other people? All I wanted now was to play for a few hours each day with Bubba and pass out menus while smiling graciously at customers in my "city girl" *ao dai*, the elegant, flowing dress of a proud Vietnamese woman.

After giving Al's Philippine school a good try for a month, I dropped out. Oddly enough, he didn't seem to care as long as I continued to pick up English from our housekeepers, villagers, and people at the restaurant. Like school, I had these lessons every day and got to hone my business skills as well.

Uncle Al & Aunt Thu behind the register counter at Albert's Restaurant in the Philippines

Al started me behind the scenes at his restaurant. I didn't greet customers or wait tables, but I stamped the restaurant's name on the top of the pre-printed order tickets and stocked supplies on kitchen shelves and below the cashier's counter. The restaurant could seat about forty people at ten white-clothed tables. Plate glass windows bracketed the front door with more windows on either side, making the dining room bright and friendly. The path from the entrance to the rear door was almost a straight, unobstructed line—bad *feng shui*, a Chinese waitress said, especially on a slow day—but handy for waiters hustling food from the outdoor kitchen in the back. The far corners of the interior were enclosed with a European-style bathroom on one side and a break room for the staff on the other. An out-building for washing pots, pans, dishes, and laundry was in the backyard next to a big refrigerator, with a chicken and duck coop behind that. All in all, it seemed to me a very nice place. My opinion was soon shared by the locals and out-of-towners, including servicemen from Clark Air Force Base, who began flocking to the place both for the good food and the novelty of an American running the business and greeting the guests.

Al's multicultural staff was headed by a Philippine chef who ran the kitchen with only one assistant. Aunt Thu, no stranger to feeding lots of people, marveled at how he was able to crank out superb meals no matter how packed the house. Al often volunteered to help during rush hours, but the chef always chased him away, making it clear that while the owner wrote the checks, the chef made the food, period. Our twenty-something butler/driver pitched in, too, prepping and plating food but never cooking. I was also privileged to observe when my other duties were finished, and the chef seemed to take a shine to me. He explained what he was doing while cooking, and when the staff ate their shift-meal between seatings, he prepared a traditional Philippine dish called *Pancit* (meat, vegetable, and noodle stir-fry) just for me.

All this focus on the "kitchen family" and food made me suddenly miss Grandma, Quang, and Thuy even more, though they always hovered at the back of my mind during the flood of new places and faces.

One of these new faces was a neighbor girl named Alice, which was short for Alicia. She was one or two years younger than me, with blue eyes and long blond hair that was almost silver-white. She was friendly and curious, actually speaking to me first as she stood outside our mansion's gate, where she had been waiting, perhaps desperate for a playmate, as were most of the kids in our somewhat isolated expatriate community. I was tending Bubba, and she invited us to her house—her older brother, apparently, was also starved for a companion, someone to talk to. We got permission from Aunt Thu to go next door, beginning a pattern that was to last almost as long as we lived in the Philippines—Alice calling for us at the gate and us spending the rest of the day at her home, which was at least as large as ours. It was also an excellent chance for me to practice my "kitchen English," and Alice (and her mom) turned out to be both patient listeners and teachers.

Our first visit started with an introduction to her mother—a "modern American lady," the likes of which I hadn't seen since we entertained Al's co-workers in Quy Nhon. She fed us milk and cookies before Alice whisked us upstairs to show off her bedroom, her brother's room, and the "toy room"—a room devoted entirely to playthings. In truth, I had seen cluttered rooms in Vietnam—mostly leaf huts or cement houses stuffed with junk people had scrounged from scrapyards and garbage bins for resale or to trade—but never had I seen a whole floor covered with toys, and so thick Alice had to kick a path for us to get to the main attractions: a spring-mounted rocking horse, a doll house so big I could've slept in it, and a wooden box that overflowed with goodies like a pirate's treasure chest.

But the best toy of all (and I could hardly call it that except that's what Alice said it was) was a fully functional sewing machine that even Grandma Mau would die for. This one, though, was pink and yellow with a plastic bobbin case only big enough for doll's clothes—a wardrobe of which Alice had already made and trotted out to show me. She asked if I wanted to make something on her fantasy machine, and I said, "Yes, yes, yes!" so that's how we spent many hours of subsequent visits. Fortunately for Bubba, Alice's brother also had lots of toys and games, and if her mother hadn't taken a nose count before sending us home, he would likely have been lost amid the piles of blocks and stuffed animals.

Another new face was that of an American Air Force officer who lived with us for a while. He was a regular restaurant patron, and I think someone Al knew from Vietnam. His name was "Ben," and when he moved into our guest room, he brought a huge portrait of a beautiful, long-haired Vietnamese woman wearing a blue *ao dai*. This was obviously someone who was, or had been, very close to Ben. He sometimes talked to the picture—though his Vietnamese was bad and my command of English worse, so I never really got the gist of those one-sided conversations. He did tell me that she was the woman he would marry someday when he returned to Vietnam, which may have been only a few weeks after he moved in. Ben kept the reputation of American GIs clean as far as I was concerned by always treating me kindly and being a considerate, unobtrusive guest.

All in all, we were settling into our new life nicely, except maybe for Bubba, who, like most small kids, took more time to adjust and sometimes left traces of that discomfort. Since arriving at the mansion, we slept side by side in the same bed, although there were twin beds in the room and Lord knew there were plenty of rooms to accommodate us separately. But I was still his most familiar face and, since leaving school, resumed my duties as his nanny. He was normally a jovial kid but got anxious when left alone, so the more our time together reminded him of Vietnam, the better he liked it.

Once, in the middle of the night not too long after we moved in, I awoke to a warm flood under my back. Bubba usually wasn't a bed-wetter, but maybe the changes were getting to him. This really irked me, but it wasn't the first or last time I would be called upon to be a midnight mom. I cleaned us both up, changed our clothes, and put Bubba down on the other bed. He zonked right out on the clean sheets. Good for him! I stripped the soiled bed, but the mattress was still wet, so I climbed in next to Bubba and finished the night. When I told Aunt Thu about it the next morning, she angrily accused me of peeing on the bed (after all, we had been sleeping in mine) and trying to blame her little "prince." When she turned to Bubba and asked who did the deed, he made a pouty face and pointed to me. Thu threw up her hands, slapped me on the head, and while she pulled the wet mattress from my bed, Bubba giggled, covered his mouth, then ran away. I knew this was a losing battle so I just shut up and helped Aunt Thu drag the mattress downstairs for the maid to wash. After that, I always put Bubba down first in his own bed, though most nights he waited until I was asleep, then crawled in next to me, Vietnamese family style. There would be a few more pee episodes, but the next time we handled it "by the numbers," like a fire drill, and never told Aunt Thu.

§

That December, 1968, when I was about eight years old, Bubba and I experienced our first "American Christmas"—and a thing of beauty it was.

Al had a carpenter build a big (at least five feet by three feet) facsimile Christmas card and hired an artist to paint a portrait of Bubba and me standing beside a Christmas tree on the interior. He then mounted the display on the roof of his restaurant and illuminated it with floodlights. Coupled with the real-life Christmas tree inside, which was lit and decorated in traditional fashion, it made a memorable, festive sight. Under the real tree, he put wrapped gifts for each employee—a card filled with bonus cash and a box of chocolates to share with their family. We probably had a few Buddhists among the Catholics on our staff, but everyone seemed to enjoy the gifts.

At home we decorated another Christmas tree, bigger than the one at work, and opened our gifts on Christmas morning. Bubba got a big toy tractor like the one he nearly wore out at Alice's house. I got the miniature cooking set—kid-sized pots and pans and Western-style utensils—I had wished for since living in Stucco House. I don't remember what Al gave Aunt Thu, but from her "Ooos" and "Ahhhs," it must have been nice clothes or fine jewelry. Al was a very generous Santa, and he obviously wanted our first American-style Christmas to be one we remembered.

After the holiday was over, Al moved the big rooftop Christmas card to our backyard and kept it as a lawn decoration. We stared at it through the window every morning at breakfast and played around it most afternoons until rain and sun peeled off our painted faces and the wooden panels splintered. It was a kick, though, while it lasted.

Of course, nothing lasts forever, and happiness can turn to heartbreak in the blink of an eye.

§

By the summer of 1969, Al's restaurant was a fixture in the San Fernando area. Bigwigs from nearby *barangays*—the local political townships—frequented "Alfred's" for lunch with their patrons, cronies, and henchmen. The Mayor of San Pedro made it his hangout, making deals and making promises, or whatever politicians do. Al wasn't exactly his buddy or any sort of political insider, but the Mayor always brought an entourage, and ordinary people often followed just to see the celebrities.

One evening while Thu was running the register and Bubba and I were behind the counter (Bubba was on the floor playing and I was stamping order pads), the Mayor and his friends came in and occupied several tables. They sat at their usual place to the right of the main entrance in front of the plate glass window so their constituents could wave as they passed. Faster than it takes to tell it, a car stopped out front and parked illegally, discharging four salty-looking men we had never seen before. The men ran inside, pulled out submachine guns, and without a word, began spraying the Mayor and his party. Al, who was by the servers' station, jumped over the counter and pulled Aunt Thu and us kids to the floor, covering us with his body. The staccato shots were deafening, and in the darkness under Al's makeshift bunker, the smell of his sweat and our own fear sent me back to Hong Ngu, but I held on and kept my eyes open. As quickly as it started, it ended, and the men ran out and the car zoomed off.

Silence, then groans and breaking glass. Chairs and tables scrape as survivors creep out from hiding.

I peeked over the countertop through the purple gun smoke at the all-too-familiar spattered blood, bullet holes, and carnage. I felt like I was crawling out of the bunker in Hong Ngu once again, or standing in the door of the Stucco House the morning of Tet. Everything was chaos. The wounded were crying, and the dead were doing what the dead always do... laying still in their own blood. Another Tsunami.

Al immediately rallied the staff and checked for injuries, then tried to aid wounded patrons while a waiter called police. The Mayor and his party were all dead, splayed across the backs of chairs or slumped over a table; a few tumbled awkwardly to the floor when Al tried to help them, lumps of flesh like the Hong Ngu soldiers or the casualties on our doorstep after Tet. I'd hoped I would never see such sights again—a nine-year-old with three battle stars deserved a little R&R—but fate had other ideas. The most horrible thing about horror is the moment you realize it's become an old friend.

Gangland shooting at Albert's Restaurant

In what seemed like hours but was only minutes, police cars circled the building, blue lights flashing, and uniformed men swarmed into the restaurant with guns drawn. Once assured the fight was over, the authorities took charge, but nobody was allowed to leave until everyone had been questioned, the photographers and technicians had done their jobs, and the bodies had been hauled away. Aunt Thu and us kids got home about midnight, but Uncle Al didn't show up until morning, after securing his beloved dream-business that had likely seen its last customer, at least until the investigation was over. Detectives said it would take a month.

During that time, Al restored the interior and planned a grand reopening, but that was not in the cards. Aunt Thu put her foot down and said she had not fled one war zone to put herself and her family in another. She and Al argued about whether a business could ever be safe in a country as corrupt as this one. Yes, Vietnam was also corrupt, she said, but there we at least had the support of a big family and relatives in the police and armed forces. Like mice in a jungle, we knew how to find small spaces and deep holes for evading predators.

Finally, Uncle Al gave up his dream, gave notice to our mansion's landlord, and put "Albert's" up for sale. While the buyers shopped and agents haggled, Al took a salaried job with Pacific Architect and Engineering Corporation, an American company headquartered in Los Angeles but with worldwide operations. Not by coincidence, but by Al's request and Aunt Thu's insistence, his first assignment was as a facilities engineering supervisor in the Vietnamese seaside village of Nha Trang. I was not sad about leaving the Philippines. I knew I would miss Alice and our beautiful home, but Vietnam was my life, war and all. At least there, I would be with my grandmother, and my brother and sister.

CHAPTER 8

INTO THE DRAGON'S DEN—1969

Even warriors need time off, and for many American GIs, Nha Trang was such a haven with broad glistening beaches, roaring surf, and bracing air from the South China Sea. That was our destination, but only after a stop to collect more family at Phu Nhuan.

Grandma hadn't changed a bit. Quang was a little taller and looked well-fed. Sister Thuy still tried to blend in with Grandma's knees, the furniture, or the trees whenever she could, but once she knew we were at the door, her shyness eased and she welcomed back her big sister. That was great, because Hoang and I became chatty houseguests while Al and Thu went house-hunting in Nha Trang. Another year, another house! Maybe we'd get lucky with another villa and generous neighbors like Alice—without the blood and bullets—but I didn't count on it. What counted was that, for the first time in five years, all of my parents' kids would be in one place at one time. Grandma was very happy. It may have been the middle of summer, but for us it felt like Tet.

In late June, Al and Thu rented a two-story house near the beach. It was big enough for all of us, so we helped Grandma, Thuy, and Quang move out just as Uncle Chieu and Aunt Que arrived to take possession of their Stucco House—one reunion Thuy and I worked hard to miss.

The Nha Trang house faced the main highway to Saigon, so despite the seaside setting, it felt like city living. Civilian and military traffic flowed constantly, and wherever you have travelers, you have street vendors and pedestrians. People are always fleeing or arriving. Some are lost souls just passing through, hawking their wares or knocking on doors looking for relatives or a handout. Aside from the wonderfully cool and constant sea breeze, the upside was that for the first time in a year, Grandma had no worries about feeding or clothing her grandkids—or protecting us from a brutal war. Because Al made a generous American salary, he could afford both a housekeeper and a cook, over whom Aunt Thu now lorded as she had our servants in the Philippines.

Grandma got to act the Matriarch again and let others do things for her, enjoying her grandchildren instead of slaving on their behalf. In return, we got a grandmother who was now relaxed enough to teach us more than how to make a day's meal last a week or survive on an urban street. She taught us to be polite as well as stoic, how to care for others as we cared for ourselves, and to appreciate the labor of those who helped us. She was an admirable woman.

Since we were near another big U.S. base, Al often brought home American food, such as Washington apples, Florida oranges, and grapefruit from the great Southwest at the Exchange or the dining hall where he was a friend of the catering manager. These were exotic fruits to the Vietnamese so we shared what we couldn't eat with our landlord and his family, who lived behind us. This alone made us feel special, and it was a treat to finally live in a Vietnamese neighborhood where community spirit overcame political suspicions. Outside that neighborhood, though, the world was a different place.

I thought Aunt Thu would enroll us older kids in the nearest public school, but she didn't. I never asked her why—partly because I still remembered my bad experience in the Philippines, and partly because the parents always made such decisions. It was useless to second-guess them. The real reason turned out to be more complicated than her usual indifference to education. First, Al's assignment was temporary and our rental month-to-month, so it was pointless to get involved with a school we might have to leave as soon as we got started. More importantly, despite Nha Trang's reputation as a destination for R&R, the war was creeping closer. Distant explosions and occasional gunfire interrupted our sleep, and although there had been no fighting or sabotage in the city itself, the adults kept us kids on a short leash. Playtime was confined to our house or immediate neighbors, and we never went to the beach without an adult. Even then, our sand-and-surf adventures were only on weekends when Al and his male friends could go with us. These excursions often turned into full-blown beach parties with a barbeque, beer, and sodas. On one such outing, I tried my first carbonated drink—a can of Dr Pepper. It was sickly sweet and hard to swallow, but I pretended to enjoy it. When no one was looking, I poured it onto the sand. Quang got good at drinking his soda fast and burping for our amusement, but it was a taste and a skill I never acquired.

This combination of no school, free time, and virtual house arrest brought out the mischief-maker in all of us. Quang and I were the chief offenders, with Hoang as our apprentice. Shortly after our arrival, he used a new slingshot Al gave him to shatter a shop window across the street. Aunt Thu paid the merchant for the damage and confiscated the weapon, sternly telling us all to "shape up," whatever that meant. If her beloved prince could act so stupidly, what were the rest of us barbarian orphans capable of? She wouldn't have to wait long to find out.

We children were supposed to take naps right after lunch in our upstairs bedroom. Like dutiful kids, we trooped upstairs and waited until the adults got busy, then Quang and I scouted up something to do. Our first choice was hanging over the balcony to watch the traffic, flinging old fruit at cars and motorbikes as they passed—pretty stupid, I know, but to bored little kids, the rules of proper behavior were made to be broken, just like plate glass windows.

The noon hour was always busiest, and one day we spotted some older students walking to afternoon classes. We had some squishy rotten apples from a batch Al brought home from the mess hall a week before, so we saw our opportunity. Leading the pack was an attractive high-school girl in a flowing, white *ao dai* and traditional conical straw hat.

"You go first," I challenged Quang.

The girls had passed beneath us when Quang said, unexpectedly, "No. You."

So, with the girl's back in my sights, I threw out the first pitch, not really expecting to hit anything. Instead, my first shot mashed the edge of her sun hat, splattering stinky, overripe pulp all over her dress.

For a split second I covered my mouth and laughed noiselessly, then turned to give Quang's arm a victory slap, but he had already hit the dirt—or rather, was hugging the balcony floor since a dozen eyes had suddenly turned in our direction. I hit the concrete, too.

Target practice—Nha Trang

What happened next was almost as bad as waiting for the shelling to stop on Tet. The victim didn't scream. She didn't curse or call out for me to show myself so she could knock my block off. She just sobbed uncontrollably in the arms of her girlfriends who tried to comfort her. Apparently it was a special day at school, which called for a special dress that I'd just ruined. I heard her run back the way she came while her friends rushed on, not daring to be late. I had no idea who the girl was or what special event I had spoiled, but I felt lower than the apple-mush splattered on the sidewalk. I had learned about *bad karma* from my old friend Truc while I was still wearing my black patch and bumming free lunches from her kind mother.

I wondered now how fate would even the score with me for this cowardly, thoughtless act. Then, recalling my own weird history of good and bad fortune, I decided it was probably best not to know.

On the brighter side of our "captivity," I did have time to learn more about cooking from Aunt Thu and especially from Grandma Mau. Because Al loved barbeque, Aunt Thu put me to work making its tangy sauce, a Vietnamese specialty. She showed me how to thin-slice the pork and chicken, flavor it with fish sauce, and sprinkle on the right amount of sugar and other seasonings. I learned that the secret to great kabobs was getting the little pieces on the skewer just right so they'd grill evenly. Although Aunt Thu was seldom satisfied with anything I did, Master Chef Al liked my work, and, for the moment, that was what mattered.

§

In Nha Trang, living a very comfortable middle-class life style was something so new and different that even remembering it now seems surreal and almost like another world. There I began a life-long love affair with ocean beaches, warm surf, and soft sea breezes. Grandma was the happiest and most content I ever remembered her being since Mama died. This Oasis of Time was for her a well-deserved, hard-won respite from some long, difficult, dangerous, and scary years. None of us went hungry, and we were not touched by fear or the war. For a while, life was good.

§

In 1970, six months after arriving in Nha Trang, we left. Al's company transferred him to the biggest American base in Vietnam—Long Binh Bien Hoa, or just Long Bien, as the GIs called it, about twenty miles north of Saigon. It was a noisy beehive compared to Nha Trang, and being closer to the capital, we all took a psychic deep breath for a return to the world of war and worry.

Our rented house in the residential section of Thu Duc was a block from the main highway, which helped a little with noise, but gave Al a thirty-minute commute. It was smaller than our home in Nha Trang, so Grandma, sister Thuy, and I shared one bedroom. Bubba and Quang had another one, with Al and Aunt Thu taking the third. Though the floor plan was different, it at least had an indoor bathroom, and we were grateful for that. If nothing else, big Vietnamese families get very good at taking turns.

School was in session when we arrived, and since Al anticipated a long-term assignment, I asked Aunt Thu about enrolling. Another lecture was sparked about the irrelevance of education for young girls on the "mama path" and how, with the government's poor record keeping and our multiple birth certificates, nobody would even know what grade we belonged in. That stopped the discussion until Uncle Hai arrived to save the day.

Since Thu Duc was not far from his Naval Station, he was one of the first relatives to visit. In no uncertain terms, he reminded Thu that Mama had believed in education for women, and that if Thu and Al couldn't raise us according to our mother's wishes, they should put us in an orphanage where school was mandatory. With Grandma backing him up, Thu relented and took us to the local Catholic school about a half-hour's walk away. When we returned, I was a registered third grader, Quang a fifth grader, and Thuy a first grader. While the "mama path" wasn't exactly out, the world of books and pencils was at least restored to its margins.

Zoom—Moto ride with Uncle Chieu and his girlfriend after school

One of the next relatives to visit was Uncle Chieu, who nobody but Al was particularly anxious to see. Chieu had apparently split with Aunt Que—again—and came to Thu Duc almost weekly to show off his new 1967 Honda motorbike and new girlfriend. Since Al depended on official vehicles for transportation and those trips seldom included us, we kids jumped at the chance to ride with Chieu—to the market, to school, or even into Saigon's far-north suburbs for a snack or just to see new sights. Our seating arrangements would not have passed muster for any conscientious parent. With Chieu on the driver's seat and his girlfriend behind him, we kids wedged ourselves onto or between anything we could—the gas tank, the luggage rack, the front fender over the wheel. We returned from these outings with only a few scratches, and our opinions of Chieu began to change. He became the "fun uncle."

Fortunately, Al invited Chieu to the weekend "team building" luncheons he threw for his staff. Aunt Thu dutifully cooked mountains of barbeque for these events, and I dutifully volunteered to help her. With all the people laughing and drinking, it reminded me of Al's Philippine restaurant, although the specter of armed gunmen breaking in was always at the back of my mind—this time Northern soldiers instead of gangsters. After all, this was still a war zone, though the shooting hadn't reached Thu Duc. The parties always ended with half of the men drunk and doing the "elephant dance" (conga line) in our yard or on the street. I was uneasy about the level of drunkenness, but at least the guests were having fun.

Being close to Hai's Naval base, we also enjoyed visits with Aunt Nga, Uncle Hai's wife, whom I seldom saw in earlier years. Uncle Hai met his wife when he was stationed in Can Tho in 1967, and now they lived near his present assignmen at Bach Dang Port, in Saigon. Nicknamed "Mo Nga," she was petite and polite and always a model of good manners.

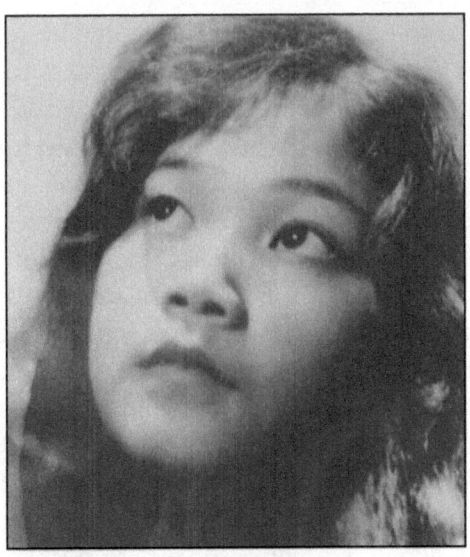

Beautiful Mo Nga (Aunt Nga), Uncle Hai's wife before their marriage

Their daughters were way younger than us: Tam was two, Yen one, and Suong a mewing infant. Because this brood of tiny kids was a handful for one person, Aunt Nga often stayed with us when Uncle Hai went to sea. They were beautiful children, and Thuy and I loved to mother them, but Mo Nga took after her spit-and-polish husband and fretted constantly about them dirtying their clothes or putting dirty things in their mouths or touching dirty things—including us. This irked me at first and reminded me of the way Uncle Hai warned me off on his first visit to Stucco House before taking me to Ben Thanh market. Then, he was wearing a clean white Naval uniform and such precautions made sense. Now, Aunt Nga just seemed to be searching for excuses to keep us from handling her girls. Grandma told me, "Oh, that's just how some mothers are," but it may also have been that Mo Nga viewed us as *dirty orphans*—a stain that I learned long ago no soap was going to wash off.

Returning to third grade made me remember why I liked school so much. Once again, I donned my white blouse and blue skirt, just like Papa put on his old uniform when he returned to the Army. This time, I was not a lone soldier but a crusader against ignorance with Thuy and Quang beside me. We felt like a formidable force.

We all enrolled in the morning session, and so walked to and from school as a unit until we linked up with other Catholic kids in the neighborhood. Some things had changed since second grade. First, classes were bigger because as the war progressed, more and more families were displaced from the countryside and found refuge near the capital. Second, I realized that our uniforms were more than a way for us students to look nice for the teachers. By looking all the same, distinctions in wealth and family status were erased and forced us to concentrate on what was important: studying hard and showing what we had learned. Rich kids had no special advantage, and poor ones bore no special burden. Everyone had the same opportunity to excel or, if they weren't up the challenge, fail. I was determined that the third-grade student called "Van" by some relatives and "Hien" by others (even though Al and Bubba still called me "Sissy" at home) would again become an exemplary student. Mama would've settled for nothing less.

By January, 1971, I was eleven years old and back in the academic groove, making new friends right and left. One reason for this was another change I'd noticed: I was no longer the runt of the litter. In fact, after a couple of years of regular meals and nourishing food, I was somewhat taller than average, which led many students to treat me with the respect they normally saved for older kids. Many teachers viewed me as a "natural leader"—demanding a bit more from me but rewarding me, too, for my extra effort. Overall, it was a pretty great year.

One of my new friends was a third-grade girl named "Cuc," which was short for the Vietnamese word meaning chrysanthemum. Her mother was married to an American civilian who, like Al, had recently been transferred to Long Binh. They lived in Thu Duc, too, but in a section called University Village—a trim, well-landscaped district with a college hidden at its center like the peanut in a green M&M. I passed this neighborhood each day on my way to school and always envied the people who lived there. Cuc enrolled as I did, at mid-term, so she was happy to have an old hand and "class leader" befriend her and show her the ropes. Unfortunately, my position atop that ivory tower didn't last long.

We were playing jump rope one day at recess when she whispered in my ear, "Van—you have blood on your underwear!"

I paused, tangling the rope around my feet. "I don't think so," I replied. It was more of a wish than a statement. "What do you mean?"

She pointed down at my blue skirt. "You know. Maybe you're having your period."

The only period I knew about was the one at the end of a sentence. If I was bleeding, something must be wrong. I had never seen blood on anyone when it didn't mean something awful.

"Okay," Cuc said, taking my hand. "Let's go see the nun."

But recess was over, and the last class was about to start. I didn't hurt anywhere so I skipped the nun and tried to concentrate on the task at hand, which was mostly worrying if I was sick. When class was over, Cuc walked me as far as her house, then I ran the rest of the way home. Inside, I found Grandma in her bedroom. Making sure no other kids were around, I blurted out my story.

Grandma only chuckled and gave me a hug. "Don't fret, Van. You're just growing up. Come with me."

Aunt Nga happened to be visiting, so Grandma took me back downstairs, figuring a younger woman might be needed for this job. She whispered my secret in Mo Nga's ear, and Mo Nga smiled her pretty smile. Together they told me about the birds and the bees—not everything, but enough to reassure me that I was fine and the embarrassing little episode was just one more step I had to take in the process of becoming a woman. There would be others, they assured me.

After that, Cuc and I became like sisters. She waited at the gate to her house for Quang, Thuy and me to pass each morning, then walked to school with us. One day she wasn't at the gate. I knocked on the door, and her mother said she was ill but would return to school the next day, so we went ahead. It was just as well she missed this trip.

As we neared the edge of University Village, an area heavily landscaped with trees and bushes, I told Quang and Thuy to wait because I had to pee.

"Can't you hold it until we get to school?" my brother asked irritably.

"Nooo. I gotta go *now*!"

"Okay," he sighed, and pointed to some bushes. "You can go over there. But make it snappy!"

They started walking while I ran into the bushes, squatted, and did what was necessary. I stood up, pulled up, brushed a couple of twigs from my skirt, then turned to join them when I almost tripped on a human arm. Only a human arm, with no body attached to it.

"QUANG!" I screamed as if I was the one who'd been murdered. "Come here!"

He came running with Thuy right behind him, then stopped when he saw I was okay.

"What are you yelling about?" He was really irritated and probably assumed I had just seen a snake.

"Down there! Look! It's somebody's arm!"

He didn't even bother to look but held out his hand to me. "Just forget about it. Come on."

He turned with Thuy, who likewise seemed less than curious, and started down the road. I picked my way around the severed limb—not too freshly severed, given its mottled blue look—but somebody was definitely missing something important from the elbow down. Vivid images filled my head from Hong Ngu, the street in front of Stucco House, and even the bloody tables at "Albert's"—but my stomach didn't turn. I didn't feel faint, and I didn't need a guardian angel to talk me off a dead man's chest. Maybe life for me had become too normal, too clean, too comfortable with Al's household so that images like this, rising out of nowhere, had regained some of their shock value. But they were old hat for Quang and Thuy, who were used to going to sleep to the sound of artillery and firefights in the streets, in the poorer neighborhoods where the VC not only felt safe, but often lived. It wasn't that Quang didn't care; he just cared about other things more. Like wise-owl Uncle Thanh, he knew when to keep his beak out of dangerous places and when it made sense to squawk. I ran after them, and by the time we arrived at school, my world was back to normal. It was if the monstrous arm was just another fading, terrible dream.

Unfortunately, dreams or any other kind of sleep didn't come easily in the next few months.

The first problem was the war, always lingering nearby, like a noisy shadow. Bien Hoa was too big and tempting a target for the North to ignore as their units marched steadily farther south. Although the residential district of Thu Duc remained unscarred, battles rumbled more frequently in the outlying areas. But despite their advances, a Northern victory was still deemed impossible. Peace talks had finally started between the U.S. and North Vietnam in Paris. Everyone from nuns and priests to cab drivers, street vendors, and neighborhood police—even Al's co-workers from the base—seemed cautiously optimistic while keeping one eye on their backyard bunkers.

The second obstacle to my peace of mind lay closer to home: Al himself. I don't know if it was the party atmosphere of his recent assignments, his fatalism about the violence that seemed to dog our every move, or the simple fact that the little girl he had adopted was slowly ripening into a young woman, but his attitude toward me began to change, and not for the good. It was a side of him I'd never seen—and hoped vainly that I would never see again.

It began on one of our "party nights" after the other guests had gone home. Al was a little tipsy and the whole family was still energized by the duties and pleasures of hosting a jovial group. Although we were tired, none of us (except Grandma, who promptly went to bed) wanted to quit just yet, so Al suggested we play Hide-and-Seek. With Aunt Thu and us kids assembled in the living room, he shut off the lights, then said that one person would be "It"—starting with himself—whose job was to find the others in the dark. The first one he touched would become the new "It," repeating the process until everyone had taken their turn.

Predictably, we all scampered away and hid behind furniture or in a corner or against a wall. Al growled like a tiger and said, "I'm gonna get you!" as he stumbled around the room, drawing squeaks and giggles from Hoang and Thuy and laughter from Quang and Aunt Thu, who easily evaded him. I wasn't so lucky. Al found me curled up beside a chair and his strong hands clasped my waist, tickling me as he pulled me up. I laughed and assumed the round was over, but Al's fingers didn't stop. The tickles moved higher and lower until I knew with great certainty that something other than a kid's game was going on. My laughter turned into a shriek, and I twisted away, running from the room. Behind me Al said, "Okay, Sissy is out! Who's next? Oh, here's Bubba—got him!" Hoang screeched, and the game was on again, presumably according to Hoyle, but definitely without me. I went searching for Grandma, wanting desperately to ask her about the whole experience, but she was asleep. Anyway, I was too terrified and ashamed to do so. This was something completely new and confusing—and, I knew, down deep, terribly, terribly wrong.

The next day, nobody said anything about our new "game," least of all Al or me, although we were to play it several more times over the next few months. With my creep-detector activated, I put extra distance between me and Al when he was "It," usually pushing Quang or Bubba out front so he would find them first and not bother me, but there were other avenues for him to satisfy this new, guilty pleasure. If I was reaching high up to clean, for example, he would find some excuse to "help" or show me how to do something better—such lessons always involving a touch or a pat or a squeeze that had nothing to do with the job. If I squirmed or tried to move away, it only seemed to encourage him, so I either just endured it or said quickly, "Oh, fine, thanks. I've got it now," or something else to signal that the *game* was over. Compared to what was happening in the countryside around us, I never really believed Al's weird, inappropriate behavior was a serious threat, but it sure felt like one. Eventually, it just became one more thing I had to put up with, and like every other danger that demanded vigilance and respect, I got very good at avoiding it.

§

Finally, in the summer of 1971, Al decided it was time to move again. Emboldened by God-knows-what, he said that this time, he would not do things halfway but be in charge of his own destiny. He said he loved Vietnam and loved Aunt Thu and wanted to embrace them both for the rest of his life. He applied for dual citizenship, to combine his U.S. citizenship with citizenship in the Republic of Vietnam, and so formalize his marriage to the land and people he loved. Dual citizenship would also facilitate the other half of his plan: to open a new business in our homeland in an area less threatened by the war and well-positioned to prosper once the war ended. As one of his friends in the Philippines had said, entrepreneurs are nothing if not optimists. I guessed I could learn to be one, too.

Chapter 9

Fish Farm—1971

Al and Aunt Thu finally found what they hoped would be *Nirvana* near the village of Da Minh, a hamlet west of Long Binh about an hour from Saigon. The property, formerly owned and operated by a Catholic priest, covered about five acres adjacent to the main highway, QL15. Al was adamant on this last point, and it explained why—at least in Vietnam—all of our houses were near big streets. If "the balloon went up," as Al put it, we could escape our neighborhood fast. The fact that everybody else would be running from a battle, too, apparently didn't figure in his calculations, but that was his theory.

This particular property, with a residence and a collection of smaller sheds and barns, lay behind a gas station (another plus in an emergency), and three of its four sides were enclosed by a living bamboo wall. Inside the enclosure were nine fresh-water fish ponds fed by a stream outside the bamboo fence and controlled by a series of wire-filtered sluice gates. The stream flowed year-round and emptied into the Dong Nai River which, at this location, was itself affected by tides from the South China Sea. the stream's constant flow, the tug-and-pull of the tides, and sluice gates he could open and close at will, Al could produce fresh-water fish for markets and paying visitors without the use of pumps, cement-lined canals, or other expensive equipment. That, too, was his theory. Since he was experienced with all kinds of machinery and an entrepreneur at heart, I had a lot more confidence in his fish-farm idea than his plans for escape-and-evasion.

Another benefit of so much acreage was the free-ranging livestock (ducks, chicken, quail, even a small herd of pigs) that roamed the grounds and the variety of fruit trees nourished by fresh water: mango, jackfruit, sugar apples, water apples, guava, several species of banana, and even a stand of sugar cane. There was also plenty of fertile ground to grow vegetables, and it slowly dawned on me that even if we didn't have to escape a battle, we could live forever on the fish and produce we grew ourselves. And what we didn't eat, we could sell at the local market, but Grandma was way ahead of me on that.

"Do you think we could start a business with the stuff Uncle Al doesn't use?" I asked.

She puffed on her pipe and looked out thoughtfully over our new plantation. "We'll see," she said. "We'll see."

The residence was a short walk from the main gate. It wasn't in very good shape, but Al fixed that within weeks of our moving in. His carpenter was a "mountain man" (Muong) named Mr. Phuoc who had worked for Al at Long Binh. He braided his long hair down to his waist and always dressed in white—an odd choice for a man who worked in dirt and sawdust—but it was apparently part of his religion, *Dao Cao Dai*, the cult of the One-Eyed God. He was a very serious guy who didn't smile much, so I took it as a personal challenge to cheer him up, learning in the process all I could about his craft and his fascinating religion. Al didn't like this since he thought I distracted Mr. Phuoc from his work (which I probably did), but after a while I was carrying his tools and fetching his wood and nails so, in addition to finishing my own chores first, our team actually became more productive. He taught me that *Dao Cao Dai* was a mystical sect of Buddhism, and he believed in most of the things I'd learned from Truc: veneration of ancestors, non-violence, vegetarianism, and strict observance of ritual prayer. Unlike other Buddhists, though, they thought killing for *any* reason was forbidden. Once, while he and some local workers were eating lunch, one of them swatted a fly, and Mr. Phuoc burst into tears. He told the worker that all living things were entitled to live unhindered by human action. It was a nice thought, but I wondered if he knew what Uncle Al had planned for the fish that swam in our ponds.

When the work was finished, our "new" house looked like new. Al added a separate dining room (most Vietnamese families ate their meals in the main room of the house), which was built out over a pond, as well as a modern "island" kitchen with plenty of cabinet space around the sink and stove. He also built two new bedrooms: one master suite for himself and Aunt Thu, the second oversized for Grandma and us kids that he divided into a girl's section and a boy's section with a big double-sided armoire for our clothes. Best of all, he constructed a modern indoor bathroom which, as was the case at Long Binh, became the most popular room in the house.

After living there a few weeks, it became obvious why Al put such effort into the dining room and kitchen. He still missed his restaurant, and although Aunt Thu was a good and willing cook, Al was the master chef and determined to hook us on American food. Whenever he cooked—pancakes for breakfast, hamburgers and hot dogs for dinner—we always used the formal dining room. This may seem odd for what Americans considered "street food," but to us these were exotic foreign dishes so we just shut up and expanded our palates. When Aunt Thu or Grandma cooked traditional Vietnamese meals, we ate them in the screened-in porch just outside the main door.

The nice refurbished house was not the end of Al's new empire. Connected to our room additions by a screened walkway were two duplexes, each self-contained and, though fairly small, could accommodate a whole family. Because we were now even closer to the capital, Uncle Hai moved Aunt Nga and their three girls into one duplex when he left on a year-long training assignment with the American Navy in Guam. The other Al rented to a handsome young Vietnamese Air Force officer with whom I immediately fell secretly and clumsily in love.

The officer was a little younger than Aunt Thu, though as far as I could see she never flirted with him and kept their relationship strictly business. This may have been because the young man was "billeted" to our duplex as an informal security measure. Al knew his commanding officer from Bien Hoa, and they concluded that the presence of a uniformed Southerner would somehow insulate us from harassment by the VC. This didn't make a whole lot of sense to me—I had, after all, had a front row seat at two battles where the VC seemed not only undeterred by Southern soldiers, but actually sought them out—however, in this case it worked. We had no troubles the whole time he was there, commuting to his job at the air base early in the morning and returning late at night.

One of my chores was to clean his room, and in his case, I was happy to do so. He lived a neat and orderly life, so his duplex was always "ship shape." I only had to sweep and mop the floor and dust the shelves, staring dreamily at his handsome face in his small collection of family photos. I was less thrilled about my other household duties, which I had to complete after school. I always wondered why Aunt Thu never assigned at least a few of them to her two paid household servants, who would've done them faster and better, or even to sister Thuy, who spent most afternoons playing with Bubba. This work included hand-washing clothes and even helping out with pond maintenance when Al was short-handed. When I finally complained to her about it, she replied, "The chores I give you are only the things a girl must know before she gets married," and that was that. As far as Thu was concerned, I was still on the "mama path" and not the "scholar's track," despite my accomplishments as a newly enrolled fifth-grader in another nearby Catholic school, this one run by nuns in conjunction with an orphanage. If I was ever going to break out of the "mama path" with Al and Thu, it would have to be by showing my worth in some other area. That's when I learned about farming.

§

Although the priest and parishioners, who worked the property before Al bought it had lived frugally and toiled hard, they never really made the business pay. They harvested fruit and livestock mostly for their own use and fed human waste to the fish—a common practice in the countryside but not one that led to plump, well-fed fish. One of Al's first changes was to remove the Asian-style toilets from over the ponds and replace them with American-style outhouses on solid ground. This started the fish on a healthier track but improving the stock would take time. In the meanwhile, he focused on making the other livestock more productive.

Beyond the duplexes was a barn with twelve pigsties and three sheds for storing tools and fodder. Grandma set up one small kitchen inside the barn and a larger one outside. She used the inside kitchen to brew tea for the workers and our family. The outside kitchen she used to boil down water lilies, banana tree pulp, and dried corn into bran powder to feed the pigs—Al's first cash crop. He didn't like the barn's pigsties and built new pens between two ponds, giving Quang the job of washing down the pigs once a day. The fresh water he used for cleaning was pumped from one pond and the runoff went into the other. This "gray water" was then used to irrigate our garden so all the fresh water went to the house, the pigs, or the fish. It was a tidy, practical system.

Quang, cousin Ngoc, Bubba and Fish Farm hired hands at work butchering a pig

One person who liked the old pigsties was Uncle Chieu, an early visitor after our move. One of the enclosures had been converted to a small bedroom for the resident gardener, Mr. Ba, a man who came to work for us from my home village of Rach Gia and had a "green thumb" if there ever was one. His pretty daughter, Mai, stayed there, too, although only for occasional visits. She got along well with the family and made custom clothes for Aunt Thu, teaching me how to measure and cut cloth without a pattern. On one of Mai's visits, Uncle Chieu happened to drop by and was smitten by her at once. They struck up a romance, and after that both visited often. With his daughter around a lot more, Mr. Ba put his own money into fixing up another former pig-stall so that Mai could have her own space. Unfortunately, that's where she and Uncle Chieu liked to have their romantic interludes, so when Mr. Ba discovered them, he became furious and would have probably beaten Chieu with a shovel if he hadn't been Aunt Thu's brother. Fortunately, Chieu convinced Mr. Ba that he loved Mai and would look after her, which he did. They drove away one afternoon on his motorbike and we seldom saw them again at the Fish Farm. Except for the pigsty part, I always thought it was a beautiful story.

Just as typical of Uncle Chieu, and not uncommon among Vietnamese families, he tried to place a relative on our payroll—and this time, I was happy he succeeded. Cousin Ngoc, about Quang's age, had been my friend and confident at Leaf House. When Al's new business got off the ground, Chieu asked Aunt Thu if his son, Ngoc, might have a job as a houseboy or laborer in exchange for room and board plus a small wage. This wage was important, he said, because Ngoc's mother, Aunt Que, looked increasingly to her eldest son for support, especially for her daughters. Que was a *butterfly*, as flirty women were called, and since separating from Chieu, she had put those talents to work as a professional escort. This embarrassed her whole family, especially policeman Chieu, but there was little he could do about it. She parked their children with a relative about a half-hour's drive from Fish Farm and badgered Chieu to convert his friendly relations with Al and Thu into a paying job for their son. Fortunately for Ngoc and me, he did.

Like Quang, Ngoc was a hard worker and seldom complained, except once when he admitted to envying us for going to school and having a solvent, reliable American "dad" to give us security in an insecure world. This doubly bothered him because both his parents were still living, yet his life remained poor and miserable, unlike Quang and Thuy and me, who were technically orphans but lived in comparative luxury. He had a point, but those were the cards we'd been dealt. Aunt Thu was not charitable by nature and shared the good fortune of her marriage grudgingly, mostly as a duty to Grandma and her departed sister. When I asked her why she never enrolled Ngoc in school with us, she snapped back, "He has parents. They can look after his education if they want to." That was the end of that. From then on Ngoc was viewed as just another resident groundskeeper, paid the wages he was promised and given a mat to sleep on and a roof over his head. He was never invited to dinner or share any family functions.

Once, with Aunt Thu's permission, I accompanied Ngoc to his home in Binh Da, a small rural town near the American Long Binh military base and the town of Tam Hiep. Binh Da to Fish Farm was about an hour's walk. He had to take the money home to his mother, he said. He didn't say much about his home circumstances whenever I asked questions, and it took some convincing before he agreed to let me go with him.

Ngoc and his sister Lien cooked for me that evening. The first thing I noticed was a new child, a blond-headed Amerasian boy named Tuan who Aunt Que had apparently birthed during the intervening years. Aunt Que was of course not at home. She was out working as an "Escort" again, and all the children were fending for themselves, although it was obviously a condition they were quite accustomed to. They had no electricity, no in-door plumbing, not even a clock in the house. They told time by the shadow of the stick stuck in the ground. They lived poorly, very much like when we lived together at the Leaf House in Phu Nhuan with Grandmother. I was reminded of those days as I sat watching them prepare a meal. They did not have enough food that day for a guest. So Ngoc went next door to borrow some low-quality brown rice, while Duc went into the backyard pond and pulled out the fish he had caught that morning. I helped Lien and her brother Thang gather water spinach and garlic for a stir-fried meal to go with the fish and rice. I talked some to Lien as she was stir-frying the spinach. I last had seen them right after we returned from the Philippines in 1969. Their situation now was worse. Lien said they were really on their own almost all the time since they moved to Binh Da in 1970. They rarely saw their mother or father, and of course none of them attended school. They learned to survive on an acre of land that their mother left them. Later after dinner, Ngoc and I walked silently together back to Fish Farm. I wondered to myself with a heavy heart:

What was worse? Having parents who were dead, or parents alive, who did not care?

§

My first contribution to the business came after Al built a new cage to house the previously free-running quail. It had a slanted floor that let their eggs roll forward, making them easier to collect. The feed trays, water bottles, and even a special incubator made especially for poultry were imported from America. His flock quickly increased to just under a hundred birds. Although we ate a lot of the eggs ourselves (one of Al's hobbies was pickling them for snacks), we occasionally sacrificed the non-breeders for our table or to plump up market receipts. My job was to collect the eggs, feed the hens, and clean out the cages. This was on top of my household chores, but somehow it felt more important—a way for Al to notice that I wasn't just a bride-in-waiting or a floor mopper or a teen-toy for him to ogle when the spirit took him. On some occasions, though, his attention backfired.

With so much open land, so many people coming and going, and so many natural predators living around the water, some of the smaller animals inevitably vanished. When it came to the chickens and quail, Al always blamed me for these losses—even when I was the one who reported a missing bird. He'd call me "careless" when cleaning the cages and "stupid" when I gathered the eggs, slapping me on the head so that his lesson would sink in. This bothered me a lot, since I tried to be extra conscientious in the hope that my contribution would stand out and he would treat me with more respect. Finally, I got so fanatical about proving him wrong that I was determined to keep the cages so clean that we could eat from them. That's when I checked under the coops and saw a lot of dried grass had collected there. Without thinking, I started scooping it out with bare hands only to feel my fingers slip over something cool and slimy and long, like a hose. I jumped back, and a big grey and black snake uncoiled from the shadows toward me. Now very afraid and still without thinking, I grabbed Mr. Ba's hoe, which was leaning against the cage, and chopped at the snake furiously. After a frenzied minute or two I stopped, dripping with sweat, then ran to get Al. He followed me to the cage, saw the mangled snake, then inspected Mr. Ba's hoe, which I had bent. He poked around the coop with the wooden handle, examined a couple of loose boards and holes in the chicken wire, then said, "Well, I guess the snake has been here. I'll get a hammer and nails and see if I can fix it."

He didn't apologize for the slaps or the chewing out, but he didn't change my duties. If I learned anything from the incident, it was to regularly check everything I was responsible for—and if I ever had to poke around in tall grass again, do it with a stick.

§

My next challenge was the fish—the whole purpose of the farm.

Originally, Al had a crew of five, including Ngoc, to take care of the ponds, which mostly involved flushing them occasionally with fresh water, cleaning mud and weeds from the sluice gates, and generally keeping things in working order. By the summer of 1972, after we'd lived on the property for a year and invested a lot of heavy labor into fixing things up and making things work, cleaning out mud from the fish ponds, and expanding our living space. We were ready to reap some rewards.

Al was now known in the community as "the Catfish Farmer" since that mild, hearty fish was the backbone of our business. Our ponds also produced tasty alternatives like fresh-water tilapia, "mud fish" (basically, a smaller cousin of the bigger catfish), and fresh-water shrimp. I originally assumed we would catch the fish ourselves and take them to either the Tan Mai or Bien Hoa markets, which only showed how much I had to learn, mostly about not thinking small while Al was thinking big. His grand plan for the place was to make it a recreational garden, which he accomplished with considerable success. American servicemen, foreign contractors, and local Vietnamese would bring their families, wives, and girlfriends for a pleasant day behind our bamboo forest, lounging by the ponds and catching their own lunch or dinner—which they could take with them or we would prepare on the spot—or enjoy the "petting zoo" of our livestock with their kids. Al had this down to a science: one price, $5 USD paid upon entry, would buy you a day to fish and relax, with a guarantee that you would leave with five pounds of fresh catfish even if you had no luck with your hook.

From the day it opened to the public, it was clear most guests preferred the big pond in the front, mostly because the surrounding shade trees were the highest and the small pier jutting out from the main building made an ideal place to drop a line. While Al played host to this radically new "Albert's," the kids, women, and a few spare workers would clean, gut, and fillet customer orders, then grill them to perfection if requested. Sometimes we dipped a few catfish in a batter of cornmeal, flour, salt and pepper, and began handling them out as samples, although only Americans seemed to like these. If bad weather or rumors of impending violence slowed attendance, Al and his helpers (mostly Quang, who proved to be a whiz-bang fisherman) netted a few dozen of each type and drove them to nearby military mess halls and local restaurants that were always in the market for a fresh "Catch of the Day."

While this was going on, sister Thuy and I sold sandwiches, beer, and soft drinks from our screened-in kitchen porch while Quang kept us supplied with merchandise and cleaned up the grounds after picnics in addition to his other outdoor duties like feeding the pigs and skimming the ponds. Little Bubba got into the act, too, following Quang around and helping squeamish females put worms on their hooks or shuttling orders from our kitchen to the guests. Best of all, Al allowed us to keep half the profits from the concessions, minus the cost of the ingredients, of course, plus a modest markup for "the house." Any tips we got, too, were ours and went into a jar that we divided evenly at the end of the day. Americans, in particular, were good tippers. Quang spent his loot mostly on store-bought haircuts and new clothes and, eventually, a new bike—a shinier version of the old one we rode when he gave me a lift to school and a precursor to the used bike he later bought for me when I learned to ride one myself. All in all, it was the best deal I had since my M&Ms racket, and it was a lot better than scrubbing floors and beating snakes with a hoe.

Grandma also had the entrepreneurial itch. Just as she had cooked up trade with the Muong at Binh Duong and figured ways to put vegetables in our pot in Saigon, so she saw gold in the fruited trees around our property. She specialized in bananas, which were easy to grow, easy to transport, and easy to sell. Her trick was to cover the ripening clusters with their own leaves, fooling the birds that often got to our fruit first. This trick once yielded a bunch over seven feet long with a count of 173 bananas—too much for even all of us together to lift, but a sign of bounty that made the effort seem worthwhile.

Selling bananas at Tan Mai market

We took her produce in a wheelbarrow to the Tan Mai market a half-mile away. Believe it or not, I was the horse who pushed our cart, having learned the principles of balance and leverage by helping the workmen move cement and other materials around the property. At the market, Grandma found an empty slot among the vendors and wasn't shy about hawking "Catfish Man" bananas to everyone who passed. As the day wore on and shoppers dwindled, we took any remaining stock down the aisles of other vendors and Grandma offered to sell them wholesale, the price getting better with the setting sun. Still, she was a canny bargainer, and we always went home with an empty wheelbarrow and a clinking bag of coins and cash.

§

School was a different matter. Had it not been for Aunt Nga, all us kids might've stayed home and perfected the arts of housekeeping, cleaning, and manual labor.

From the day we were adopted and moved in, Aunt Thu continued to show her indifference to education, at least for us girls. It was only when Mo Nga arrived at the duplex and lobbied continuously, and successfully, that we all went back to school. I did not know until then that Aunt Nga had taught elementary school in her hometown of Tra On, and could thus assure Thu from experience that our spotty paperwork and confusing birth records would not be a barrier to enrollment. All four of us kids went down with her and Aunt Thu to the Principal's office to sort things out. As Mo Nga predicted, our age and appearance were all that mattered. Bubba was youngest, but very bright so he was sent to kindergarten. Thuy was obviously third-grade material, and (maybe because I was tall for my age) I was sent to fifth grade without having to bother with fourth. Quang was finished with elementary school, so he was sent to Vinh Sang, a Parochial Junior and Senior High where he enrolled in the seventh grade. If you're going to tackle the system, it helps to have someone whose been there. Mo Nga was a very beneficial advocate for our continuing education.

Between school in the morning and Fish Farm chores in the afternoon, my only free time was after dinner and after dark. I still had a passion for reading and used most of the money I earned from working the snack bar and selling bananas to buy books. My favorites were from the "Purple Flower Book Closet" series written by Vietnamese authors for teenagers, and *Quynh Dao* romances translated from Chinese. Al thought my reading was a complete waste of time. His objective for my education was strictly to learn English, which I still spoke poorly despite a few years of casual interaction with Americans. According to Al, anything that took me away from gainful labor showed laziness at best, and at worst, disrespect for him as head of our household. The first time he caught me reading, in fact—after I had cleared and washed the dinner dishes—he snatched the book out of my hand and told me in a combo of broken Vietnamese and English, "*Di di mau!* Get to work!" I cringed, expecting a whack on the head. I didn't argue but made tracks to find Quang or Grandma who, if not doing something productive, were usually out of doors and out of sight around twilight.

The next time I wasn't so lucky. The Fish Farm was closed for some reason, and with the men and Quang out tending the ponds and the housework finished until dinner, I took the opportunity to knock off a couple of chapters. Not a good idea.

Al suddenly loomed over me like a thunderstorm, grabbed the book, and ripped out a handful of pages.

"Di di! Di di! Get to work! Now!"

I scampered away like a cockroach, tears welling in my eyes. I truly had no idea why Al's irritation about my reading had suddenly turned violent. I knew he had a lot of responsibilities—an extended family to care for, a payroll to meet, bills to pay, property and livestock to maintain—but he also had lots of help beyond my own two puny hands. Maybe the Paris peace talks were going badly, and more war was brewing around us. I wouldn't know because adults never discussed such things in front of kids. Maybe he was frustrated by my growing ability to foil his unwanted advances in his sad, sick game of "It!" I didn't know. All I knew was that Al now spent his days like a walking volcano, searching for reasons to erupt. I refused to give up my books though, which was my way of escaping any bad situation, but I also decided that it was best to keep my distance.

From that time onward, I confined my reading to the indoor bathroom or one of the outhouses, whose privacy even Al respected. I also looked for places in the house where I might hide or could at least spot trouble coming. The best spot turned out to be on top of the big armoire that divided the boys' from the girls' sections of our bedroom. It was crowned by a decorative cornice that pretty much hid anything on top, especially a skinny pre-teen girl. I discovered I could spend an hour up there looking like a pile of dirty laundry while kids and housekeepers—even Aunt Thu and Grandma—could pass through the room without noticing. Unfortunately, Al was taller than all of them.

"What the *hell* is this?" he bellowed, reaching up to grab my hair. Al *never* came into the kids' room, and I could only guess he was searching for me. He jerked me down like a rag doll and left the armoire teetering. Still hanging by the hair, he gaffed me once, twice, on the side of the head and dropped me on my knees. He then turned back to the armoire, groping around the top until he had collared all of my books, which he then confiscated. I never saw them again, and frankly, I was afraid to look or even bring up the subject with Aunt Thu or Grandma. In Al's private war against books, I was the VC, and he had all the American firepower.

Bubba later told me he watched Al manhandle me by the armoire and destroy my book collection. Al didn't do it as a lesson for his son—little Bubba was just standing around—but it affected him nonetheless.

Remember, I was Bubba's "mama figure" for a couple of years before Aunt Thu returned to claim him. Like a dutiful son, or loving little brother, he decided to make things right on his own. Secretly, he stole some fishing gear from the utility barn—nothing big, just some hooks and weights and nylon line—and traded it to a neighbor boy for some books the boy's older brother had finished and no longer wanted. These Bubba brought to me a few days later, beaming like it was Christmas morning.

"Here you are, Sissy," he said proudly. "I got just the ones you said you like—Red Flower detective, *Kiem Hiep* Swashbuckler, you know. Don't be sad. Daddy doesn't hate you."

I took the books with a big lump in my throat. I literally couldn't answer.

"I made a deal to get more books so you won't have to buy them. Just keep quiet about it, okay? Or both of us will get in trouble."

It was, of course, more than a deal. It was the first time my "little brother" showed his character, and I could only be proud that I was responsible for at least part of it. He never told me where he got the books. I didn't know until a few months later when the neighbor boy found me at school and demanded them back, saying his older brother still wanted the books and would raise a stink about it with my parents. That seemed like a persuasive argument, so I gave back all but a few of my favorites without demanding the return of the fishing gear, so everyone was happy. I told Bubba what had happened and asked him not to engage in any "black market book buying" in the future. He promised he wouldn't, and he didn't. It was not the last time "Sissy" would turn to Bubba in an hour of need, and from that moment on, we were convinced that we could read each other's minds—or at least knew instinctively what was in each other's heart.

§

With my world of books imploded, I tried to make the most of my time at school. Quang's school was in the opposite direction so the rest of us had to walk about a mile, a hike that got our blood pumping for morning classes. We left the house about 7:00 a.m. after a breakfast of leftovers, which often included hot French bread (Al loved the kind that came from a bakery only half-a-mile away) or Grandma's garlic fried rice reheated from the night before. Bubba, on the other hand, was a finicky eater, so Thu gave him money to buy hot rice crepes from a vendor who worked the school entrance. As Bubba's unofficial nanny, it was my job to make sure he got his crepe breakfast, then wait for him to eat it. Unfortunately, he was often so pooped from the walk that he just plopped down in front of the vendor as soon as he was served and ate it on the spot, blocking the counter for other people. This should have annoyed everyone, but Bubba looked like a chunky little Buddha while he ate, swaying back and forth with a big grin on his face and chanting "Yum, yum!" to the vendor's cart. After a while, people came to enjoy his little act, so I gave up trying to move him. How often Thuy and I would've loved a fresh, hot crepe ourselves, but a house can only hold so many "royals." Our little Bubba was the "Prince" in ours.

Since little waited for me at home beyond more chores and abuse from Al, I hung around school after the final bell and looked for things to do. I went out of my way to make new friends and finagle invitations to their houses, where, in addition to gabbing and exchanging hair-care tips, I could do a little reading. One of these after-school buddies was Thom, whom I nicknamed "Skinny Thom," because no matter how much her parents fed her, she never gained weight. This was no small trick, since her family of five lived at the Tan Mai market about a half mile from Fish Farm. Her mother sold food of all kinds, from beans, rice, sugar and spices to C- and K-Rations scrounged from GIs who were sick of eating them. One of her best sellers was Hormel canned ham, which had more fat in one serving than most Vietnamese ate in a month, but her customers couldn't get enough of it. Thom, in turn, called me *Chi Van*, or "Big Sister," because I was taller than her. Thom's house was a safe place to hang out and shift gears from the rigors of school to the labors of home, but we didn't really become *best* friends until an unhappy incident near the end of the school year.

Another girl in our class, Lien, lived in the school orphanage. There but for the Grace of God went I, right? So I tried to treat her kindly, but she would have none of it. She had a chip on her shoulder the size of Al's quail coop and, with a gang of other girl orphans, decided early on that I was her sworn enemy. I certainly gave her no reason to think this, other than the fact that the whole school knew I was an orphan, too. But, my situation was better than hers by living with an American's family in a snazzy house with lots of property and close relatives around me (Of course, she had no idea of the constant fear I lived with because of Al and Thu. If she had, maybe she could have been nicer). Pre-teen girls can be cruel at the best of times, but when circumstances turn against them, they can be as treacherous as snakes. Where was my hoe when I needed it?

Lien's harassment began with small raids on my sanity. At first she and her gang threw wadded paper and chalk at me from the back of the classroom, then pretended nothing had happened. I "retaliated" by being nice, offering her cuts in line at the water fountain and inviting her to play hopscotch or jump rope with Thom and me on the playground. But she just grunted and turned away. Since she was struggling with writing and arithmetic, I even offered to tutor her after class, but she treated that as an insult. My friends said she was a "lost cause" and "bad news" and would wind up getting us both in trouble just to make me go down with her ship, but I persevered. Not only did I understand her loneliness, confusion, and frustration, I still felt them in my strained relationship with Al and Thu ("We can always dump you at an orphanage," was their favorite last-ditch threat), and my endless question about my father's fate. These were things I learned to live with, and I knew how much better Lien's life could be if she would only do the same. Fat chance.

Things came to a head in what, without exaggeration, I could only call an assassination attempt. The morning session had just let out, and we fifth-graders were leaving our second-story classroom and had reached the head of the stairs. Out of nowhere, I felt two hands push hard against my shoulders, and I tumbled forward. The stairs were crowded, but once I got going I made a pretty big hole. I bounced between kids like a billiard ball until I cartwheeled into some kindergartners at the bottom of the stairs. The little ones screamed, but a big girl behind me was laughing—not Lien, who was still at the top of the stairs, smirking and heading down the hall—but one of her goons, a muscular girl named Lanh. I whirled, not knowing if anything was sprained or broken and not thinking more than a split-second about the matter, and I punched Lanh square in the face as hard as I could. That year of pushing wheelbarrows, pulling mops, and raking muck off the ponds had paid off. Lanh fell back onto the stairs, then got up quickly, staring back at me wide-eyed over the tops of the bloody fingers that covered her nose.

The little kids had now scattered, and my classmates at the top of the stairs took off. Lanh stabilized herself with the handrail, and I raised my fist for another punch. Lien had started things, but if only one of us walked away from the stairwell, I was determined it would be me.

Lanh stared at me a second, then sat on the stairs and cried.

All this excitement was bound to bring the nuns, so I turned and walked briskly toward the school gate. Almost immediately, Thom and some playground pals fell into formation beside me. We made it out ahead of the authorities, who swarmed sympathetically around Lanh, but we all knew my luck wouldn't last.

Back home, I dove into my chores with single-minded determination—undoubtedly a surprise to Al and Thu until a stranger rang the bell at our gate. It was Lanh's mother.

Though I was closest to the gate, I ignored her. Sister Thuy moved to answer it, but I told her to stay put. It finally occurred to me that this strategy was probably doomed, especially when Aunt Thu breezed in, saying, "Why in Heaven's name don't you girls answer the bell?"

I stopped her long enough to give a brief, sanitized version of my story. "Fighting at school!" Aunt Thu frowned, then I quickly added that since Lanh was a bully, her mother might be, too, so if she chose to answer the bell, she might call Al or one of the workmen or at least carry a big stick. Aunt Thu went to the gate and peered through, but didn't open it. The lady on the other side screamed when she saw me.

"There's that filthy kid! She broke my daughter's nose! What are you going to do about it? You know how much a doctor costs?"

To her credit, Aunt Thu started to tell my side of the story, but the woman cut her off. "Is this the way you raise your daughter? Teaching her to be a thug?"

Lanh now crept out from behind her mother. "Mama, Van doesn't have a mother. Her parents are dead."

The woman paused, mentally regrouped, then pounded the gate again, "Well, that proves it! She's just a worthless, stupid orphan who belongs with the nuns. Now who's going to pay my daughter's doctor bill?"

"Van will be punished, you can count on it," Aunt Thu said. "But—"

"No buts!" The woman shoved her arm through the bars at me. "Send out the little brat, and I'll take it out of her hide!"

At that Aunt Thu grabbed my arm and took me into the house, leaving Lanh and her boxing coach screaming outside the gate. I got a lecture from Thu about how fighting was bad and hadn't I seen enough of it in my young life to know it was wrong? I said yes, I agreed with everything she said, but I felt no remorse. Lanh should not have pushed me down the stairs. She was lucky that I had only a few bumps and bruises from my tumble. What if I had been really hurt? What if one or more of the kindergarten kids had been hurt? I didn't say it to Aunt Thu, but Lanh had that punch coming. For the sake of peace in the family, Thu said that she would not tell Al about the incident. She was sure right about that, and I once again thanked my guardian angels.

The next day I went to school expecting the worst—from Lien, from Lanh, from the principal or from the parent—but nothing happened. Apparently there were too many witnesses to the shove, and Lien's and Lanh's reputations were well-known. Besides, if anybody had a reason to complain, it was me and the kindergartners Lanh had endangered. The principal thought it best to just let the whole thing blow over, allow God to move in His mysterious ways, and leave playground justice to playmates. That ended the crisis, and more importantly, Lien's campaign to make my life miserable—at least for the time being. Our final showdown wouldn't come until the last day of school.

§

Every grade school in Vietnam had a year-end awards ceremony, and ours was no exception. Students are not only graded on report cards, but also ranked against each other in a way that mimics the real-life competition for jobs, promotions, and mates. For us, rankings were more important than grades in determining who was admitted to what high school, and later who made it to college.

To this point in my short academic career, I had managed to come out first in student rankings for every grade I attended. Aside from the prestige, which admittedly didn't mean much to first-and-second graders, schools gave out prizes befitting the student's age. The top students got the best prizes, which could range from an entirely new uniform for first place to various kinds of school supplies as the rankings descended. At the ceremony, all students convened in an auditorium or lunch hall, and the principal gave out awards in reverse order, building suspense until she got to number one.

My name was called for Third Place.

While my friends clapped politely, I walked to the principal's table in a state of shock. I received a couple of notebooks and a few pens and pencils held together by rubber bands. I suppose there was a second- and first-place winner, but frankly, I was too numb to hear who they were. I only knew that Number One hadn't been me.

When we were dismissed, I went straight to the Principal's office to protest.

"What are you talking about, Miss Van?" the head nun asked politely. "We tallied the semester scores very carefully, and you came out number three in your whole class. You should be very proud!"

"I would be very proud if I was first, which I think is where I belong. I think there's been a mistake. Please recount my scores."

The principal indulged me, and I took a seat while she retrieved my file from the cabinet behind her desk. After a few moments she closed the file and said, "No, there's no mistake. The original count was accurate. If you still think we've made an error, you can bring in your old papers, and I'll double-check your grades."

She knew, of course, that nobody kept all of their old homework, reports, and exams for a whole year. She again congratulated me for finishing third and told me that if I wanted to rank higher next year, just work a little harder and be sure to save my papers. *Right.*

Thom was waiting for me when I left the principal's office, and she could tell things had not gone well. She knew one reason I pushed so hard for first place was that the prize—a new school uniform—changed when the students reached sixth grade. Instead of the old blue skirt and white blouse, girls in Junior High wore a white *ao dai* over white or black pants—the flowing, traditional outfit of Vietnamese women. I doubted if Al and Thu would fork over the cash needed for this new outfit, and I probably couldn't earn enough from working the Fish Farm concessions and hauling Grandma's bananas to buy one. I needed a miracle.

I was thus in a very bad mood when we passed through the gates and were confronted by Lien and her gangsters. The school year was over. They no longer had to play nice.

Without a word, Lien simply lunged at me, grabbed my hair with both hands, and used the full weight of her body to throw me to the ground. I spun away and got up, but her hand locked onto my blouse, tearing off every button to the waist and ripping off one sleeve. She was a tiger, a maniac. Then three of her goons joined the fight.

Fortunately, I was still the tallest kid in the class, boy or girl, so my punches had a longer reach. Despite my lucky hit on Lanh four months earlier, I really didn't know how to fight and swung as wildly as anybody. A few landed, but most didn't. I never knew who I hit or where. I just wheeled back and forth like a wounded water buffalo and struck out at whatever was in front of me. A second later, one of those figures was Thom. She jumped on one of Lien's girls—maybe Lien herself—and began pummeling her head and shoulders. They both went down. Strangely, the Thom I knew—a sweet girl like Mr. Phuoc who wouldn't hurt a fly—became a biting, scratching, punching machine. This was not what Lien and her demon army expected. Just as quickly as they attacked, the bad guys ran off.

When I turned, I saw that it wasn't because of Thom's berserker defense. Three nuns were running at us full tilt through the stunned crowd by the gate.

This time we didn't try to escape. The nuns questioned and chastised us, but I never heard what they said. A friend told me later that Lien was apprehended by the nuns (after all, where could she go?—she was an orphan who lived at the school!). The other girls were disciplined, but it was the end of the school year and everybody, including the teachers, just wanted to go home. Thom helped me pick up my prize notebooks and pencils and carry them to my house since I needed one hand to hold shut my buttonless blouse. I did not even want to think about what Thu or Al would say. But my private little war was over, and thanks to Thom's help, there was not much damage. As far as I was concerned, my troubles with Lien were over for good. I would not have to deal with her in the next school year because we would be going our separate ways. I hope her fortune changed, and that she enjoyed some happiness.

§

With promotion to Junior High, I joined Quang, two grades ahead of me, at the Vinh Sang Catholic school. A lot of my former classmates opted for government schools because private education at the junior and senior high levels, while partially subsidized, was just too expensive for their families. Among new expenses for girls was an *ao dai*, which I still didn't have. Aunt Thu complained enough about tuition so I didn't dream of asking her, and that was when Grandma again came to my rescue. She had enough money from her banana business to buy fabric for a slick, rose-print outer dress and almost-silk black pants, both of which were tailor-made by a seamstress in town. I felt more than grown up: I looked like a genuine princess. Unfortunately, Thom's mother could afford none of those extras, including tuition, so she wound up in the public school. We promised to keep in touch, though it would be difficult. Al now watched me like a hawk and said that unless I was at school or at the market, I must be on the Fish Farm doing some work. Thus my visits with Thom all occurred by her mother's food stall at Tan Mai. Lanh, the girl whose nose I broke, was a different matter. She was going to Vinh Sang, too, and when I bumped into her, she apologized for all the hubbub and said she wanted to be friends.

I was astonished. "I don't know," I said. "Do you promise you won't attack me?"

She laughed. "Yes, I promise. Besides, I know you could beat me up!"

That didn't really sound like a compliment, especially to a bookworm like me, but she seemed sincere, so on those occasions when our paths crossed during the semester, we got along and eventually became good friends. My first visit to the principal's office, however, produced a different kind of crisis.

Each new student had to interview with the principal, during which the nun or priest running the school reviewed your records, accomplishments, and discussed any problems you might cause or encounter. My "deportment" (always a big deal at Catholic schools) wasn't an issue because my battles with Lien weren't reported on my fifth grade transcripts. They did mention, however, my ranking at the year-end Awards Ceremony—officially, *third*—while the certificate I brought to the interview said "first," a pen-and-ink correction I felt I owed myself. The priest compared my obvious forgery to the school's official record, thought a moment, then handed the certificate back without saying a word. I guess my stellar grades belied the official rating, and since I didn't seem to pose any special risk except maybe overachiever burnout, the principal decided to let sleeping dogs lie. I was glad he decided quickly before I fainted from shame by his desk.

§

School settled into a familiar routine, which was fine with me. Quang's gift of a used bike saved me the two-mile walk to Junior High, and I signed up for afternoon classes so I wouldn't have to get up so early and could finish most of my Fish Farm chores before it got too hot. Studies were harder (math included algebra and geometry now, along with some biology and chemistry), and the books we read in class were more challenging. This at least kept my mind occupied during the endless hours of cleaning, mopping, and muckraking that preceded school. Not all of my teachers, though, thought I was God's gift to their classes.

Mr. Hung, my math teacher, had studied to be a priest but flunked out. This gave him a dour outlook even worse than some of the other nuns and priests, who saw the world as being full of sinners. He resented anyone with scholastic ambitions, particularly people who might actually succeed—and especially girls. In this he had a lot in common with Aunt Thu, who would've agreed there was nothing a woman couldn't do better, provided she was barefoot and pregnant. I did not understand why he stayed in teaching, except that maybe it kept him out of the Army.

Anyway, my first run-in with Mr. Hung was when he judged me too quick to answer questions in class. "Give someone else a chance!" he told me, then called on some girl who had no clue. After a few days of this, and at the request of some classmates, I began passing notes to my neighbors with scribbled answers to his questions. Of course, one of these was eventually intercepted, which got me into even more trouble. I was not only a "talker" now, but a "cheater" and a "disrupter." When I finally asked to see him after class, he didn't want to talk about academics but only lectured me about "striving harder" to be a "better young lady." When I asked him to explain, he said that because "orphans usually don't know their place," I should work harder to fit in. I didn't know what this had to do with math, but I did know it had everything to do with how he and a lot of other people still looked at me.

As it turned out, one of those people, Mr. Thai, my language teacher, was Mr. Hung's brother-in-law. He taught both Vietnamese literature (which I loved) and English (my worst subject—sixth grade was the first year students took it in organized classes), but I at least got to hear it spoken at home, an advantage over most of my classmates. Thai was Dr. Jekyll to Hung's Mr. Hyde. He encouraged me to read (imagine that!) and gave me advanced lessons after class. Since I felt I'd found a teacher who finally understood me, I asked him why Mr. Hung disliked me so much. Maybe it was because they were in-laws and Mr. Thai had to keep peace in the family, but all he said was, "Well, don't worry about it." Perhaps to make up for something neither of us could help, he asked if I wanted to volunteer for the party-planning committee, which he headed, and help get decorations at the local market. I said "Sure." I was already class Vice President and had organized several student events, including the annual intramural cooking contest and a folk dancing group, so the other kids trusted me with such duties. But, I added, I would need my family's permission. Mr. Thai went home with me and talked for a few minutes with Aunt Thu. They got along well, and she said yes, so we left right then for the market. Mr. Thai was a careful shopper and good custodian of Parish funds. I got back to Fish Farm about 7:00 p.m. that night.

As soon as I walked in, Al blew his stack.

"What the hell are you doing out after dark with a stranger? And a grown man at that!" I told him Aunt Thu gave me permission, but he didn't care. "From now on, young lady, you come home immediately after school—no extracurricular activities, no parties, no sports, no girlfriends, no boyfriends, no nothing! You come straight home, understand?"

I said, "Yes," although I didn't understand most of his words, and his harsh attitude was a complete mystery. Days later, Grandma hinted that things were tense in our district because although the treaty supposedly ended the war, the soldiers from the North were still in the field and tightening their grip around the capital. Maybe Al was worried about a family member wandering around after dark, or maybe he was behaving like an overly protective Vietnamese-style father, but I had other suspicions. Perhaps he resented Mr. Thai as a prospective adult male rival in the "It!" game. With Al, you never knew. Anyway, I took the "grounding" as just another punishment for being who I was, where I was, and there was not a lot I could do about it.

§

By the summer of 1974, I had turned fourteen, and Aunt Thu decided I must learn the ultimate Vietnamese housewife's art: cooking rice on a coal stove. The secret to cooking rice in any fashion is even temperature—not too hard in a pot on a modern stove, black magic when the source of heat flares and fades like burning coal. People the world over had been cooking like this since iron was discovered, but for a girl my age, when there is a first time for everything, my debut was a total disaster. Aunt Thu put me in charge of lunchtime rice for the entire Fish Farm crew, so we're talking lots of grains, lots of water, and a really, really big pot above a coal-fired stove as deep and dark as Lucifer's cave. I was doomed before I started but gave it a shot.

Of course, coal takes time to heat, and if you wait too long to spread the lumps, it roars like a blowtorch. The foamy, starchy water boils over, and the sickening smell of scorched rice fills the kitchen, killing appetites. Lunch was protein-poor that day, and after being slapped silly by Thu, I spent the rest of the afternoon scouring black soot from the pot. "Tomorrow, you'll do better," she said, her words sounding more like a threat than encouragement.

The next day in my crash-course on Vietnamese housewifery was the proper cutting of greens called *rau day*. This time, Aunt Thu would handle the cooking but harvesting the vegetables—the key to the dish, she said ominously—was up to me. This key was slicing the greens off precisely three inches above the ground. Not only did this ensure greens of proper taste and texture, it did not kill the plant, which would continue to grow and provide for future meals—never a minor concern in a culture where hunger is a constant companion. This was also a big deal for Thu personally, since she never allowed other people in her garden. This was the test of tests.

Full of dread, I entered her sacred garden and proceeded to measure from the base of the plants, precisely three inches, or the length of her index finger (the middle finger for me) and performed the required surgery. I took the cuttings into the kitchen, plucked the leaves from the stems as she had shown, making sure not to take too much of the outer layer, then presented the stalks for her inspection. To my relief, they passed muster. She put them into her soup and again set me to making the rice—a pop quiz!—but this time with Grandma's help. An hour later we enjoyed a delicious lunch, with no bruises to cheeks or egos—or so I thought.

I started to clean up while Aunt Thu went to her garden. A few seconds later, she slapped my head, left and right. I dropped the pot I was scrubbing and cowered.

"Stupid girl!" she shouted. "Stupid child!"

"What did I do?" Both forearms now covered my head.

"You killed my plants—that's what you did! Pulled them up by the roots!"

"No, no. I cut them just as you said. Three inches from the ground!"

"Don't talk back!" She belted me again on my sheltering hands. By now Grandma had put her soft-puffing pipe aside and came to restrain her daughter.

"Thu," she said firmly, catching her flailing arms. "Stop it. Stop it right now."

"But this stupid girl killed my plants!"

"She did no such thing." Grandma took me under her arm. "And even if she cut too short, they'll grow back. They're just plants, for heaven's sake. What's gotten into you?"

"What's gotten into me?" Thu fumed. "That little brat's gotten into me. She got me into this mess! If Hien had stayed alive instead of chasing after Tinh at Hong Ngu, I wouldn't have to play mother to three orphans! I wouldn't have to pay their school money! I wouldn't have had to clean other people's toilets! I wouldn't have had to marry an old-man American! Is that enough for you?"

This outburst stunned me more than the blows to my head. I saw they rocked Grandma, too, but her face revealed nothing. Or maybe she just knew, as mothers know, that her daughter had regrets about the man she married, in this case Al Strauss—the savior of our family—and taking responsibility for another woman's kids. This was not about *rau day* or burned rice or my habit of reading books or anything else that had made me the household's whipping post.

I folded my hands over my heart and said, "I am sincerely sorry for everything, Aunt Thu," and meant it. "But I am not my mother. I did not do these things to you. Even Mama did not do these things to you—"

Thu pulled away. Her face contorted with her anger, her fists clinched to her side as if to hold back from striking me again. "So, now you're my mother, too? I don't need two mothers. The one I have is enough!"

She looked at Grandma, who stood with me.

"What??" she screamed. "You want me to beg her (pointing at me) for forgiveness? To apologize?" She feigned a sorrowful, mocking expression and dropped to her knees, sobbing in her anger.

"I'm sorry!" she wailed. "I didn't mean any of that! Forgive me! God in Heaven, both of you, forgive me! All of you forgive me!"

She was now talking to no one and everyone, and I had no idea what to do next. I could only stare at her, and I don't think Grandma did, either. Then Al came through the door. He saw his wife on her knees in front of me, pushed between us, and picked me up by the shoulders. "What the *hell* is all this?" he bellowed, giving me a good shaking.

Grandma put an arm in front of him, but he brushed it away, then slapped me across the face with the back of his hand. "I asked you a question, Sissy! What the hell is going on?"

I started to sob incoherently, that nasty metallic taste of pure terror in my mouth, along with a little blood. Al dragged me out the screen door, snatching a loose two-by-four from the porch, and threw me down to the dirt. His first blow hit me on the shoulder. I covered my head, and the second blow hit my arm. I ducked and weaved, but he kept at me. I thought of running—maybe out to the ponds, maybe *into* the ponds, maybe into Mr. Ba's strong, protective arms, but the board found me again. The edge bit into my forearm, gashing to the bone, and I curled into a ball. Blows rained on my back and ribs and hips and then it stopped. Grandma had thrown her body over mine. Al waved the big piece of wood menacingly a few times, then threw it down and stomped into the house.

After a minute to make sure the storm had passed, Grandma helped me up and we went into the screened-in porch. Al and Thu had gone to their bedroom, and shut the door. Grandma dampened a rag and sponged my cuts and bruises. She put something sticky on the big gouge on my arm—I had no idea what it was or where she got it, or even how it stuck, since I was sweaty and dirty and shaking like a leaf. After a few minutes, I became aware that she had been talking the whole time. I have no idea what she was saying. After I had been bandaged and the blood wiped away, I got up and stumbled to my bed and cried harder than I can ever remember. I was so tired of being brave, tired of being hated because I was alive and an orphan, tired of being tortured by Al and ignored by Thu. Neither my Grandmother's love nor my own love for Quang and Thuy and Bubba could sustain me any longer. In that selfish moment I did not even think of them. I had nothing left in my heart other than sorrow and a wish that I had never been born. No hope, no promise of a future, no mother or father to kiss those hurts away. I spotted a new bottle of aspirin on Grandma's bedside table. With out hesitation, I opened the lid and swallowed all the pills. Sometime later, I have no idea how long, Grandma came to check on me and found me doubled over with cramps, sweaty, and throwing up. Once again, Grandma had the task of cleaning me up. I know that if she could, she would have emptied her heart into mine. Through the fog, I heard her whisper:

"*There now. That's better. You're almost old enough to find a husband. That will save you. That will get you out of this house. That's what your mother would want...*"

Chapter 10

Mouth of the Dragon—1974

For the next few weeks, Aunt Thu and I didn't exchange a word. Al didn't talk to me either, though both made clear with frowns and gestures what would happen if I neglected my chores or ignored their rules. Even Grandma faded into the woodwork after Al's savage attack. She spent more time in her kitchens at the barn or just sitting outside with her pipe, staring at the ponds and the trees and muttering to the animals. She was in the world but above it. I envied her greatly.

My body healed from the beating fairly quickly, but not my heart. I kept going over things in my mind, what I could have done differently that day to spare me—and Grandma—Al's brutality with the board. What led directly to the beating was Aunt Thu's accusation that I'd killed her plants, which was just not true. But my protests of innocence—and Grandma's calm defense of me—only sent Aunt Thu further over the edge of the abyss of her long-buried and unreasonable rage and resentment, rage and resentment I now understood to be toward my mother.

My aunt was furious with my mother for dying.

Did she think my mother *wanted* to die? That she died on purpose, just to make Aunt Thu's life miserable? Was she also furious with my mother for being happy—truly soul-deep happy—in her too-short marriage when she—Thu—had been disappointed in love and felt forced to marry a man she didn't love, didn't want to marry, in order to be able to provide a secure life for herself, her fatherless son, and her aged mother, and, on top of that, her "unnecessarily" orphaned nephew and nieces? I realized that not only would I never fully understand the now-unresolvable issues Thu felt she had with my mother, but also that I could do nothing to change how Thu felt about me, and, to a lesser extent, about Quang and Thuy. She blamed us for our very existence. When she unmercifully slapped my head back and forth, she was slapping my mother, her sister, not me. It wasn't about me. It had never been about me. And because it wasn't about me, there was nothing I could do to fix it.

My saviors in this desolate time were Quang and Thuy. Quang carved a little sign for me in his woodworking class bearing my middle and first names: *Bich Van*—a fitting reminder that I had not always been "Sissy." He also bought a small rosary for me and told me to keep it with me always for protection, so I did.

Thuy was a different matter. Her duties had always been lighter than mine, so we had more time to talk. It appeared that I was not the only one singled out for Al's unwanted attentions. Since she spent more time with Bubba and both Al and Thu still revered their "little prince," she basked in their goodwill. However, as time went on and I became less accessible for the "It!" game, Al began paying more attention to Thuy. Though she seldom drew his anger or a swat, she told me *he sometimes handles me* in a way that was wrong for a father-figure or "uncle" or even a taskmaster. She was too shy to tell me much, but I knew firsthand what she was talking about. Al had singled her out for his creepy game of touch-and-tickle—an unsavory ritual that in recent months I'd either evaded or been spared. But this was too much. First me, now my younger sister. This was the last straw.

I told Thuy we must do something about it—*now*.

At a time when Aunt Thu seemed more approachable than usual, Thuy and I stood before her, hand in hand, and I told her we had something gravely important to talk about. Thu gave us a suspicious look and continued folding the laundry, but said, "Okay, what's on your mind?"

I told her.

"Liar." That was all Thu said. She said it firmly but didn't shout. She didn't raise her arm to hit me. She obviously wanted the issue to end right there before Al arrived on the scene, a risk that none of us—even Aunt Thu—was willing to take.

Fortunately, Uncle Hai and Aunt Nga were staying with us at the time. Hai just happened to be nearby in the screened-in porch, preparing his duffle bag for another cruise. He heard Thu call me "*Liar*" and came to see what was wrong. With Thu still in the room and quietly ignoring us, I told him what I'd told her. Hai took time to hear me out, his face getting darker with every detail. Just as I finished, Al came into the kitchen.

In a stream of Vietnamese invectives, Uncle Hai read Al the riot act. Al, unable to speak our language, understood none of it, and Aunt Thu wasn't about to translate. Still, through tone and gestures, Hai got the message across.

Al muttered something to Aunt Thu, who nodded, then he left. She turned to me and said, "Al wants you out of the house today. Right now. Go pack your things."

This was supposed to be punishment? "Fine," I said. "That's exactly what I plan to do. But Thuy is coming with me."

"Take her." Thu sniffed and went back to work. "That's one less mouth to feed."

Uncle Hai started to argue with Aunt Thu, then stopped. He was enough of a man of the world to know that he wouldn't change Al by reasoning, and that to leave us girls at Fish Farm now that he knew the facts would make him complicit in our abuse.

We all walked back to the duplex, where Hai explained the situation to Mo Nga. I expected her to offer my sister and me a motherly hug or at least a word of sympathy, but she just gave us a blank stare. Maybe she was embarrassed or ashamed, or just worried that this development would wreck the handy deal she had with Al and Thu, who gave her lodging while Hai was at sea. At any rate, she simply turned, got pencil and paper, and jotted down Uncle Chieu's new address in Saigon.

"You get along fine with Uncle Chieu and his girlfriend, Mai, don't you?" Uncle Hai asked.

I said we did, maybe with fingers crossed. Chieu was a better man now that Aunt Que was out of the picture, though he could still be a little undependable. Mai was a "city girl" at heart with her own ideas about things, but she had always been friendly to us. As Chieu's brother and one of our favorite uncles, I knew Hai wouldn't needlessly add to our peril.

Thuy and I packed our few things that afternoon and put the Fish Farm gate behind us well before dinner. I was fourteen and Thuy thirteen, but as far as the world was concerned, we were two determined young women on a mission. Inside, however, we knew our world was turned upside down. Thuy held back tears the whole way to Saigon, and I, too, put on a brave face, though my insides felt like jelly. We got off the bus still trying not to look like exactly what we were: a pair of runaways with an orphanage snapping at our heels.

§

We knocked on the door of Uncle Chieu's rented leaf house a few hours later. He was at home, but Mai was out. We gave him a condensed version of the facts (another adult who seemed to be unsurprised!), and he showed us where to put our things and where we could spend the night. His son Ngoc still lived with the hired workers at Fish Farm, but his daughter, Lien, who had befriended me years before, and the other two younger sons, Duc and Thang, still lived with Aunt Que in a situation arguably worse than mine. Here, we were the only children in the house. We cleaned ourselves up and had something to eat while Chieu pondered his next move.

"You know, I want to help you, but it's not all up to me. I have to talk to Mai about this. She might object to having two teenagers living in the house. As you can see, we don't have much room. And the landlord—I have to talk to him and see how much he'll charge for extra lodgers. And I should talk to your uncle Hai. This is a big change for everybody. Why don't you girls get some sleep? We'll talk about this in the morning."

We did and with the morning sun came Aunt Nga and her kids. Apparently she and Hai decided that the atmosphere at Fish Farm was too poisonous for them to stay, so they were moving, too—an opportue time, with Hai leaving on another cruise. Mo Nga and her children would return to her home town of Tra On, a suburb of the larger south-central city of Can Tho on the Mekong Delta, to live with her mother. They would be well taken care of, but first she wanted to check on us.

While Mo Nga talked about her plans, Mai came in. We were asleep when she returned late the previous night and had no idea how she felt about the situation. We did not have to wait long to find out.

"Tra On!" Mai said enthusiastically. "That would be a wonderful place for Thuy, don't you think? I mean, Chieu and I really don't have room for both of them. Van's the oldest and I can use her help around here, but Thuy would really be better living with your girls."

"I don't know," Mo Nga said. "The sisters really want to stick together—"

She and Mai haggled like two pig farmers until a deal was struck. While they were talking, I saw Thuy's face cloud up, so I took her aside.

"Look, I know you want to stay with me, but we can't have everything, okay? We've got to take what we can get. At least we're away from Al and Aunt Thu. Mo Nga's a good person and you like her daughters. I'll look for a job and after I've made some money, I'll come and get you. We can live on our own in the city, okay?" Thuy's eyes filled with tears, but she finally nodded. As for me, I clamped down hard on the pain in my heart and refused to let my own tears even form.

I knew my plan was pure wishful thinking, but it gave both of us hope and was enough to get Thuy out the door with a family we could trust. Now all I had to do was make the rest of our little fairy tale come true.

§

I spent the first on-my-own night at Uncle Chieu's tossing and turning, covered with mosquitos, occasionally crying silent tears, and listening to distant gunshots. I was exhausted and still in shock, needing to sleep, but my mind was wide awake. That morning, which now felt like a lifetime ago, I'd been living with my grandmother and my siblings. Tonight I was living in a stranger's home, where I was not made to feel welcome, not knowing what my life would be like from now on. How would I explain everything to Uncle Chieu? Did I have to tell him all of the reasons why Thuy and I left Aunt Thu and Fish Farm? Perhaps it was better to wait until he asked. (He never did ask, nor did Mai.) Oh, so much to think about!

When Thuy and I had first arrived, I'd been too upset to look around, but in the cold light of day, I saw that my "life raft" from Fish Farm was really much more raft than a place to start a new life. I felt depressed and utterly alone.

Chieu rented a fair-sized room in a four-room hutch of typical low-income construction—bamboo structure with tightly knit leaves for insulation. The elderly landlord and his wife, plus a nephew, lived in one room by the entrance, rented out the next two rooms behind it, and used the fourth—which overhung the river—as a combination kitchen and bathroom. Chieu and Mai shared the last bedroom next to the common area, and all occupants had to pass through their room down an open, central hallway to cook or use the toilet, so they didn't have much privacy. The other couple worked, and I glimpsed them only rarely. Overnight guests were permitted, but adding a third full-time resident (and an almost-woman at that) put a strain on everyone's resources—more cooking, more water, more bathroom sharing, more noise—and that meant a boost in rent. Uncle Chieu negotiated a second bed, which he placed against his far wall on the other side of the open passageway. He told the landlord that I was well-behaved, quiet, and relocating to Saigon to attend a better school. I don't know if the landlord believed him, but the fact that Chieu was a member of the National Police force didn't hurt.

Once I was up and washed and had breakfast (Chieu had gone to work and Mai was still asleep behind the curtain around their bed), the landlord's nephew came to the room, introduced himself politely, and offered to help me find a new school. Chieu said before he left that the nephew was "a good guy" so I was inclined to trust him, and well, I simply had no other plan. We visited some neighborhood schools that looked like old prisons, then settled on Son-Ha Junior High and High School, a public school that looked the best maintained. It was also the shortest walk from Uncle Chieu's apartment, which, after the previous night's clattering gunfire, seemed like a good idea.

A few days later, I enrolled myself in the eighth grade. Even though it was a government school and I had no birth certificate or ID or school transcripts, they accepted me without question and told me to show up for class the following day. On the way home, I stopped at a local bookstore and used some of my savings to buy a folio case for my pens (the first one I ever owned!), a notebook, some pencils, and a bottle of purple ink—a favorite color for cool teenagers, so I hoped to impress the crowd. Most of the kids at Son-Ha wore public school uniforms: black or blue slacks and white shirts for boys, *ao dai* and white or black pants for girls. I didn't want to waste cash on clothing, so I simply wore my *ao dai* from parochial school, which still fit just fine. My biggest concern was money. Uncle Chieu had a good heart, but Mai controlled the purse strings. She had no regular job beyond running numbers in a popular betting game, mostly for her friends and neighbors. It was risky, but she had fun and enjoyed an occasional payday that may or may not have made up for her losses. I had no idea how long my welcome would last, and I sure didn't want to live on the streets or commit myself to an orphanage. I had also promised to "pick up" Thuy someday, whatever that meant, and I knew that whatever it meant would cost money. I had to find a job.

After a month in school, I thought I'd found my chance. Back in the Phu Nhuan Leaf House, when Aunt Thu briefly ran her shaved-ice stand, she had a regular customer named Loan, a friendly, good-looking girl a few years older than me who always greeted me with a hug and had spending money in her purse. Grandma treated her respectfully and even allowed her to take me to market and buy me lunch at a nearby restaurant.

I recalled her now because she said back then that she lived in the Ba Chieu district, where Uncle Chieu and Mai now rented their room. I don't know why Loan's name and face popped into my head—after all, it had been eight years and a lot had happened—but I took it as a sign that a Guardian Angel, perhaps my mother, was looking out for me. Undeterred by the long odds of finding a half-forgotten person in a jam-packed neighborhood, I started knocking on doors. My Guardian Angel stuck with me.

Following leads for a week, I found Loan living with several other young women in a cramped shack in a very poor neighborhood. One of these young women answered my knock on the door.

"Does a woman from Ba Chieu named Loan live here?"

The young woman looked me up and down with heavily made-up eyes, then, seeing that I was just a kid and not a threat, invited me in. "Yes, Loan lives here. That's her over there." She pointed to a young woman sewing embroidery at a small table. Despite her own fine clothes, makeup and jewelry, Loan looked exactly as I remembered her.

"Loan—it's me, Thu's niece, Van!" I then remembered she would only recall my original name, so I added, "I mean Hien. Thu's niece. Remember? I used to watch baby Hoang while Thu sold sweet ice in front of our house."

Loan looked at me cautiously. Okay, I get it—Saigon is a war zone, you have to be careful—but come on! We're old friends. Practically sisters!

"Don't you remember me?" I asked incredulously. I got a sinking feeling. Despite her bleak surroundings, she was obviously doing well—nice clothes, jewelry, makeup, styled hair. If anybody could refer me to a good job, it was obviously her. I filled in the blanks about the intervening years as quickly as I could and watched her face gradually soften. "So," I said finally, "you are a seamstress? That pays pretty well. Do you need any help?"

"Sister Hien, you don't want to do what I do for a living," she said flatly. "This is just my day job. The real money you make at night, and you don't do it sitting in a chair."

I glanced at the other young women, and none would look me in the eye, preferring instead to read a newspaper, file their long fingernails, or sip tea as they quietly talked.

"Take my advice and get out of here," Loan said. "Go back to school. There are a lot of things you can do with your life, and this isn't one of them."

I was pretty good at math, so I put two and two together and went home.

§

The weeks turned into months, and my routine stayed the same. Days were split between school and job-hunting—a wide-ranging search that took me around much of the city. I spent most nights trying to make myself small in a room scarcely big enough for two, but if Chieu and Mai's relationship suffered from my presence, they never showed it. I helped Mai prepare meals and cleaning up afterward to repay my hosts at least a little. Mai insisted on doing all the cooking herself, which was fine since she made excellent meals. The one dish she let me try, tomato-lime fish soup, was "too Northern" for her tastes, but at least my exile from the stove wasn't because she tagged me as a "stupid orphan." Food was simply too expensive to risk with my basic lack of culinary skill, and Mai was mostly unwilling to spend much time teaching me.

One day I accidentally burned the back bottom of my *ao dai* when I was ironing with the charcoal iron. I didn't know how to fix my mistake and was terrified that I'd ruined the garment. From watching Grandma and Aunt Nga, I knew a little about patching, but I was concerned about how it would look. It would be an embarrassment to go to school with a hole in my dress or a poor repair job. I remembered Grandma telling me many times that being poor was no excuse to not be clean in body and dress, to always look to my appearance. So I went to the market window-shopping to get some ideas for my mending project. At one of the stores I found embroidered felt patches on display in a glass-covered case. An idea came to mind, and I bargained for a pink, grey, and black elephant patch—the only one I could afford on my tight self-imposed budget. I stitched my barely-big-enough patch over the quarter-sized burn, and although it looked sort of goofy, I was happy with the results. My friends at school thought I did it for "decoration," and in no time, some of the other girls added patches to their long dresses. I had never envisioned myself as a "trendsetter," and this meant a lot to me, because in the world of an orphan, respect and acceptance were sometimes hard to come by.

There was still fighting at night, and we were starting to occasionally hear the rat-a-tat-tat gunfire during the day, sometimes joined by the distant *whoomp* of artillery. We had no bunker or public shelter handy so we just covered our ears or talked louder. Chieu was a policeman, and if he didn't look worried, I figured I should stay calm, too. I never sensed from the adults around me—including my teachers—that things were any different than what I'd experienced my entire life. The growing signs of anxiety I saw around Saigon during my job search didn't seem to deter anyone from the activities of daily life, so I didn't worry about that either.

§

In the fall of 1974, I got a letter from sister Thuy. I hadn't heard from her since seeing her off with Aunt Nga and her girls at the Saigon bus station, so I opened her envelope with jittery, expectant hands. What I read shocked and depressed me.

After some half-hearted pleasantries (Aunt Nga's family was treating her fairly although Thuy had been required to surrender her savings to Mo Nga's older sister to help with expenses), she said she was still counting on my "picking her up" and wished we were living together. She was also running into problems at school:

> *The other day, my French teacher spanked me for wearing damp clothes to school. He didn't even ask me why or allow me to explain. He punished me by slapping me on the palm with his ruler, and my left hand is all red. I told him afterward that I have only two sets of school uniforms and that I washed both sets that morning before school and neither of them dried in time because of the rainy weather. I did not want to miss school, so I decided to wear the damp clothes.*

She said the French teacher passed word of Thuy's infraction to her Literature teacher, perhaps to make sure she was punished again or maybe to ensure that she wasn't. In any event, the Lit teacher showed compassion for "an orphan" and invited Thuy to lunch at his house, where his wife rummaged around her closet and gave her some old clothes so that she would not have to face the "damp clothes" dilemma again. Sometime later, the Literature teacher gave Thuy some money, explaining that it was a "reward for good studies" although Thuy had never heard of a school doing that and her grades so far had been poor. While she appreciated his kindness, she knew he acted out of pity, which made her feel even worse. There was a bit of Grandma's stiff spine, apparently, in both of us.

Thuy's letter went on to describe more about her life in Tra On.

Mo Nga and her daughters lived on one side of a duplex, built something like Uncle Chieu's house, with her mother and older sister living on the other side. The kitchen and bathing area was mounted on stilts over a river, though Thuy was not allowed to use them. Instead, she wrote that she was forced to bathe and relieve herself at the riverbank, which, as a young teenager, she found most embarrassing.

> *Lucky for me, I met a friend from school named Thy. She is also my next door neighbor. Whenever her parents are away, she allows me to bathe at her house. I am glad and grateful for her kindness and friendship.*

But this was not the worst of it. Although she no longer faced danger from Al, my sister's safety was threatened in other ways. The war at Tra On was a lot closer for her than for us.

> *Living down here in the country is very scary. At night, when I am in bed, I can hear people outside crying for their loved ones. I am afraid to be alone in bed. Every night I hear fighting, shooting, and big explosions. I think folks find their loved ones' dead bodies in the river and they carry them home to bury. One night I had to go pee badly, and I saw someone's shadow in the back room. I knew that if I went to the back room to pee, I would get in trouble, so I forced myself to go pee by the river. I heard a gun go off somewhere near and felt the bullet brush through my hair. I was frightened and fell over and didn't move. I thought I was dead. But after a little while, I got up and ran inside as fast as I could and jumped into bed, hiding under my blanket and shaking with fear. I am so glad I didn't die.*
>
> *...my heart is aching because I am lonely and miss you. I can't wait until you make some money and come for me. I want to be with you, sister. I am sad that we're not together.*
>
> *Well, it is getting late and I have to get ready for bed. I'm not allowed to use the kerosene lamp after a certain hour. Please sister, don't forget about me. Don't forget to write.*
>
> *Your loving sister, Thuy*

I broke down in tears. I thought that by sending her off with Aunt Nga, as Mai wanted, she would be safer and happier, but neither of those things had happened. I had sent her to a slightly different version of "orphan's hell" and back into the teeth of the dragon, no better off than we had been at Stucco House during Tet. I felt like I had let Mama down and that her spirit—the Guardian Angel that best looked after me—had for some reason abandoned my sister. There was only one thing to do. Since I couldn't take care of Thuy myself, I must at least get her back to Grandma's, despite all the dangers that might entail. The only way I could be sure that I was not throwing Thuy from the frying pan into the fire was to go back to Fish Farm myself and make sure the coast was clear.

§

In October, I took the bus from Saigon to Fish Farm to visit Grandma and retrieve my bicycle—a treasured gift from Quang—which I'd had to leave due to my hurried departure with Thuy. Fortunately, Al and Aunt Thu were making deliveries when I arrived so Grandma answered the bell at the gate. She looked a little thinner and moved a little slower than when I saw her last, but that didn't strike me as odd. Like everyone else in their household, Al and Thu drove her hard, but not as hard she made herself work. While Grandma enjoyed a peaceful smoke and a fine sunset, she filled her otherwise idle hours with one task or another, just to keep busy. Over the years, though, it became clear that while her spirit was willing, her flesh often needed a break.

We stepped quickly into her bedroom so that others on the farm wouldn't see me and report my visit to Al and Thu. Aunt Thu, Grandma said, seemed to have mastered her demons about Mama, at least for the present; then again, Thuy and I weren't around to remind her. After I explained Thuy's circumstances in Tra On, Grandma agreed that, if for no other reason than to escape the encroaching war, she—Thuy—would be better off under her care. She pulled a wad of bills from under her mattress and gave them all to me, along with the tiger-stone diamond ring Al had given her for Christmas the previous year. "Here, take this for expenses and bring little Thuy to me. The ring is for emergencies when people may no longer take cash. Keep it safe until you need it."

I could not conceive of a time when ordinary people—vendors, cab drivers, government workers, laborers, even policemen and soldiers—would not want paper money, but maybe Grandma knew something I didn't. I thanked her and stuck it under my blouse.

"Now get going." She glanced around. "You should leave before they get home."

I went to the porch to get my bicycle and saw Quang working at the edge of a pond. He looked up at me and I waved, but he just lowered his head and went back to work.

"What's wrong with Quang?" I asked Grandma, genuinely surprised.

She only shrugged. "He's been like that since you left. I don't think he knows what's going on. And if he does, maybe he feels bad that he didn't protect you. What could he do? He's only a boy. Just make sure Thuy gets here safely. I'll take care of things after that."

§

The following month, I told Uncle Chieu that I needed to go to Tra On and escort Thuy back to Fish Farm, that it was all worked out with Grandma and I had enough money for the trip. All I needed was directions.

The route involved a three-hour bus ride from Saigon to the city of Can Tho, then a thirty-minute journey after that to Thuy's house in near-by Tra On. I arrived about lunchtime, and Thuy greeted me with tears of joy. I explained that I had come to "take her home," leaving out for the moment that meant a return to Fish Farm and Grandma's custody, but we would have plenty of time to talk about that. For the moment, it was too late in the day to start back, so we spent the rest of the afternoon saying good-bye to the teacher who had helped her and visiting her best friend, Thy, who lived next door. Mo Nga, though always pleasant and polite, seemed noncommittal about Thuy's leaving. I think Mo Nga's mother, the matriarch of the place, and Mo Nga's older sister were happy to see her go. Thuy and I spent a final night together in her small bed, then left at first light for Fish Farm, where I assured Thuy that things had changed for the better. Thuy was disappointed that I wouldn't be staying, too, but I honestly think she had been spooked enough by surrounding battles and disheartened enough by her second-class "orphan" status to welcome some familiar faces, even in a setting that held bad memories.

Arriving hours later at Fish Farm, I accompanied her to the main gate where Grandma greeted us. I saw Al and Thu in the house behind her, so I didn't try to see Quang. When I returned to my little bed at Chieu and Mai's in Saigon, it was almost midnight and the nightly fireworks on the edge of the capital had already begun.

§

If things were changing around Tra On, they were changing, too, in

Saigon—but more slowly, like a disease that first shows up as aches and pains, then leads to fever and death. One of these small changes happened in Saigon's streets, which were never completely safe from muggers and pickpockets and recently made worse by the growing influx of people fleeing violence in the countryside.

I was riding my bike to school, enjoying the fine weather of the dry monsoon, on a dusty congested street. Suddenly, a little boy and his father crossed in front of me on their bicycle. The little boy was giggling with joy. This brings back the memory I had with my father back in 1964.

Papa and Uncle Thanh as young men

Just before Papa left on his assignment to Hong Ngu, he has a sudden urge to see his side of the family all together. The gathering at Uncle Thanh's house included Aunt Thoi, their children, and us. To celebrate the Nguyen reunion we commissioned a photographer to create a group portrait, at the party papa told us that we should all realize in wartime, life is not only precious, but that each moment could be your last. Mama dismissed his concerns as normal deployment jitters while others seemed to agree. Mama, stays back at the house with Thuy and Grandma to prepare the banquet meal. Off we go, Quang tagged along with Aunt Thoi and her family in a taxi while I hopped onto the rear fender of the bike behind Papa. Uncle Thanh carried Lan and their youngest girl, Ha, on the back of his bike and set off beside us. As the taxi sped away, Thanh and Papa began to pedal fast to keep up. Papa smiled and told me to hang on. He then leaned toward and shouted. "Let's see who can get there first!"

As Papa coasted to the curb in front of the shop, Thanh shouted from behind us, "Tinh—stop! Stop! Hien's sandal is caught in the wheel—her foot is bleeding!"

Papa stopped immediately and looked back at me, then at my foot. My left sandal had been tangled in the spokes and my ankle was bleeding. I was so excited from being close to papa that I failed to notice what I'd done.

Papa carried me into the studio where Lan blotted my wound. The photographer gave me a banana to shut me up so he could get on with the picture. In seconds, he had us all in front of his lights and the camera snapped, immortalizing not only my small accident and the half-eaten banana, but a tender moment now frozen in time I will never forget.

The only surviving picture of me (bottom right), Quang (center, from right, middle row), with Papa (back row, right) and his siblings taken shortly before he left for Hong Ngu assignment

Suddenly I heard a girl's voice behind me.

"Sister, sister—stop! Turn around!" A girl a few years younger than me was peddling her bike fast to catch up.

I stopped and leaned on one foot. "What's wrong?" I asked.

"Some guy just stole something off the back of your bike." She pointed to the little rack over the rear fender where my school supplies were normally stored with a bungee cord. My notebook was still there, but my nice folio case was gone, along with the pens and money inside. *Oh, no.* My heart sank. I looked around the foot traffic in the street but didn't see anyone suspicious.

"I yelled at you for the last block. Didn't you hear me?"

I shook my head. "What did he look like?" As if that would make any difference.

"I don't know. It was just some guy. I gotta go or I'll be late." The girl pedaled off toward the grade school a few blocks away.

Bicycle ride to school, Saigon

I was mortified. I prided myself as a street-wise "sharp cookie," and to let myself get pick-pocketed—*while on a moving bicycle!*—was unforgivable. What was the world coming to? The big problem was not the case and the pens, but my cash, which I always kept with me because of the strangers in Uncle Chieu's house. Now that was gone as well. I had planned on using some of that cash to buy a new rear tire for my bike, but that was out of the question. And I didn't even have pens for homework!

After school, I told Uncle Chieu about my misfortune.

"It wasn't your fault," he said. "There's a lot of that going around. The guy was probably after your cash. The whole city's changing. Too many strangers. Nobody knows their neighbors anymore. We've got to look out for each other."

At that, the landlord's kind nephew stuck his head in the door and said, "Don't worry, Van. I have an old Pilot pen you can use. Just be careful with it, you know? Seems like everybody's trying to steal something!"

The next day, before Uncle Chieu left for his shift, he glanced around to make sure Mai wasn't watching, then pressed some bills into my hand. "Here you go. You're a young lady now, and young ladies shouldn't be on the street without mad money."

I didn't know what "mad money" was, but I was happy to have it.

"But won't Auntie Mai—"

"What Auntie Mai doesn't know won't hurt her." Chieu smiled. "I spend an hour or two after work running my Honda as a moto-taxi. A little here, a little there—pretty soon it adds up. But that's our secret, okay? Just keep it someplace safe."

He dashed off to work, and I could feel my tears building. Chieu had always been a nice guy—playful, even, with us kids—but he never seemed sentimental or very responsible about anything. This was the first time in a long time I felt cared for by somebody else, especially family. He never hit me, or even raised his voice, and now this special gift of money along with kind words...that was a moment I've never forgotten.

So I got my new rear tire and replaced my stolen pen, returning the Pilot to our neighbor. But I also received something else, and it would be worth a lot more than money in the weeks and months ahead.

§

Son-Ha Junior High was a friendly place. Whether it was because the many displaced families now flooding Saigon were hungry for security or because older kids simply knew they had to look out for each other, I don't know, but nobody hassled me about being an orphan. One of these friendly, helpful people was a girl named Phuong. A bit taller than me and very mature for her age, she reminded me of my old friend Thom, whom I hadn't seen since last summer. Phuong's family owned a storefront at the market near our school, which meant they were comparatively well-off. Because Uncle Chieu's house was so crowded, I was always happy when Phuong invited me to hang out with her after school.

She was a girl with wide experience, I discovered, and was aggressively "into" boys. She seemed to know the background and personality of every male in our class and flirted shamelessly when our teacher wasn't looking. One young man in particular, her cousin named An, confessed he was crazy about me ever since she introduced us at her parents' shop. I think she wanted to play matchmaker, because she asked more than once if I shared his feelings.

"I don't know," I said, blushing. "We're only in eighth grade. Don't you think that's too young to get serious about boys?"

"Boys are serious at any age." She winked. "Come on—you must have some opinion about An."

"Gosh, he seems kind of old for me. How old is he?"

"Twenty-three."

"*Twenty three!*" I almost choked on my tea. "That's eight years older than me!"

"So?"

"Well, why does a man his age want to date an eighth grader? It just doesn't seem right."

Phuong sucked the straw in her soda until it gurgled. "Don't worry about it. He's my cousin. I've known him all my life. He's not some kind of pervert or creep. He's a cool guy. Besides, you write his name every time you sign your own."

"What do you mean?"

"I mean whenever you write Van, you start with a V then finish with An, right? Come on. That's an omen. You've got to meet him again. He'll just keep pestering me if you don't."

I thought a moment about my only pre-teen crush, the one-way romance I conducted in my imagination with the handsome Vietnamese officer who lived for a few months at Fish Farm. He was older than An, but only a little. I remembered Grandma and Mo Nga telling me about the birds and the bees when I first got my period, but they left out a lot of other stuff that suddenly seemed relevant. My hormones said yes, but my brain told me no. Fate finally made the decision.

A few days later, I was leaving school, and An surprised me at the gate. I pretended not to notice him, but he sidestepped into my path.

"Hi, Van!" he said engagingly. "I was just talking about you to

Phuong. Let's go get a soda or some tea. I promise I won't keep you long. There's a little shop down the street. How about it?"

I suddenly became aware of a dozen eyes watching me. Despite her other qualities, Phuong had a big mouth, so lots of other girls probably wondered how I would respond to this juicy situation. For that matter, I wondered exactly what Phuong had told him to give him such encouragement. It was all too much, too fast, but the next thing I knew we were standing in front of a refreshment stand around the corner. He ordered us both a sugarcane drink, and we found some shade under a Royal Poinciana tree.

"You know, I asked Phuong all about you but she didn't tell me much," An said.

"Phuong didn't tell me much about you, either," I replied, "except that you are her cousin."

An laughed. "Fair enough. Well, I work for my parents, who run a delivery business. Actually, I do most of the work and make a pretty good living. They always ask me when I'm going to take a wife and I always answer, 'When I find one!' Up to now, I haven't had much luck."

I didn't like the direction this was going, so I tried to change the subject. "Well, family is very important."

"I know. Phuong told me you live with your uncle and used to live with your aunt and her husband. She says you look after your younger sister and are a good student. She says everybody in school likes you. Can you blame me if I do, too?"

Okay, that was it. "Look," I said. "I have to get home and cook dinner. Like you say, my family is counting on me. I don't want to let them down. Thanks for the cold drink."

I let him have a quick handshake, then lost myself in the crowd as fast as I could. To my great relief, An didn't wait for me again at the schoolyard gate, nor did he make any effort that I know of to contact me. In fact, the only one who kept flogging that dead horse was Phuong, who couldn't believe I wouldn't go out with a good-looking, eligible guy. "Look, if you marry him, he'll take care of you," she said. "Isn't that what you want?"

"What I want is to finish school and find a good job. I don't have time to think about boys." I was right, of course, though maybe for the wrong reasons. I never thought of myself as a timid person, but I had learned through the school of hard knocks that jumping into things before you are ready is a sure road to disaster. I had nothing against An. Lord knows, Papa was twelve years older than Mama when they got married, but they were different people living in a different time. So much of the world—of my world—had changed since then and was changing faster still. I needed some stability in my life, not new troubles to rock the boat. Eventually, even Phuong let it go, although our friendship never recovered its old warmth. I think in a way she was like that delinquent, Lien, at my previous school. She didn't just want friends; she wanted disciples, a posse she could control who shared her own passions. That just wasn't me.

§

Christmas 1974 saw more strange doings in Saigon. Americans—GIs, contractors, office staffers and aid workers—once everywhere on foot or in vehicles, were increasingly rare. Their favorite bars, restaurants, and other hangouts were either closed or now catered to locals. The distant rumble of jet aircraft, once almost comforting, like pounding surf, was noticeable by its absence. The planes that still flew in and out of Tan Son Nhut were now mostly airliners. Artillery and rockets still *whoomped* through the night, but explosions seemed to start earlier and continue longer, often well after sunrise. Still, you would never know anything was wrong by the demeanor of families or teachers or the other kids at school. We were in our own little cocoon, and everyone was afraid to peek out.

I spent the holiday with Uncle Chieu and Auntie Mai. Unlike other Christmases with Al, I attended midnight Mass with school friends, not with family, at Nha Tho Duc Ba, Saigon's largest cathedral, modeled after Notre Dame. Once again, I felt very alone in a very big world. I spent most of the school break, though, visiting with classmates and still looking for a job. Mai had her own family, and Chieu was filling in for vacationing colleagues as well as running his moto-taxi business. In a way, I thought this was great—no screaming or threats or sick games or beatings or extra chores to accommodate guests. On the other hand, when one has to work too hard to make things feel like a holiday, the holiday feels like work. I missed Thuy and Quang and Grandma, as well as Bubba—the "little prince" who had become my little brother. I wanted to see them, but it was more than an hour by bus. I could ask Uncle Chieu for bus fare but did not want to risk running into either Al or Thu. I had the freedom to come and go, but found no real joy in my liberation.

Part of this problem was Mai. At the beginning of the fall term, she'd been fine, even supportive of me, and we had found a way of getting by without stepping on each other's toes. By the end of Christmas, though, it was clear that almost everything I did annoyed her. She was especially vexed when I spent time with Uncle Chieu, who had become like a real godfather. It may have been because I was a budding teen, and although I was Chieu's blood relative, no woman wants "her man" beguiled by a little serpent with her tempting apple. It may also have been because she learned, somehow, that Uncle Chieu's after-hours moto-taxi catered mostly to prostitutes, who liked having a policeman as their driver and tipped him accordingly. I don't think Chieu indulged himself with these women, but he didn't report his true earnings to Mai, either, let alone the occasional "allowance" he slipped to me. On top of all that, Mai was pregnant with their first child, a development that made Chieu very happy and Mai very moody, and suspicious and jealous about the attention I received from Uncle Chieu. With all the scary vibes around the city, it was not a good time to start a family, and Mai was definitely worried about their future.

Anyway, more things now pulled me away from Chieu's household than drew me to it. I delayed coming home after school as much as I could, hanging out with friends like Phuong and going to soda shops, joining study groups, lingering at libraries and bookstores, sometimes just knocking around the streets on my own, looking for "Help Wanted" signs and asking proprietors for a job. Nobody wanted to hire a young person my age, especially a girl, and particularly since the city was now filled with too many young men and women with shifty eyes, peasant clothing, and a certain purpose to their walk. Most of them seemed to have no visible means of support, yet none were starving. Most were well-muscled, like soldiers, and I seldom saw them with babies or grandparents—odd for Vietnamese at any age. Once, a group of these scruffy, hard-eyed street people passed the glass storefront where I was interviewing, and the owner pulled down his shade. "Infiltrators," he muttered, "or deserters," and wouldn't say more than that. Apparently, in my government-style school uniform, I was above suspicion, but I didn't get the job—nothing new about that—and I started keeping more distance between myself and these newcomers when I made my daily rounds.

There was, in my observation, still no sense of impending doom, none that was evident to an eighth grader, anyway. I didn't know it, but I was exploring Saigon—the Paris of Asia—in its last days. Others knew, though. I remember so many earnest-looking young men and women, whose eyes would not meet mine, who did not quite fit in with vibrant city life. Half or more of these young people must have been Viet Cong, waiting for what I did not know. Others I was sure were deserters from our own military, desperately looking for a way out. Yes, they knew.

I also saw homeless men, women, and children wandering the streets, hungry. The sight of them made me grateful for the life I had. I didn't have a mother or father, but I was not homeless. I was not one of them.

Early in 1975 before Tet, Uncle Chieu told me he'd received word that Uncle Hai had been admitted to Tong Y Vien Cong Hoa General Hospital for evaluation of an undisclosed ailment that might result in his discharge from the Navy. His symptoms were serious—uncontrollable hand tremors resulting from some sort of nerve damage, maybe from chemicals, maybe from disease, but in any case, rendering him unfit for further duty. This alarmed me greatly so I visited him as soon as I could. He was surprised and happy to see me, and while I enjoyed feeling like a little girl again in his presence, the actions of his ward-mates made it clear those days were over.

"Hey, sister," one bandaged soldier called from the next bed. "When I get out of here, let's you and me go to a movie, eh?"

Uncle Hai barked at him like an old sea dog. "Watch your mouth, buddy! That's my niece you're talking to!"

The other sick or wounded soldiers laughed, and I laughed, too, promising the poor man that if he made a speedy recovery, I would take him up on his offer. Of course, this was just a joke, and even Hai laughed at it. All the soldiers in the ward were there for serious reasons, and half would never leave. Uncle Hai himself was soon diagnosed with Parkinson's Disease, and although he was released—making him one of the "lucky ones"—he was never again quite himself.

In late February, after a tense but uneventful Tet, Mai and I had our first fight. I came home from school to find that someone had pawed through my belongings, leaving my clothes in disarray. I immediately suspected the quiet couple next door, or even the "nice nephew" who lived with the landlord. I had learned from Grandma, after all, that being nice was sometimes just a tactic to survive. My main concern was for Grandma's tiger ring, which I had wedged into the lining of an old skirt. Unlike my cash, which I could carry in my folio case and keep with me at all times, the ring was too large for me to wear, and even if I could, the diamond would attract unwanted attention. Sure enough, someone had discovered my hiding place, and it was gone. Just then, Mai entered the room with a laundry basket.

"Did you take my ring?" I asked pointedly. She didn't deny it, just averted her glance, and began folding her laundry on their bed.

"Why did you take it?"

"Who are you to ask me about anything?" she said bluntly. "The only reason you're here is because of me and my generosity. If it wasn't for me, you'd be living on the street."

As I watched her fold the laundry, I saw Grandma's ring on her middle finger.

"What's that, then?" I pointed to her hand.

She flipped it up, casually glancing at the stone, then went back to work. "This is just something I borrowed. I need to wear it when I go out. People bet more money with you if you look like a winner. You'll get it back."

"You should've asked my permission first. That belongs to Grandma, and she entrusted it to me. You have no right to take it."

"I do what I like in my own house, young lady. If you don't like it, you can leave."

This was getting nowhere, and I was not about to knock her down and take it, so I decided to bide my time. I thought about telling Chieu but realized that, too, would amount to nothing. He was a policeman, true, but he had proven many times he was not above cutting corners and, after all, Mai was his lover and soon-to-be mother of his child. There was no question whose side he would take, even though the prize was my life savings and emergency fallback for a time when cash was no longer king.

I got home early the next day and returned the favor, going through Mai's drawers and extra purse and all the secret places I knew she kept precious things. Unfortunately, she came home early, too, and caught me in the act.

"Okay, that's it!" she declared. "Get out of my house!"

The ring was still on her finger, and I knew instantly it would stay there forever. I had not only crossed some final bridge with her but burned it behind me. I went to my little bed and threw the few things I owned into the straw bag that had seen me through many such retreats. I felt like stalking out right then, and probably would have despite a lack of money, or a plan, or a place to go.

"Oh, don't be so dramatic," Mai said, though her tone was still as hard as stone. "You can leave in the morning after you've said good-bye to your Uncle Chieu."

Chieu worked very late that night, undoubtedly raking in loot from his moto-taxi until the streets got too dangerous. I didn't want to spend the evening staring at Mai, so I went to bed early, covering my head to blot out the songs on our neighbor's radio. I started to cry, then stopped. I didn't want to give Mai the satisfaction of hearing her victory. I was frightened, and at the same time, determined. I would leave here. I would not go back to Fish Farm. If I could not find a place to live, I would live on the streets, find a job, and survive. Still, I cried a little more, silently. I felt as if, finally, I had no place to turn, no safe place to be, no family I could be with. If I ever needed a Guardian Angel again, it was now.

Mama's voice came to me in the darkness, calmed me, gave me strength.

> *Your purpose is to live, whether in a house or on a street. Your mission is to survive, whether a princess or a pauper. Your work is to serve God, whether planting rice or selling vegetables. You will live because you are a daughter and a sister, and the grave is not your goal.*

All of a sudden, the ring didn't matter. Mai didn't matter. The future didn't matter. All that mattered was me on my mat and the peace that enveloped me as I slept in my mother's arms.

§

The next morning, I left my packed bag on my bed and went to school. During the first break I told Phuong what happened and that I would no longer live at my Uncle's house, even if it meant living on the street. For once Phuong's head came down from the clouds, and she gave me some useful advice. She said, "Wait here," and went to the Giam Thi, the school supervisor responsible for student discipline and welfare. He was an older man, at least Papa's age, and more like a kindly grandfather than a disciplinarian. He struck me as a practical man who had seen it all and really cared about us kids. I had only met with him once, to discuss my eventual "eleventh grade" exams, which were key to getting a high school diploma, no matter how good one's everyday grades. I worried about those exams, not knowing there was no reason to. They were not in my future.

A few minutes later, Phuong returned with the Giam Thi, saying she told him briefly about my predicament and that he knew a way to help.

"Don't worry," the Giam Thi said. "You're a bright girl and a good student, and the street is no place for you. You are welcome to stay with me and my family, and if things work out, we can do the paperwork to adopt you so you won't have to worry about problems like this again."

This was a life-ring tossed to a drowning girl, but having been down the "adoption" road before, I wasn't sure it was a good idea. So far (except for Grandma), my life had been filled with guardians who said one thing, then did another, usually because of money. But I was desperate and feared that if I turned down this kind man (and as Giam Thi, he had seen problems like mine many times), Phuong would pressure me again to take up with An and become a teenaged bride—and I just might be desperate enough to do it. I would give the Giam Thi a try.

So I picked up my things after class, not hanging around to say goodbye to Uncle Chieu, who deserved better from me. I then went back to school with my suitcase tied to my bike and followed the Giam Thi to his house. As the sun went down and gave way to evening, his family came home, and he introduced me as they arrived. His wife was a prim but friendly lady who reminded me of Aunt Nga. His two adult sons were about An's age, and they made it clear from the beginning that I would be an imposition in their house—not a good start. Their heated discussion with their father turned into a full-blown argument, and the two sons left on their motorbikes. I hadn't said a word. The Giam Thi's daughter, a quiet woman a bit younger than her brothers, gave me sympathetic glances but didn't take one side or the other. After the sons left, the remaining four of us settled down to a nearly silent dinner. My stomach was churning, so I barely ate anything, hoping that my lack of appetite wouldn't register as ingratitude to my hosts.

After I helped clean up, the daughter showed me where I would sleep. We went upstairs to the attic where exposed beams and flat boards formed the roof. The floor was two big squares of plywood that jiggled when I walked on them, and I had no idea what was underneath. At one end of the little room was a small Buddhist altar where the family gathered occasionally to light incense, observe the customary rituals, and leave gifts and prayers for their ancestors. I thought immediately of Truc, and while part of me relaxed, another part recoiled, weary and sick. Old food covered the altar (it was usually replaced every day to ward off bugs and rodents—the daughter said she had just not gotten around to it today), and the sickly sweet aroma of incense permeated every corner. She gave me a blanket and said I could pick any spot I wanted to store my things and sleep. Tired and distressed beyond words, I found a place where I felt the Buddha wasn't watching me and bedded down like a soldier in the field.

So this is how it will be, I thought. One night at a time, one day after another. I will live. I will survive. The grave is not my goal.

The next morning, March 4 1975, I got up early after a fitful night's sleep and told the Giam Thi that I would miss school that day to visit my grandmother and tell her where I was. I authorized him to prepare the written statement he'd said at dinner that I would need: namely, that I was living at his house voluntarily, was not being coerced or mistreated in any way, and that I wanted his family to adopt me. He said fine, the document would be ready for me to sign when I got back, then wished me a safe trip. I waved good-bye to him and his wife as if I were already their daughter, then lit out toward the nearest bus stop like my bike was on fire. I felt better knowing I had a lifeboat if I needed it, but I dreaded another night under the Buddha's unblinking eyes. I wanted desperately to clear my head and get Grandma's advice.

I reached the bus stop just ahead of the bus and hauled my bike aboard. The route ran to Da Minh, but without a bike, it would be a long walk to the Fish Farm so I took it with me. We finally stopped at the Tam Hiep freeway intersection, and I disembarked by a big water tower at the entrance to Binh Da industrial park. It reminded me of my old *Monster* at the plantation, though now it just gave me a chuckle. I picked my way through the whizzing traffic to the safety island and lifted up the front wheel. I thought back on the long road I'd traveled since that seminal day when I defeated *The Monster's* deadly shadow and—

The horn blast and the truck came out of nowhere. The whole world hit me, and I was caught in the arms of a silent Angel. She floated with me through the air and laid me gently down on the grassy edge of the road. I recognized her—she was one of the two Guardian Angels I saw over our roof in Phu Nhuan when I was four years old. She was so beautiful and loving! She smiled at me, and I, at her. Then, at last, I had a good sleep.

§

A tube of light grows brighter and a halo of voices chorus around it.

> *I don't know. That looks pretty bad. What about this? Okay, increase the drip. What did she say? Oh, I thought she said something. Jesus Christ, how did she live through that? The leg's probably going to have to go. We need another pressure pack...*

Slowly, still unable to see anything but the doctor's flashlight scanning my eyeballs, images begin to re-form. People are standing over me, silhouetted against the blue sky. Now I'm on a Lambretta but stretched out—not on a seat. Now I'm in bed—no, on a gurney in a hallway. For a long time, it seems. Lots of people pass me. Lots of noise. I raise my hand to my cheek, which burns and aches, but find only a gooey hole. I swallow, but it's like swallowing sand and pebbles. Somebody covered my hand with red paint. Some joke! I go to sleep again.

Now the tube light goes away, and I see a couple of white-jacketed men talking in low tones over the side-rail of my bed. A woman in a white apron dabs my face with a cloth and the pain almost knocks me out. She stops. I figure I better pay attention to what the two men with concerned faces are saying.

> *Crushed mouth. Loss of blood and teeth and bone. Not much tissue left on that calf. Does anybody even know who she is? Okay, another Jane Doe. Better keep an eye on her. Try to keep her comfortable.*

Comfortable?

Another face looms over my bed. I recognize it as the Mayor of Da Minh, a frequent visitor to the Fish Farm and a friend of Al's. I try to speak, but I can't. The Mayor turns to a woman with a clip board. "Yes, I know this girl. Her father owns the catfish farm just off the highway. American guy with a couple of daughters. This is the oldest one. Her name is Sissy or Sissu or something like that. I'll get word to her parents."

Then somebody grabs my leg, and the lights go out for a long, long time.

§

Reality returned, but only as a guest for short visits. One of those early, lucid visits was with Al and Aunt Thu, probably the first evening I was in the hospital, but maybe a day or two later. Other than a vague recollection of seeing their solemn faces, I have no recollection of what they said or if I said anything back. Time had no meaning for me except the interval between pain pills, occasional injections, and bouts with the nurse who doused my left leg with mercurochrome, which stung like a million bees. I began to recognize my doctor, who always tried to manage a half-hearted smile each time he came to my bedside. "No broken bones. No infection. Amazing!" was his usual mantra, occasionally shared with other doctors who tagged along to see his freak.

Finally, I was well enough, and the doctor knew enough about my status and prognosis to give me a few straight facts.

"Believe it or not, you're a lucky girl," he said, looking at my chart. "You have the usual contusions and hematomas we expect from trauma like this, but no broken bones and no injury to your internal organs, so that's good. You lost a lot of muscle from your left lower leg, but if you continue to avoid infection, it should heal and function just fine, although you may have some back problems when you get older. Your left-side mandible and maxilla were badly damaged, and most of your upper front teeth are gone, with some of the lower ones chipped and broken, so you won't be eating solid food for a while. We can treat the wounds and stabilize your jaw with gauze, but we have no facilities here for reconstructive surgery, so your parents will have to arrange for that. They said they were willing to pay for a private room until you're discharged, but we don't have any to give. This is a community hospital with only public wards. However, I'll tell the nurse to put screens by your bed so you can have a little privacy. You won't feel like getting up or talking for another week or two, so plan on being our guest for a while." He got up and started to leave, then turned. "Oh, I also suggest you stay away from mirrors after the dressing comes off your face. You'll get used to your appearance eventually—we get a lot of battlefield injuries and amputations and all of them do—but it can be a shock when you first see it. Better to just take things one day at a time." His straightforward words were hard to hear, but to this day, I remember his kindness as he delivered what had to be a terrible report to give a fifteen-year-old girl.

One day at a time. One night at a time. I will survive. The grave is not my goal.

I told no one of my dreamy flight through the air and gentle landing with my beloved Angel.

After the doctor's no-nonsense report of my condition, I rested and began getting used to the hospital's noisy routine. I also tried to adjust to the idea of avoiding mirrors, like a vampire. One by one, my friends from school and my family from Fish Farm—including Al and Aunt Thu, but for some reason not Grandma or Thuy—came to visit, but they never stayed long. They didn't look shocked, just sad. One surprise guest was the mother of the truck driver who hit me. She came almost daily, bathed me and brushed my hair, massaged my back and shoulders, and helped me turn over when the nurses were too busy. I assumed she was just a good person and maybe a devout Buddhist seeking to build good karma. She was genuinely kind and caring, but eventually it became clear she had another agenda.

"My son is a good boy," she said one day as she tended me. "He feels terrible about the accident. He's a very careful driver and has never had an incident before! It would be terrible if this situation got worse—you know, like trouble with police or lawyers or anything like that. It's just not worth it, is it? Not after what you've been through."

She was a nice lady, but she was obviously terrified that I or my parents would sue her son or the company that owned the truck. She added that they were a poor family and her son's job was their only income. If he lost his license, they would all be out on the street. Why make a bad situation worse? It was a compelling case, and since I couldn't speak with my jaw wrapped shut, I could only nod—whether in sympathy or agreement, she would have to decide for herself.

In the little journal I kept during my hospital stay, I made an entry on March 11, 1975, about a visit from a fellow patient named Thao, who told me her story. Her younger brother was flying a kite and got it stuck on a power line in front of the house. From the balcony, she used a broom to try free the kite. The live wire broke and struck her, and she was severely burned. Still, she was very spirited and happy, always smiling and trying to cheer me up. Her mother would come and clean her wounds and promised that they would take her to France for cosmetic surgery. I loved Thao—she was courageous and I knew that her physical pain was much greater than mine. We were both discharged on the same day—March 24, 1975, at 12:25 p.m. She gave me her address, but my life was going to change very dramatically—again—in a very few days. I never saw her again.

Finally, the bandages came off—a necessary part of the healing process, although with the whole mirror thing at the back of my mind, I would've just as soon kept them on. I was discharged with some containers of pills and a page of doctor's instructions, all written in French. The gauze wrap came off my jaw, which was a mixed blessing. I could only drink soup, and it hurt my lips and sutures to use a straw, so I was hungry most of the time. But the nurse's instructions were firm: take it easy, don't talk too much or try to chew, and come back right away if you start to bleed from anywhere. The driver's mother gave me cab fare as a parting gift, along with a final lecture on the virtues of forgiveness, so I considered the case closed. As I walked stiffly out of the hospital—alone—I passed a seemingly unending parade of people with raw wounds going in on crutches or canes, on rolling flats, in wheelbarrows and on produce carts, and more than a few on stretchers and gurneys. Something really bad had happened—or was still happening—for the month I was in the hospital, but people refused to talk about it. For once, I was happy I couldn't ask questions.

Even with the money from the driver's mother, I couldn't afford a car-cab, so I flagged down a Lambretta and told the driver to take me to the Fish Farm—he knew very well where it was. Why I went there and not back to the Giam Thi's house, I can't say, except I missed my brother and sister and grandmother and thought my recuperation would probably go faster in seclusion behind Al's big bamboo wall. I was also afraid to let Phuong and my other friends from Son-Ha see me in this condition, which, as far as I knew, was permanent. It was bad enough to be Cinderella without a glass slipper; now I was Quasimodo as well.

When I arrived at the Fish Farm, the gate was open so I just went in. The whole family was at home, and everyone greeted me like a long-lost sister, which I was, except for Al and Aunt Thu. Their coldness told me immediately that I was not welcome, but I felt I had nowhere else to go. That was okay for the moment. Quang was happy to see me, and Thuy gave me a tearful hug and refused to leave my side. Grandma immediately began to dab dust and sweat from around my wounds and ordered Thuy to set up a sleeping mat in her room and safely store my take-home medications. She also told Aunt Thu, in no uncertain terms, that I was to stay until I was able to be on my own again. Many of the Fish Farm staff who were otherwise my friends, like cousin Ngoc, continued to keep their distance, taking their lead from Al and Thu.

That evening we had a nice family meal in the living room (Al and Thu ate on their own in the dining room). Quang made me feel less a freak when he joked about me slurping my thin rice soup through the right side of my mouth. Mr. Ba was first to break ranks with his employer's boycott and promised that if I ate all the minced shrimp he prepared, the muscle in my leg would grow back quickly. It went on this way for three weeks. I got stronger and spoke better and could finally make myself understood. Al and Thu still avoided me, though, just as I avoided them. It was clear both expected me to leave as soon as Grandma gave the word that I was able.

Midway through my recuperation, Uncle Chieu arrived with my bag, which he had retrieved from the Giam Thi's house. Thankfully, he was pretty laid-back about the whole thing—typical Uncle Chieu—and I now realized how much I loved him for it! He said that when I didn't come home after my fight with Mai, he went to my school and was told I had moved to a foster home owned by one of their administrators, so not to worry, I was in safe hands. Not satisfied with that, Chieu sought out the Giam Thi and had a man-to-man talk with him, partly to size him up and partly to arrange to see me. When the Giam Thi said I had not returned from my grandmother's house in Da Minh, Chieu got worried and contacted Grandma, and that started the ball rolling. Everyone they knew went out looking for me, which meant checking the hospitals and police stations, so eventually Al's friend, the Mayor, identified me as one of the community clinic's "Jane Doe's." Chieu assured me that he apologized for my disappearance and the inconvenience the whole episode caused the Giam Thi's family. I thanked Chieu for his efforts and understanding and for bringing my belongings to Fish Farm, which, meant I wouldn't have to return to Saigon and extricate myself from the Buddha-attic and Son-Ha Junior High. If I were to start a new chapter in my life, it would at least be with a clean slate, and I could choose a road that led away from Al and Thu in any direction. I prayed to God and Mother Maria and my newly re-discovered Guardian Angel for guidance and help to untangle the mess I was in.

By mid-April, 1975, my lips had healed well enough to sip soup normally. The gashes on the inside of my mouth and outside of my cheek and on my nose had closed sufficiently for me to bear looking at myself in the mirror. The gums where my upper molars used to be had also toughened up enough to allow me to eat some of Mr. Ba's minced shrimp instead of sucking it as a paste. I was finally getting all the protein I needed to recover. Best of all, as Mr. Ba promised the big hole in my left calf had begun to re-inflate like a balloon—not from infection, which the doctors and nurses feared most, but solid muscle that quickly began to support its share of my miniscule weight. I wasn't ready for my bicycle yet, and Lord knew I would never be a soldier, but somehow, wherever he was, I knew Papa was proud of me. I had survived, and I once again thanked my beloved Guardian Angel.

Chapter 11

Escaping the Dragon—1975

The next three weeks passed rather quietly at Fish Farm as I continued to recuperate, except for the regular shelling and gunfire at night, which now carried on throughout the day as well.

Then, on April 18, we were eating lunch in the big dining room when the gate bell rang at about 1 p.m. A housekeeper answered it and returned to tell Al that a man from the U.S. Embassy was there to see him. Al told her to show him in.

The man was tall and slim, wearing a crisp white short-sleeved shirt and a weary, worried expression. I could tell by Al's greeting that he knew the man from somewhere—how could he not, having spent so much time on so many bases with so many officials around the South? The visit, though, was anything but social. After speaking with him quietly for a moment by the door, Al brought him to the table.

"We have some very bad news," Al said. "The NVA has started a full-scale offensive to take the capital. Right now it looks like they'll succeed. Saigon and South Vietnam will probably fall."

The visitor took over as we sat in shocked silence. "All American citizens and their dependents are ordered to report to Tan Son Nhut for immediate evacuation. There are no exceptions."

I was sitting in my usual place next to Grandma and instinctively took her hand. I had understood some of the American's English words, but I could not fully grasp the enormity of what had happened. I just knew it was something about the war, it was bad, and it had to do with leaving Fish Farm.

Al gripped the back of his chair. It looked for a moment like his legs would buckle. I had never seen him like this—stunned, filled with genuine, utter dismay. He'd always been the man in charge, the person who knew what to do, even if it was wrong, the patriarch who could not be reasoned with, only obeyed. He loved Vietnam, loved his Vietnamese wife, loved the Vietnamese people. He had planned to make Vietnam his home for the rest of his life, and his Vietnamese neighbors his family. Now, all that he had worked so hard to build was, in an instant, worthless. Now he was reduced to just another refugee, fleeing with the clothes on his back. Now he was an orphan, just like me.

Saddest and most ironic of all, Al prided himself on his ability to talk his way out of any bad situation. After all, he ran big organizations for U.S. companies in a country filled with corrupt officials while a shooting war ebbed and flowed around him. He had started two successful businesses that depended on catering to vastly different customers and satisfying them all. He was pals with politicians and street vendors, bankers and laborers, engineers and car mechanics, and always got what he wanted. I'm sure he thought down deep that, if the unthinkable happened and the communists took over, he would somehow cut a deal with them and come out on top, like he always did. But this time he wouldn't get the opportunity to talk himself—and us—out of what was coming. Now he was like me in my hospital bed a month ago, listening to doctor's orders, knowing his life had changed forever, and there was nothing he could do about it.

The embassy official continued. "Pack only one change of clothes. Work quickly and travel light. You must be at the airport no later than sundown. Any questions?"

We had a thousand, but Al asked the only one that mattered to me. "What about my wife's mother?" He pointed to Grandma.

The man shook his head and looked at the floor. "Too old," he said quietly. "I'm sorry."

Instantly, I realized all that was happening. We were being told to leave our home without a moment's delay, and Grandma could not come with us. I cannot describe the emptiness, the total and complete abject sadness that gripped me. I stared at her, speechless, my heart pounding, my hand squeezing hers. Grandma understood more English than she let on and had no trouble guessing what had been said. She stared stoically straight ahead. I would not leave her side, nor release her hand.

The embassy official wished us luck and set off immediately to visit the next expatriate family. Like robots, Thuy and Quang began clearing the remains of our half-eaten lunch, knowing full well we could not take a dish, a pot, a chopstick or a spoon with us, but old habits die hard. Al and Thu spoke quickly but quietly in a corner of the kitchen. Like Grandma, Thu was hard-headed and practical about many things, and I was sure that she, if not Al, had squirreled away some valuables—gold leaf, jewelry, loose diamonds, jade—in a safe place for just such a moment, the same reason Grandma had guarded her tiger ring and given it to me.

"No—they wouldn't let me! Not one *dong*!" I overheard Aunt Thu tell Al how the Vietnamese bank where they kept the Fish Farm deposits refused to permit withdrawals during the last few days.

"Okay, don't worry," Al said in a tone that did not inspire confidence. "I have some cash in the bill drawer. Not much, but it will get us to Saigon. We'll leave a little for your mother."

"Thuy, Quang." Aunt Thu turned to us. "Forget the dishes and grab your clothes." They dashed to obey. She did not address Bubba, who had no clue about what was going on. We all ran to our duty stations.

Thu approached Grandma, who still sat at the dining table as if she'd had a stroke. I was still by her side, my hand still glued to one of hers. Her daughter took her other hand and put a few scrunched-up bills in her palm.

"Here," she said. "This will have to do until the bank reopens. Your grandson Ngoc and Mr. Ba will help take care of you."

Grandma spoke at last. "You won't forget me, will you? You'll come back to visit?"

"We'll come back to get you, Mother, just as soon as we can. Don't worry about a thing." Thu grabbed Bubba's hand and ran to the back of the house to throw their things together.

The tears in Grandma's wrinkled eyes began to slide down her cheeks. She gently pushed me away. "Get going, Van," she said with remarkable calmness. "Go pack, and make sure you stick with the others."

Until that moment, it never occurred to me that I might not be included as a dependent and a member of Al's family, which, of course, all paperwork said I was. I toyed briefly with the idea of staying behind at Fish Farm, mostly to help Grandma, but also to have a home and a job and some security under the new regime. After all, I had done just about every job there was to do on the place, and our workers had nowhere to go—especially cousin Ngoc. and Mr. Ba, who by now were as much fixtures of the place as the ponds and birds and trees. Besides, it was an old Vietnamese tradition to look after one's relatives, even distant ones like cousins, as well as loyal employees. I could see the wide-eyed terror on the faces of Thu's two housemaids as they discovered their only role now was to stay out of the way and take their chances with the invaders. Somebody from the family ought to stay and speak for them.

"Come on, Van, shake a leg!" It was Quang passing through the kitchen toward the courtyard. His voice was enough to pull me out of my trance, out of my fantasy. As he did at Hong Ngu, he talked me off the dead bodies and back to the world of the living.

On my way to the kids' room, I noticed Al by the front door, talking to a woman I remembered from one of his parties at Bien Hoa. Her name was Bobbie, an American with two grown-up adopted sons. Her husband, a Vietnamese Air Force colonel, had been away from their house when the evacuation order arrived, and she was beside herself with fear that they would be separated. Al tried to calm her down. "Just go home," he said. "If he can get away, that's where he'll go. Your boys, too. Now get going. None of us has much time." She pulled off in a big American station wagon toward her house a few miles away.

Back in the kids' bedroom, I ran around the armoire and got out my little suitcase, barely unpacked from my stay in Saigon. As Thuy quickly sorted through her mostly American clothes, I shoved in my *ao dai* and one change of everyday clothes consisting of a plain blouse and pajama pants. I packed my journal, too, which I'd kept off and on since the Philippines, the rosary Quang gave to me, and a few dog-eared, yellowed photos of Mama and Papa I'd hung onto over the years. A skilled and practiced packer, I was done in a minute, then turned to give Thuy a hand.

My sister was agonizing over a pair of nice dresses she'd received from Al's American family at Christmas. Which to take? Which to leave? I said, "Take both—just shove them in your bag. As long as it's one suitcase, nobody will care."

"What about this nice purse?" Thuy held up a small white handbag.

"Pack it, too, if it will fit—"

"No!" Aunt Thu breezed through the room, grabbing some shirts and shorts for Bubba. "It's too much. Just one change of clothes and your toothbrush. Now hurry."

She left and Thuy's face began to cloud up. She really loved that white purse.

"Here," I said, stuffing it into her suitcase. "If they don't see it, they won't know it's there."

"No," Thuy said with a sniff. "I don't want Aunt Thu to hit me. I'll just leave it. Maybe I'll get another."

I let out an impatient breath, fearing that she would one day regret being so obedient about the purse (and she did.) "Okay. But take these—they're small." I put a couple of pictures of Mama and Papa, different from the ones I had, under her blouses. "There. You're done. Now let's get out of here."

I led Thuy through the main room on our way to the gate and saw Grandma still sitting at the dining table, as immobile as a church or temple, weeping noiselessly like a statue in the rain, as if she already had one foot in the grave. What was she thinking? What feelings of loss was she suffering after having lost so many of her family already? Were her thoughts of her old home in the North, her dead children who had been left there, her flight to the South twenty years ago? My mother's death in Hong Ngu? And now, she faced the sudden departure to a strange land thousands of miles away of her only remaining daughter and four of her most cherished grandchildren, who she had raised as her own. Undoubtedly, she was thinking that she would never see any of us again.

Silent tears ran down my cheeks, too. There was such a feeling of finality weighing on me, like an end of times, like the end of the world. I thought about telling Grandma good-bye again, but she seemed to be in another world so I left her and returned to mine.

Outside, the family had assembled in the courtyard with their single suitcases. Al pulled up in his small Honda hatchback, which was never intended for so many people and so much stuff. Grandma then appeared at the door, like a weary hostess saying farewell to guests who had overstayed a party. I went to her one last time, as did the other children. I cannot remember what words we may have exchanged, if any. There was nothing I could do for her. I did not know enough about what was happening to argue about leaving her behind. Events were too chaotic and moving too fast, and I blindly followed the orders of the adults around me.

As an orphan (I never considered myself to be "adopted"), there was such a deep emptiness in me, a sense of never belonging to anyone, that had been filled only by this very brave, very loving, and determined woman. Now she would be gone from my life. I was desolate beyond words. We gave each other a final hug.

Then Al flung open the doors and we all shuffled toward the car. I was last. I felt like the nurse tugged me again from my mother's arm at the Hong Ngu clinic, a force just as irresistible toward a future just as blank.

At that moment, Bobbie's car appeared again at the gate. She got out with her youngest son, and Al went to speak with her. I don't know what she said, but by the time it was my turn to squeeze into the Honda, it was obvious that we all wouldn't fit, even without the suitcases. Al came over and pulled the keys from the ignition.

"Okay, everybody out!" he commanded. "Get into Bobbie's car. Her husband and oldest son aren't home yet and nobody knows where they are. She volunteered to drive us to the airport, so let's get going."

Before I knew it, I was jammed in the back with the luggage, and Al was behind the wheel, laying rubber outside our gate. The Fish Farm, Grandma, and now Ngoc, who was beside her, disappeared in a cloud of dust.

Because Bobbie's house was on the way to the airport, Al stopped so she could check again for her husband and son. No luck with her husband, but as Al pulled away, her oldest son rounded the corner on a bicycle. In what must be seen as the luckiest moment of his life, he leaped off the bike, letting it fall, and jumped into the car next to his mother. In seconds we were back on the highway, now filling with other vehicles. Apparently Bobbie's husband got a phone message to his oldest son that he would meet them at the airport. It was good thing he was in the Air Force, I thought, because the only way anyone was getting through this thick traffic later would be by helicopter, though I kept that observation to myself.

Our next stop was Uncle Chieu's house in the Ba Chieu district, also on the way. He was the only member of the family we could reach to tell that we were leaving. It was also important for Chieu to know that his mother and son were alive and well at the Fish Farm—at least for the time being. The others waited in the car with the engine running while Aunt Thu and I ran in to give him the news. He came out with us to the street and did not look at all concerned. He was also not in uniform.

"I'll check on Mother Mau when things settle down," he said laconically. "I'm glad Ngoc is with her. We'll all keep our heads down for a while. We'll be okay. All of you take care."

There were more painful good-byes, all the more so because none of us could presume that we would ever see each other again. I realized that Uncle Chieu had done all he could for us in difficult times, and that I loved him. Handshakes turned into outstretched fingers as we forced our way into traffic.

We arrived at Tan Son Nhut late that afternoon. The commute had been hellacious: speeding along at the limit for only a few minutes before traffic congealed into a mass of trucks, cars, demilitarized vehicles, Lambrettas (that couldn't navigate the white line), and motorbikes (that could), infuriating Al beyond words. At the main gate (actually a series of checkpoints, with increasingly serious barriers farther in), half the vehicles were eventually turned back and things sped up, if only for a few moments. If a vehicle held Caucasian faces, it was usually waved through. The cars or bikes with mixed couples and Vietnamese-American families invariably got stopped, though only long enough to check IDs or until someone in authority passed them on.

Astonishingly, despite the noise of revving engines, desperate voices and futile arguments, crying babies, and wailing grannies—not to mention pedestrians scurrying up and down the line of vehicles looking for relatives, friends, or just a charitable ride—the chaos seemed remarkably contained, like a tea kettle kept on the verge of a boil. There were some resolute and dedicated American Embassy personnel and American soldiers who stood guard, and South Vietnamese soldiers who tried to keep order and the yelling and screaming to a minimum.

Not all of the Vietnamese who reached the airport were permitted beyond the entrance gates, even though they were with American "sponsors." As we waited in line at the gate, I witnessed countless crying, screaming, and heartbreaking family separations. It was like the end of the world, and the damned everywhere were seeking, for the last time, God's salvation.

Initially there seemed to be one ARVN soldier for each American GI, though that ratio changed as we proceeded toward the terminal, where we saw fewer Vietnamese with guns. Harried U.S. officials and other civilians ran to and fro, most with radiotelephones stuck to their ears. If the NVA shelled us at that very moment, I doubt anyone would hear.

When we got to the final checkpoint, Bobbie couldn't produce title papers for her station wagon, so the MPs ordered us out. This was probably wise, as the "infiltrators" I'd been warned about before my accident were known to plant explosives on anything with wheels, often without the driver's knowledge. Consequently, we prepared to walk with our luggage for the last quarter mile to the terminal, without Bobbie and her sons. Al tried to keep them with us, but her reason for staying behind made sense.

Her goal was to rendezvous with her Vietnamese Air Force husband, and unless he flew onto the field, he would have to come through the main gate like everyone else. Her big American station wagon would act as a beacon, and, she reasoned, they would somehow find each other. Again, flawless logic, but Al knew that eventually the base perimeter would collapse and the terminal building would become the "castle keep." Bobbie and her sons were on their own.

We had only walked a dozen yards when another of Al's old colleagues, a man named Bill, flagged us down with his clipboard. After exchanging some quick words with Al, Bill told us to wait. He disappeared into the crowd and soon returned with a "borrowed" mini-bus used to shuttle air crews around the flight line. In an official vehicle with a honcho at the wheel, we zoomed past more checkpoints and went directly to passport control. Bill dropped us off and told us which window to visit first, then said "See you later!" in a hopeful tone and vanished with his little bus.

Inside, we sat like pigeons on a wire with the rest of the crowd while Al collected a stack of documents from the window. He filled them out diligently, several sheets for each of us, then turned them into the clerk, and came back to wait. Outside, the shadows lengthened and the crisp blue sky turned amber and purple. Inside, anxious conversations turned to whispers, then went silent as the sky turned dark and the fluorescent lights came on. The government-issue clock on the far side of the room hit 20:00 hours—eight o'clock. Bubba had been restless for an hour and now draped himself across Aunt Thu's lap. My own stomach was rumbling, reminding me that the last food any of us had was our unfinished lunch.

Finally, Al went to the counter and called the harried clerk. "Look," he said firmly, "we live in Da Minh and don't have transportation. We've been here all afternoon, and the kids are getting hungry. You've had our forms for two hours..."

While he talked, the clerk looked at us and maybe took pity on this fellow countryman who obviously had more problems than paperwork. "Okay, okay," he said. "Sit tight. I'll call you up in a minute."

Within the hour, we formed a line for our "instant" photos. Al collected the precious documents—updated passports for himself and Thu, me and Bubba, and new ones for Thuy and Quang. We were mostly "good to go," the clerk said, but not quite yet since most of our family were Vietnamese and not American citizens. "You still have to out-process with the Ministry of Internal Affairs. They're closed now, but you can be first in line tomorrow. Their office is on the other side of the terminal."

Al was exasperated, but there was nothing he could do. We were in the system, with its bureaucratic wheels turning slowly, and not even the approaching communist avalanche could speed them up. This was doubly frustrating, since the Embassy official who had visited us at noon said that all Americans and their dependents were definitely leaving the country, no ifs, ands, or buts. Who cared, then, if this paper or that got stamped with the right color ink? We had made it to the airport safely, which by itself was a miracle. The big airplanes—transports and airliners—shuttled in and out, risking very little time on the ground, so why should we be any different? We were the reason they were here! To make things worse, I saw plenty of old people among the refugees. I knew the official who told Grandma Mau to stay behind was just doing his job, but numerous families had ignored the rules and more joined them each hour. I was sick with regret that I hadn't insisted Grandma come with us, not that there was any guarantee Al would have listened to me. Victory may go to the strong but survival, as always, favors the fast and clever.

Fortunately, the processing building stayed open all night, and, along with hundreds of other families toting their gear, we sought choice spots to sleep—flat benches, folding chairs, places where tired backs could rest against the wall. A few families had dinner—mostly snacks they brought from home. Others sent scouts to find one of the few remaining food trucks and vendor carts still allowed on the base. Thank God the drinking fountains and toilets kept working! Finally, my sister and I curled up like two kittens with our heads on our bags, and I drifted off to sleep. When I awoke, the crowd in the waiting area had tripled, impatient voices our alarm clock.

Like lemmings, the "old timers"—first arrivals like us—shuffled to good slots at the head of the line that quickly swelled to a snaking Lion Dance. Unfortunately, papers collected in one line only entitled you to wait in another, so the lines broke and reformed at a steady pace as the GI wall clock unwound. While we waited, I heard other Vietnamese dependents—a few had been local government officials or American operatives themselves—grumbling about the process.

This is bullshit. In a few days the only people reading these records will be NVA colonels and secret police, finding out who left town and who's still around to be arrested. They should be burning records, not making new ones!

Good point. The creation of all the new paperwork was about as useless as re-arranging the deck chairs on the HMS *Titanic*.

By late afternoon on April 19, our family had almost reached home plate, but the bureaucrats decided to call it a day. City buses had been organized to take the anointed few—at least several hundred people in our immediate vicinity, but who's counting?—into the city center so they could eat and get a night's sleep. Our bus deposited us at a hotel on Truong Minh Ky Street, where we all shared a room and filled our bellies with Pho and vegetable rice from a food stall down the block. While we ate, Aunt Thu voiced a thought about going back to Fish Farm in a cab to get Grandma. Hope exploded in my heart. Quang volunteered to go in Aunt Thu's place, but Al nixed the whole idea.

"No. It's too easy to get separated, and there's no guarantee that who goes can get back. Besides, Chieu's son is with her, and Chieu said he'd go there himself and keep an eye on things. If they're in trouble, he'll know what to do. Our job is to sit tight and get on that plane."

Now my heart sank, but he was right, of course. While traffic was light leaving the city, it looked like the whole country was trying to get in. Every highway, byway, canal and foot path was packed with refugees, and right behind them were columns of NVA regulars and VC insurgents. Besides, at seventeen and stoutly built, Quang looked to be of military age. He could easily be shot or arrested by either side. The risks were just too great.

The morning of April 20, the city bus deposited us at the main gate. We showed our special passes to join yet another line, this one for a shuttle that would take us to the customs and security office that would be our last stop before the tarmac. There, we formed another line along tables where we opened our suitcases for a final check. That made sense because we had been off the base overnight, and there was always the chance that a saboteur had slipped an explosive into somebody's bag. Everyone around us checked out clean, so we were directed to a waiting room with windows overlooking the runway where big jets now came and went in a steady stream. Optimistically, we started a line next to the double door that led to the ramp, but nobody—no flight attendants, no ticket agent, no ground crewman, no police, nobody—came to open them. At least Al's friend, Bill, who had expedited our entry the day before, now showed up with single suitcase, traveling alone. Somehow he had found us in the maze of lines and buildings. We could only hope Bobbie and her sons had equal luck in the desperate search for her husband.

An hour later, we were still sitting on the linoleum, leaning against the wall. Bubba had to go to the bathroom—again—so we all took turns holding each other's places while we shuttled back and forth to the toilets.

I was terrified that I would be in the restroom when our flight was finally called so I held off as long as I could, but nature won in the end, as she always does. I needn't have worried. We would remain in the waiting room for the rest of the day and well into the evening, learning every crack and crevice in the floor and on the walls. We were practically on a first name basis with the security officers who strolled through regularly to give nervous passengers the illusion of safety.

Then, at precisely 22:23 hours on the wall-mounted GI clock—almost 10:30 p.m. on an overcast and gloomy night—a squad of tired-looking clerks, officials, and security guards came into our area, marked the end of the line, and the double gates to our prison swung open. An American civilian started reading names, beginning with "Alvin Strauss and family."

We were on our way.

The heavy night air on the tarmac engulfed us as we walked on stiff legs to the converted school bus that would take us to our plane. "A C-130 Hercules," Al said, squinting ahead through the windshield, "workhorse of the war." There was a wistful pride in his voice. He'd been around these big four-engine cargo planes a lot during his years in my homeland, and this was probably the last way he had envisioned himself leaving. The bus pulled into what I could only compare to rush-hour traffic. Buses, vans, tow trucks, fuel trucks, and staff cars—many with flashing red or amber lights—darted everywhere, and beyond them in the night were row after row of huge airliners and military transports, ground-power units whining, engines howling, big fuselages invisible except for rotating beacons and long lines of windows glowing from the inside out, like the stripes on a tropical fish.

During that short bus ride was when it hit me: I was really leaving Vietnam, and I was really going to America. My homeland would be my home no longer. Would I ever see Grandma again? I knew now that she could have been with us, and that made my sadness all the more unbearable. I was very worried about her, thinking of the now inevitable communist victory, because I remembered her stories about how her home in the North had been confiscated, and she was kicked out, leaving her to depend on relatives in order to survive. I knew she feared it was going to happen all over again, and, I later learned, in the end, it did.

As sad and worried as I was, I have to admit that I also felt an expectation of a very Great Unknown, an adventure that I could not begin to imagine. That Unknown was the day after this one, and the day after that. A kernel of excitement started to grow in me, and suddenly I was very eager to see an American cowboy, like the ones I'd seen on that old black-and-white TV so many years ago.

Al checked his watch as we disembarked and headed for the loading ramp at the rear of the plane. It was just after 11 p.m. Like Noah's animals, we filed in two by two and took places on the canvas troop seats that lined the interior. Quang and Thuy had never seen lap belts before, so I sat between them and lashed them down. Between the roaring ground power unit, the pungent smell of jet fuel, surreal flashing lights, and big American crewmen scurrying around like space men in their headphones and flight suits, Bubba freaked out and started crying, although his wails were lost in the hydraulic whine of the big cargo ramp retracting and the turboprops coming to life. Almost immediately, the big plane rolled forward, lurched briefly as the pilot tested the brakes, then taxied again, zig-zagging this way and that until it lined up on the runway. The big engines roared, and we all tilted sideways as it accelerated. In what seemed like no time, the nose came up followed by the rest of us, including my stomach. The landing gear clumped into place. The line of blue lights outside the small window quickly fell away and Al looked again at his watch.

At exactly 11:15 p.m., our Vietnam War was over.

Chapter 12

Home of the Brave—1975

We landed at Clark Air Force Base in the Philippines in the wee hours of the morning. Since our flights into and out of Manila years before had been during the day, the constellation of lights surrounding the airport made no sense to me—it felt like neither getting away nor coming home. It slowly dawned on me that I had probably seen Grandma, my cousins, aunts and uncles, and school friends—not to mention my mother's grave and very likely my father—for the last time. Knowing now that life was precious and often short, the idea that these losses might be permanent made them more acute, even for a fifteen-year-old. To be honest, aside from this nagging ache in my heart, I felt neither more afraid nor more excited than I had about my other moves. I did know that life outside my homeland would be radically different from anything I'd experienced. If we wound up in America, I assumed it would be filled with big cars, rich food, and cowboys and Indians, at least if American TV was any guide. In fact, as we got off the C-130, I didn't know for sure if the U.S. was even our final destination. As always, that decision would be made by higher powers.

The night air at Clark was cooler than Saigon, so I shivered as we crossed a wide field from the plane to a line of buses. We staggered aboard like zombies and found seats. Like me, none of the passengers had slept on the two-and-half hour flight, and after almost sixty bone-numbing hours spent in bureaucratic hell at Tan Son Nhut, nobody felt like talking, not about our upcoming big adventure or even what might happen next. Fortunately, what *did* happen next was a hot meal at an American mess hall, then a short ride to a refugee center lit up like a soccer stadium where we could stretch out on GI cots, change our clothes, and do some laundry. While there, I met a nice Filipino girl about my age with whom I had a great conversation in fractured English, hand gestures, and the universal language of teenage girls everywhere: combs, hair clips, and pierced earrings.

Fortunately or unfortunately, our stay at the compound was short. Al's name was called, and I said good-bye to my Filipino "sister," who had loaned Thuy a blouse and shorts while her laundry dried on the line. We rode a bus to the far side of the ramp, then climbed a two-story stairway into the belly of an enormous commercial airliner that Al identified as a 747—"the biggest passenger plane in the world!" He said it was an all-American jet chartered by the Military Airlift Command "to take us home."

At least one of us knew where we were going.

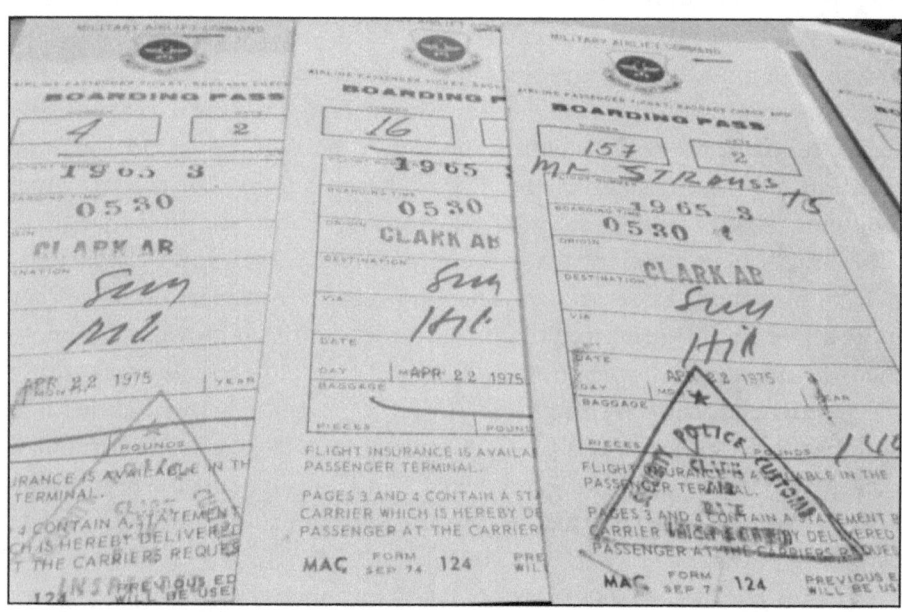

Boarding pass to America

The long flight from the Philippines to California was an odyssey unto itself. It started as all our other hurried exits had begun, with a legion of cranky, sweaty, anxious, timid, grateful, and sorrowful people shuffling one behind the other into some stuffy alien transport designed to take them from everything they knew and loved to someplace strange and mysterious.

Our giant plane climbed away from the islands through scattered clouds into a crystalline blue sky and kept the falling sun at its back until a rosy twilight descended around us. Looking down on a velvet ocean that extended to every horizon, no matter which window one used, I got a sense of how big the world really was for the first time. Our fellow passengers were mostly Asian, with a sprinkling of Americans thrown in for spice. Half the seats seemed to be occupied by kids or infants, and the babies were well organized, taking turns squawking so that at least one was crying at all times. Although we left on a beautiful morning and the flight was uneventful—even pleasurable—nobody said a word for the first two hours, as if the captain had turned on the "No Talking" light when he turned off the seat belt sign. It was here, I think, that we all realized the finality of our situation.

My path to this moment had been bumpy, but no worse than many others and easier than some. I had been out of the hospital only a month, and my accumulated aches and pains began to clamor for attention. The back problems my doctor said I *might* experience "when I got older" materialized half-way through the flight and turned my cushy airline seat into a block of concrete. My left leg was giving me fits, and on those rare moments when my body settled down, I could only think about my face. We had left a world where disfigurement and pain were common, bound for a new place of tanned movie stars, rock singers, and surfers—all paragons of beauty. Everyone assured me that once the puffiness went down and the raw scars faded, my left cheek and my lips would look no worse than anyone else's who had taken a little tumble. The only time people still averted their eyes was when I opened my mouth to eat or laugh, so I got good at tilting my head playfully to the right to chew and smiling with my fingers over my lips like the Japanese. Who needs more than one suitcase when you're a teenaged girl arriving in America with baggage like that?

The real question that awaited me when we landed was how Al and Aunt Thu would treat me. Before the Embassy official blew up our lunch and exploded our lives on that last day at Fish Farm, I knew I was on a short path out of their family, and that the gate could slam shut behind me at any time. When I moved in with Chieu and Mai, I began thinking of myself as an independent actor in life—not a happy prospect for a Vietnamese girl who grew up missing her family, but one I was learning to manage. The accident changed all that. What confidence I'd built looking for work in Saigon, navigating high school society, and finessing my way from one set of guardians to the next, had all but evaporated. And right now, if nothing else, I really wished my English was better.

As the dark Pacific slid below us, and the dimming stars shown above in a pre-dawn Grey-black sky, my thoughts again turned to Grandma. After the deaths of my parents, the only place I felt loved and safe was being with my grandmother. Even with her, though, there was a sense of indescribable loss that remained ever present, a great emptiness in my heart that even her dedication and love could not totally fill. I think it is a feeling orphans must share, even those such as I, with the good fortune to remain in the care of a grandparent. Sometimes Grandma's loving arms only made me miss my mother all the more. I often felt sad and alone when I saw other children with their parents, and especially when I witnessed a tender moment between a mother and her daughter.

With Aunt Thu and Al, I never had a sense that I was wanted as a real "daughter." I sensed only cold tolerance. Clearly Aunt Thu felt a burden of responsibility that she greatly resented. Al simply tolerated the situation, and when he no longer could, he resorted to all kinds of emotional and physical abuse. In the years before Fish Farm, none of us kids had a significant amount of real interaction with Al. He never touched any of us. That changed after he quit his position with Pacific Architect, and none of us knew why. Maybe it was because Quang, Thuy, and I were older and not so cute anymore; maybe he and Aunt Thu had more issues between them than I knew. But things became worse with each passing day. Grandma was terribly worried and hurt by the life we had to live with him, but she was mostly powerless to stop all but the worst of it. Aunt Thu proved her indifference toward her sister's children when she never, never intervened between Al and me, or with any of us kids, when he became abusive in her presence. She never came to check on me after a beating, never put a hand on my forehead to see if I was feverish...there was never any kind of "motherly" interaction, or show of affection. It was somehow impossible for her.

When I returned to Fish Farm after the accident, Al, Aunt Thu, and I continued to have little or no interaction or conversation. We spoke only when absolutely necessary, and there was certainly no sympathy for any of my pain or discomfort. Even during the events that led up to our hasty flight from Fish Farm to the airport, we did not talk. I sensed Al's hostility toward and resentment of me. He knew in his heart why I left in the first place and what I, Quang, and Thuy (but never Thu or Bubba!) had suffered at his hand. I do not think he felt any remorse or regret. His anger was due to the fact that I had decided I would no longer stay silent. As for Aunt Thu, perhaps she was embarrassed and saddened by Al's acts and actually didn't know how to treat me when I returned, knowing why I left. My way of dealing with this was to withdraw from her and not confront the issue, ever. In a way, maybe Aunt Thu was as much Al's captive as I was, until I fled. A captive by circumstance with a hopeless sense of no alternatives. She undoubtedly felt that she—and Bubba—could not survive without him.

No, I had no reason to believe that I would be welcome in Al's and Aunt Thu's family when we got all settled. I worried about Thuy and Quang, too. At least Bubba and I had a history with Al and Aunt Thu, much of it in happier days when we were living in Quy Nhon and Philippines. Quang was turning into an admirable young man: self-confident, friendly, curious and courteous, generous and forgiving, but firm in his considered beliefs, a lot like Papa. Thuy, on the other hand, though just a year younger than me, had yet to discover herself. Where Bubba was the family's "little prince," coddled and favored and loving while being loved, Thuy was often ignored or just tolerated. If Grandma had made one mistake with any of us, it was probably sheltering Thuy too well from the harsh realities of life. I worried about my sister and was afraid that I would eventually see in her all the shadows Aunt Thu imagined in our mother: short-sightedness, irresponsibility, willingness to pass her troubles onto others. In some ways, I felt like a sister to those women from those generations, but ties that bind can easily become shackles.

Sleep had eluded me for the long hours of our flight to America and I was pleased that I'd been pretty much left alone with my thoughts. My secret longings for my mother and my father and a real family and my painful missing of my grandmother now lay in a quiet place in my heart. I allowed myself some relative "happiness" and relief in our escape from Vietnam, without guilt. I felt the excitement of the coming dawn and the wonders it might bring.

We began our descent over the sparkling Northern California coast. The captain said that due to the way people kept time on a round planet, we not only had to reset our watches but repeat the previous day, April 22. Given the heartache and boredom of our endless evacuation, it was not a day I wished to experience twice, but at least the second time would be in a new land. After all that was what America was supposedly all about: starting things over and getting them right.

The first thing that struck me was the lack of jungle canopy. Flying over South Vietnam during that first year with Al and Thu, the green, flat paddies gave way to green, wrinkly mountains. Here, forests straddled craggy mountains, brown as much as green, with long slate-blue fingers of sea reaching inland from the beautiful city of San Francisco. As we descended farther toward our landing spot at Travis Air Force Base just east of the Bay, the hills and water gave way to vast yellow fields—the "amber waves of grain" Americans love to sing about. Lower still, we passed over towns and neighborhoods neatly arrayed like checkerboards, all connected by silver highways and threads of gleaming cars. Compared to the curvy, crooked, bike- and pedestrian-choked streets of Saigon and its suburbs, it looked like something from a picture book: clean, well-ordered, and wealthy. It was like landing in a bank.

After a gentle touchdown—during which all of the passengers cheered—we taxied to the terminal and "assumed the position" in another endless line, first simply to get down the aisle, which seemed as long as a city block. Then I stood in the aircraft door, smelling the air and staring out into the distance.

Hello, America!

I was overwhelmed with a feeling of intense gratitude to God, thankful beyond words. Suddenly a cold April wind swept over my body, the first really "cold" outside air I had ever experienced in my life. My thin sweater could not keep me warm. I had experienced "air conditioning" occasionally in Vietnam, mostly during brief, rare visits to base exchanges or offices where Al worked, but I never imagined it could apply to an entire country. What other wonders did this big, strange nation have in store?

I walked very deliberately down each metal stair, determined to remember those moments for the rest of my life. My feet touched American soil like an astronaut's first step on the moon. It was concrete, not dust, but that didn't make any difference. I was in America!

My elation soon changed, though, to disappointment when I did not see a single cowboy, Indian, horse, cow, or movie star! From American TV, we assumed life in the U.S. was just one continuous, low-key Tet Offensive: everybody carried guns, white settlers shot redskins, and bikini-clad girls romped endlessly in the surf. Everybody rode horses or drove big cars; nobody rode bicycles or motorbikes. None of that was true. The Americans who processed us through customs, worked behind desks, or hustled around in vehicles or on foot. They looked just like all the other GIs and U.S. civilians I'd seen in Vietnam, though maybe better fed. Waiting in one line, Quang pointed out the stunning number of blue-eyed blonds who seemed to be everywhere, and, compared to Vietnam and the Philippines, he was right. I did finally see, sort of, my first movie star: some celebrity on a program called the *"Today Show,"* which blared from several television sets mounted high on the walls of the waiting rooms—all in *living color*—the first I'd ever seen. Other minor miracles were the vending machines that appeared everywhere. Al used to complain about carrying pocket change, as if having money was some kind of burden. Now I saw Americans getting rid of their coins as soon as they got them by dropping them into "Coke" or "Pepsi" machines or other devices that spewed coffee, hot chocolate, salty snacks, or candy. With handy meal machines like these, I assumed Americans did not need markets.

§

Because Al was a U.S. citizen and none of us carried more than one suitcase, we were subjected to only the most cursory "in-processing," then were told we were free to go…somewhere. We suddenly found ourselves outside the terminal's secure area with all of America at our feet. It was here that Al revealed his secret plan for our future: He didn't have one.

This was hard to believe, since as long as I'd known him, Al never made a move without thinking things through. He was, after all, a contractor, a builder, an organizer, a manager. On the other hand, his previous plan had been to stay in Vietnam for the rest of his life, but fate had something else in mind. Aunt Thu suggested we simply stay in California. It was the cheapest option—we were already here—and we'd heard other Vietnamese talking about expatriate *Viet Kieu* communities springing up in West Coast cities. Al would have none of that.

"No way," he said. "America's big cities have been ruined. You think the violence was bad in Vietnam? Just wait till you see the Black and Mexican gangs. And where do you think all those drugs go when they leave Southeast Asia? Right to kids in American schools! No, we'll live somewhere out in the country. Maybe start the fish farm again…"

That's when Bill, who was standing behind us, chimed in. "Why don't you try my hometown, Comanche? It's an old-fashioned place deep in the heart of Texas, about an hour southwest of Dallas. Clean air. Rolling plains.

Great place to raise kids. What do you say?"

With my fractured English, I understood only half of this conversation, but I thought it was odd that Al wouldn't want to live near—or at least try to visit—his adult children, Eddie and his wife who had sent us generous "care packages" while we lived in Vietnam. Instead, he railed on about the evils of American urban life until even I started to believe him, though in a big city it was easier to get jobs. I also wondered why this man, who was so quick to mistreat me and my sister, was suddenly so interested in our well-being that he would choose to live in the middle of nowhere out of fear for drugs in school. It was not as if Vietnam didn't have criminals and drug dealers, and it was hard to imagine American gangsters teaching anything new about violence to the VC. No, it just didn't add up, but again such calculations weren't left to me.

What Al said to Bill was, "Maybe you've got a point." We all checked into a motel near Travis for a couple of days to get over jet lag and ease the trauma of our sudden amputation from our homeland. During this time, while Al shopped for an affordable used car, we immigrants cautiously explored a few American strip malls and residential neighborhoods just to get the lay of the land. My first full American meal was at a luxury restaurant called Denny's, where everything was squeaky clean, including the bathrooms, and you could have more food in one sitting than Grandma used to fix in a week. If American streets were paved with gold, as some people said, we would soon find out. At the end of the second day, Al returned to our motel room in a late model, cream-colored station wagon even bigger than Bobbie's. The next morning, we all piled in for the long, educational drive to Texas.

§

Staring out the station wagon's big window at America's evolving landscape was like watching a Hollywood movie. I missed the Indian teepees, of course, and while farms abounded in California's "Great Valley," the San Joaquin, I saw no ranch houses like the Ponderosa or cowboys herding the cattle that grazed in lazy clumps under trees along the highway. In fact, we didn't see horses at all until we entered Arizona and then New Mexico, where trail riders looked more like tourists, but this, Al assured us, was the real West. In truth, I had never traveled so far, so fast on the ground without giving at least a passing thought to jumping into a ditch to evade mortars or sweating out a checkpoint. A big part of wealth and luxury, it seemed, was simply having the peace to enjoy them.

After three days on the interstate (and many bathroom breaks for Bubba and a few more stops at Denny's, IHop, and McDonald's), we arrived in Comanche, which was southwest of Fort Worth. It was territory about as opposite from Vietnam as you could get: rolling shrub lands with "river bottom" cottonwoods that followed local creeks to small ponds; grassy knolls studded with rocks; fenced farms planted with cotton and alfalfa; and more acres dotted with cattle. Before entering the small town—a short main street lined with substantial old brick buildings—we stopped for gas, then checked into the motel next door "to get our bearings," Al said. We had barely gotten settled when there was a knock at the door.

Al opened it to reveal a short, cherub-faced older woman, well-tanned, who looked like she knew her way around a tractor.

"Howdy," she said with a soft Texas accent. "I'm Charlene Gilchrest. Welcome to Comanche!"

Al clicked into his charming mode and shook her hand. The lady peered around his shoulders to see the rest of us peering back.

"Oh, there's your family—the ones I've been hearing about!"

This came as news to us, especially Al. He stood aside and introduced us, one by one, and we exchanged polite bows, Vietnamese-style, with Mrs. Gilchrest. She wasted no time explaining that she had a Vietnamese daughter-in-law—rather odd in a small Texas town, and a fact well known to the gas station operator as she filled up. He told her that a new Vietnamese family "with the cutest little boy" just checked in to the motel, so she had to run right over and see for herself. After a brief conversation about the circumstances that brought us here and the increasingly dire news from Saigon on TV, she kindly invited us to her home a few miles north of Comanche in the town of Beattie, where she and her husband kept a rental cabin down the street from their house. If we cared to visit and liked the place, she said she would be happy to lease it for a reasonable price. Having no other prospects and no plans, Al accepted on our behalf. With another brief handshake, we all became Texans.

§

The Beattie cabin was rustic, to say the least—little more than a shack by American standards, but to us it was a godsend. Mrs. Gilchrest explained how it had been expanded to a small house for her son, Dale, and his Vietnamese wife, Hue, when he was discharged from the Army several years ago. They hadn't stayed for long, and the condition of the place showed it. The living room and the part of the kitchen that wasn't on dirt had wooden floors, and the bedrooms had patches of carpet, but that was it as far as comfort went. The boards forming the walls had gaps and cracks, letting in sunlight, breezes, and bugs. Vines grew inside the kitchen and the bathroom, wrapping around the plumbing and cabinets. Al and Thu took one bedroom, Bubba and Quang another, and Thuy and I the last.

With our few possessions and some borrowed furnishings from the Gilchrest, moving in was easy, getting the place livable took a little more time. Fortunately, Al was handy with tools and a paintbrush. Before long (and being no stranger to dirt floors and leafy interiors) it was one of the nicer places I'd lived while growing up. At least we had indoor plumbing, running water and a mostly leak proof-roof. As they say in America, you have to start somewhere, and if you begin at the bottom, there's nowhere to go but up.

§

By early May, Saigon had fallen, and the war was over for everyone, including those we left behind. Television, newspapers, and magazines ran endless photos of helicopters making rooftop rescues and landing on the overcrowded decks of American warships. Many of those life-saving helicopters were then tossed like scrap metal into the sea. Stories flooded the press about panicky crowds in the very places we'd just escaped, then all the pictures and stories stopped. As had happened in so many countries where "the people's" army was victorious, *the people* disappeared from the newspapers and TV, but not from the hearts of their relatives who make it out. Aunt Thu, Quang, Thuy, and I wondered about Grandma, Uncle Hai, Uncle Chieu, Ngoc, Mo Nga, and dozens of other relatives and friends who seemed to vanish into the abyss. Still, we didn't talk about our fears, as if merely mentioning their names would add to their peril. America went about its business, which now did not include our homeland, a place into which America had poured so many lives and dollars for so many years. We orphans now lacked even a point of origin. It was as if our lives had never happened.

Once the cabin was livable, Mrs. Gilchrest became a frequent and welcome visitor. Having a son who loved his Vietnamese wife, she empathized more than anyone in our small town with what we were going through. This was especially therapeutic for Al, who had memories and hopes from both places and now found himself unmoored from each. He had long conversations with Mrs. Gilchrest about this and that, most of which I couldn't understand. I did pick up on their agreement that it was too late for us kids to enroll in school. Al decided we would need other things to keep us busy.

Towards the end of our first month in Beattie, while Al finished the cabin, Mrs. Gilchrest took the family shopping at the Salvation Army Thrift Store in Brownwood. "It's nicer than you think," she said, as if I hadn't already concluded it would be bigger and better stocked than any market I'd seen in Vietnam. We walked the long aisles of almost-new clothes on hangers, in stacks, and in bins, and she pointed to the ones she thought best matched our petite Vietnamese sizes and were appropriate for the Texas seasons. As far as we were concerned, it was like one of Al's Christmases, except we got to choose our own gifts. Aunt Thu permitted us to buy two outfits apiece, including T-shirts, jeans, and sneakers, none of which we ever wore in Vietnam but now made us look like real Americans.

In line to check out, we happened upon another Vietnamese expatriate, an auto mechanic named Mr. Lieu who worked in the TG&Y across the street. Although he wasn't much older than Aunt Thu, we greeted him deferentially, then they chattered in Vietnamese like lost cousins. It turned out that Mr. Lieu, an even more recent arrival to Beattie than ourselves, had been one of the "lucky" few Vietnamese to narrowly escape the NVA on the very day the capital fell. Denied a seat in the endless conveyor belt of aircraft evacuating the last Americans, he clung to the skids of a helicopter until it was over the South China Sea, then dropped into the water near a U.S. Navy ship. He didn't talk about his family left behind in Saigon's black hole, and we didn't talk about ours. Orphans anywhere tend to focus on the here and now, so that's what we did. You can't change the past and tomorrow is always a blank slate.

§

We spent our first year as Americans earning money any way we could, which, hard as it was, was still easier than in Vietnam. Our first day-job was tending the Gilchrest's peanut farm. Despite a Texas law allowing owners to pay agricultural workers less than other laborers, the Gilchrests still paid us minimum wage—a generous benefit since it included all of us and was way more than we would've made doing comparable work back home. In the evenings, we laced and hand-painted cowboy belts for a nearby leather goods factory—a connection made through our new friend Hue, who lived with her husband Dale in a home they'd built between the Gilchrest house and our cabin. And local hospitality didn't end there. One of the Gilchrest's business partners, a tall, athletic woman named Kathy, lived nearby and visited us with housewarming gifts and a sunny smile. She brought sugar cookies for the kids, and after she'd heard that I'd fainted twice tending peanuts in the Texas heat, made a sun hat especially for me out of recycled denim. She became a frequent visitor and taught me how to cook a number of Texas dishes, including "monkey bread," which Bubba loved.

As the year wore on, I spent more time in the main house helping Mrs. Gilchrest. We canned vegetables, made jelly, and plucked chickens for family meals. She taught me how to bake cakes and bread and chicken-and-dumplings—another southern favorite. On one occasion, I noticed she laundered our empty flour sacks and used them to make other things for the kitchen, such as hand towels. Although the cotton fabric was coarse, it came pre-printed with colorful designs like tiny flowers and cartoon characters. I thought it would make great material for shirts and blouses for us kids. Since I hadn't tried my hand at sewing for several years, I asked her if I could have a couple pieces to experiment with. She thought that was a fine idea—"sack cloth" clothing had been around for generations in the South—so she gave me a few from a drawer. That night I cut them into sections and assembled a little shirt for Bubba and a blouse for Thuy, both of which fit surprisingly well. When Mrs. Gilchrest saw them, she was astounded that I could do so much without a pattern, instead just using Aunt Thu's scissors, needle, and thread. She went back to her house and returned immediately with a sewing machine, spools of colored thread, thimbles, and a seam ripper, plus a big stack of cotton sack cloth she'd been saving for some future project. She said I was welcome to use them all and see what I could come up with. She also gave me some patterns her daughter had used and showed me how they went together. It was like a sunbeam on a cloudy day—as if whole new world had opened! Over the next few days, I cranked out another shirt for Bubba, one for Quang, then a couple of blouses for me. It was fun, and I did it well, and, since it saved us money, even Al and Aunt Thu found something nice to say. In America, truly, anything was possible!

This discovery that my "artistic side" had some practical value was a true revelation. I already knew the virtues of hard work. I even knew my brain had value, too, though it had yet to pay many dividends beyond good grades and the occasional prize pencil box. Now, I found I could use my creativity to help my family's finances. I had no idea how deep this vein of talent ran, but I was determined to mine it to the end. I began to sketch, then create pictures using paint left over from our leather decorating business. Mrs. Gilchrest's youngest daughter, Ann (a friendly girl who taught Thuy and me how to gather wild plums without getting "chigger" bites), saw one of my early paintings and showed it to her friends at school. Lo and behold, she returned with requests for others. Emboldened by this encouragement (plus the gift of an old oil painting set for my birthday), I tried my first landscape. Mrs. Gilchrest liked it so much she gave me an old yellow photo of the house she grew up in and said she would buy me new paint and brushes if I would render it in oils. I'd received my first commission! I worked hard on it and, truthfully, thought it fell short of what I could do, but no matter. A friend of hers, a teacher at the high school I was scheduled to attend that fall, thought it was great and offered to buy me more art supplies if I painted a similar painting of her home. Since this lady would be one of my teachers, I viewed this as a serious assignment and took almost three months to finish her "Homestead Portrait." I may not have been a professional artist, but as long as I helped the family's finances, Al and Thu never complained—not that they didn't have other problems on their mind.

Since Al lacked regular employment, he became obsessed with teaching us all to "live off the land," as he put it, as if subsistence living was not already a fine art in my home country. Al contacted his son Eddie and asked him to send the gun collection that he left behind with him before he went to Vietnam. Unknown to me, but after learning that his father was returning with an "instant" Vietnamese family, Eddie (who lived in Montana) wanted nothing more to do with him. Al received a shotgun and a rifle sometime later, but to my knowledge, that was the last time that father and son spoke. If that broke Al's heart, he never showed it. Al used these guns to teach Bubba and Quang how to shoot—not too well, apparently, since their numerous safaris after whitetail deer and feral hogs usually saw them return with one or two squirrels, prairie chickens, raccoons, rabbits, and even possum (which looked like hideous huge rats) and armadillo (which looked like a monster from late-night TV). Al "dressed" these "critters" himself, which actually meant *undressing* them by removing their pelt and innards, then cooking them with his own chef's hand. Even with his culinary skills, he couldn't make the tough and skinny game less gamey, and we always looked forward to those two or three times a month when the

Gilchrests brought over fresh beef or venison.

My first kitchen duty (aside from washing up) was to make breakfast every morning. I started at 5:30 a.m. so that something hot and nourishing would be on the table by the time everyone else got up. Determined to be a true Texas girl and using techniques I'd learned from Kathy and Mrs. Gilchrest, I tried first to serve old-fashioned biscuits and gravy. I didn't even know there was such a sport as hockey until Al unceremoniously told me my first batch of biscuits could be used as pucks in the NHL. My gravy wasn't much better. After flinging one rock-hard biscuit at me and dumping his gravy into the garbage, Al suggested that we use the gravy to spackle the walls. This was not the kind of reinforcement I'd grown accustomed to with my art. Coming from a man who once ran a popular restaurant, I knew I would be in big trouble if I did not improve my cooking skill fast. This time, it was Thuy who came to my rescue.

After a month of trauma at breakfast time, Thuy stepped in and became a must needed and valuable assistant. Together, we figured out how to mix the flour and knead the biscuit dough to perfection. With her help, I was putting a passable breakfast on the table in thirty minutes or less, leading Al to promote me to more demanding meals like dinner. For a brief moment, I thought his interest in teaching me advanced cooking techniques (even with the help of Betty Crocker) was his way of rehabilitating our relationship. Not so. If the meal he specified didn't turn out as expected, he stopped everyone from eating and commanded me to finish all the food myself. If I hesitated or stopped, he stepped behind my chair and pushed my face into the plate, holding my nose and making me chew until I either swallowed the food or vomited. It was at times like these that I began to harden inside—which has in some way remained with me to this day. I wondered why Aunt Thu never said, "This behavior crosses the line!" or "Sissy is no VC prisoner to be tortured for information!" I even wondered why Quang, now almost eighteen and pretty big himself, didn't intervene and look out for me, the way he sometimes had when we were growing up. The answer was that Al had us under his thumb. None of the kids dared to interfere, and Aunt Thu had no desire to. Sometimes, seeing my sadness and tears after such an episode, Thuy and Bubba would help me with the dishes, and even that small gesture earned them an angry stare from Al.

We were all caught in a vortex of duty and obedience to the man who had saved us from the terrors of Vietnam, though what terrors his impulses might drive him to next we could only guess. It would be easy to explain our acquiescence as the natural trepidation of "strangers in a strange land," but honestly, that wasn't the case. Al simply *owned* us and behaved the way any slave master does, eventually giving in to his baser instincts.

If we were to enjoy a new life, a rebirth in this new land, it would have to come from inside ourselves.

Meanwhile, Mrs. Gilchrest remained our guiding light on the path toward becoming Americans. She was the archetypal Texas farm wife—self-reliant and skilled in homespun wizardry—but she was a modern business woman, too, who knew how to run an efficient and profitable peanut farm, her family's primary source of income. There wasn't a lot we could do to repay her kindness and wages except give her an honest day's work and share what tricks we'd picked up at places like Fish Farm.

For example, the Gilchrests enjoyed fresh fish, and Al and the boys sometimes caught a surplus. I took to her kitchen a pail of small bass and catfish with heads and skin still on so she could see what type they were. She expressed her delight, which was genuine, and admitted that she hated to clean fish and always mangled the meat when she tried to skin and fillet them. I told her, "No problem," in my growing vocabulary of colloquial English. I produced one of Al's extra-sharp fish knives to show her how we did things back in Da Minh. She was astonished at my skill, and I was pleased to return at least one of the many lessons she had taught me.

Early one morning, Al wanted to take the boys hunting, and he didn't want to delay the trip until after Quang milked the cow, but the cow needed to be milked. I overheard the conversation and volunteered. What could be so hard about milking a cow? I'd watched Quang do it many times, and it didn't seem all that difficult. So the hunters left on their expedition, and I took up the milk pail and a small stool and headed for the barn.

I looked at the cow and she looked at me, quite calmly, with her large beautiful brown eyes. I thought we had an understanding, so I took my place at the appropriate location between the cow and the barn wall. With some nervousness, I pulled on an udder with my right hand, then my left, then my right, and so on. I got the rhythm going and was pretty pleased with myself. The cow, however, was not. I guess she decided that I was pulling too hard for comfort. She gave a loud, indignant "moo!" and kicked the milk bucket over. I stood up and tried to get away, but she pinned me in midair, and before I knew it, I was stuck between her and the wall. I slapped her rump, but that just made her more unhappy. She pressed harder against me. I could not free my legs to kick her away so I did the only thing left to do: I screamed for help, loudly. Thuy came running from the house, but she did not want to approach the beast herself.

With a worried look on her face, she asked, "What should I do, sister?"

"Call Mrs. Gilchrist! Hurry!"

She ran off, yelling for Mrs. Gilchrist at the top of her lungs.

Mrs. Gilchrist soon came at a run. Once she sized up the situation, she started laughing, very hard.

I did not share her humor.

She patted the cow's flank, and the cow moved away. She then picked up the milk pail and demonstrated the proper technique for milking. "Pull gently, this way." And I did.

I'm pleased to say that I became proficient at milking, and the cow and I became friends.

§

In September, we kids boarded a bus for our first day at an American school, in this case, the combined K-12 public school in Sidney, a slightly larger "small town" where Ann herself was a student. While Bubba went off with the younger kids, Ann introduced me and Quang and Thuy to her best friends Frances and others, largely a welcoming group. She and Frances later gave me my sixteenth birthday party in the school's study hall, something I'd never had since Al and Thu didn't go in for them, not even for Bubba. Frances gave me a pair of rabbits and told me how to feed and care for them, but watch out she said: they were breeders and if you owned a couple, they would soon create a crowd, or a *warren*, as she called them. She asked what I would name them, and I admitted I was stuck for an answer. In Vietnam, we never named anything that might turn up on our table, and it was hard to imagine something with fur and a pulse lasting too long in a hut behind Al's house. Still, animal husbandry proved my forte that first year. I joined the 4-H Club and won ribbons for my rabbits. I took Home Economics and excelled in that as well, earning acknowledgement for (believe it or not) my painting, baking and, more understandably, my sewing. Mrs. Gilchrest bought my material for the final competition and cheered for me like a mom when I received three trophies from the judge. To celebrate, she gave me a pretty green sewing box and pair of orange-handled, serrated seamstress scissors. Little did she know, but I had never before received a special gift for anything that I had accomplished.

School was another matter—and not just academics. Although I had largely recovered from my truck accident, my mouth still required reconstructive dentistry so I spent my first few months in class with no front teeth. This is a bad age for any teenager, let alone a girl (and a foreigner at that), to have issues with appearance, and mine were right up front for everyone to see. Consequently, I spent a lot of time with my mouth shut, and if I absolutely had to laugh, it was always with a hand over my bare gums. Finally, Mrs. Gilchrest broached the subject with Al and Thu. She said that if they could not afford to have my dental work done, she would be happy to pay the cost herself. This was a kind and generous offer, but my guardians would have none of it. They made it clear they didn't appreciate Mrs. Gilchrest interfering in family business, so she politely dropped the subject—though it eventually registered with Al, who was shamed into taking action. Midway through my first year in high school, he arranged to have bridgework done across the border in Mexico, changing my life for the better. I don't know if Mrs. Gilchrest had any part in financing my makeover, but it wouldn't surprise me if she did—and that Al chose to keep it a secret.

Academically, my new set of choppers improved my English pronunciation, but not by much. My teachers were patient and knew English could be tricky, even for locals, some of whom spoke with thick Texas dialects and also had missing front teeth. Still, I thought of myself as an exemplary student and vowed to repay my teachers' extra help by working extra hard.

One jewel I discovered at this school was a boy named Robert, Ann's special friend with whom she often went horseback riding. In fact, the first time we met outside of class, both he and Ann arrived on horses—my first genuine cowboy and cowgirl! I declined a riding lesson, so we just sat in the shade and talked about school. Between Robert's Texas brogue and my fractured English, we didn't cover a lot of subjects, but he was a patient guy who soon made it clear he was willing to help me master English if I tutored him in those subjects that came more easily to me. It was a bargain made in heaven. For the rest of the semester, he appeared at my door after class carrying a big encyclopedia, which he said replaced the need for many other books. "Read it every day," he said, "and it will not just improve your English, it will help you research assignments." For my part, I tried diligently to speak the words I had no trouble writing on paper but just couldn't get off my tongue. Between the two of us, we slowly climbed the scholastic ladder at Sidney. By tutoring me, Robert became a better student and turned the Cs and Ds he'd been making to As and Bs. Near the end of the term, the principal called us into his office, but instead of punishing us for breaking some rule, he praised our academic initiative. Outside Al's cabin, at least, school and America began to click.

§

In the summer of 1976, Al went to work for Brown & Root, a worldwide construction company that had just won a contract to expand the Comanche Nuclear Power Plant in the riverside town of Glen Rose, Texas, an hour and a half drive from Beattie. This presented us all with a problem as well as an opportunity. Mrs. Gilchrest was too kind of a person and too keen of a human observer to let Al's behavior go totally ignored. She believed everyone had a right to privacy and to live the way they chose, but physical and emotional child abuse—if not crossing the line into child endangerment—was something she would not tolerate. Without making an issue of it, she quietly invited Quang, Thuy, and me to remain in Beattie to finish high school while Bubba accompanied his natural mother to Glen Rose. She knew Aunt Thu's "little prince" was excused from Al's aberrations and felt he would enjoy a safe and happy life once his stepfather settled into a steady job and received a good paycheck. Quang and Thuy immediately jumped at the chance to jump ship. Neither was willing to live any longer with the constant beatings and abuse from Al, whose temperament since we arrived in the United States had worsened considerably.

And, in our observation of the close-knit and loving Gilchrist family, we kids had learned that how Al treated us was not normal, that children could be raised with love and nurturing and encouragement instead of unending physical, emotional, mental, and spiritual abuse, and, in Aunt Thu's case, cold and absolute refusal to extend to us any gesture of even the most basic human consideration and care. My brother and my sister did not understand why I didn't instantly accept Mrs. Gilchrist's kind invitation, and I have to admit that my feelings were complicated. A therapist could probably explain my decision better than I could because it was difficult for me to understand, too. Why did I not take the opportunity to escape Al when a kind and safe alternative was offered to me?

I know I felt some sense of obligation and duty to Aunt Thu. When I thought back over the long years since Mama's death, I realized what a hard life Aunt Thu really lived, with troubles and responsibilities made worse when Aunt Que went off the deep end and Uncle Chieu could no longer honor Uncle Thanh's charge to care for half of his sister's orphaned family. As Thu became our mother figure, she worked hard to live up to that image, but what foster mother can? She tried at first to be a "doting Auntie," favoring me with gifts and kindness, moving back in with Grandma when she thought she could finally care for little Hoang, now called Bubba even by me. But the task was too great for an illiterate woman in a wartime world. She tried one American boyfriend after another, all scared off by the big, extended family they saw they would inherit. Except for Al. In "saving" Aunt Thu, whom he genuinely loved, Al saved us all and, in a way, saved Mama's memory, too. Try as I might, I could not blame Thu for resenting the way we three had complicated her life, making her relationship with Al—a challenge from the start—more difficult than necessary. For reasons known only to herself, she still harbored a lot of sibling rivalry with my mom, and I remained, in some way, obsessed with the desire to make amends.

Then there was my "little brother," Bubba. He watched me with big, sad eyes while all this was being decided, as if to beg me to not leave him again. Such motherly instincts that simmered inside me were kindled, I was sure, by my early years with Bubba . Even when his mother returned and this strange round-eyed man with his devilish moustache and balding head appeared with a piece of paper calling him "Papa," mine was still the face that comforted little Bubba when he was hungry, when he was scared, when he was hurt. He and I were so close, and I had played such a constant role in early childhood that, in the end, I knew I could not leave him. You can't live your life through someone else, but you can do a lot worse than giving part of that life to someone who needs you for a while.

Similarly, justified though I was, I could not blame Al for taking his failures out on us. After all, we were Vietnamese. We were the people his own nation had tried to help, and, very publicly on the world stage, had failed. By Al's own account, he had a "very, very strict father," and in Vietnam or America, abused boys often become abusive men. He was in his own way as desperate as Mr. Lieu clinging to that last helicopter. I would not be the one to push him into the abyss. I just wouldn't. Besides, I believed I could deal with Al now. His ill-treatment of me was pretty much limited to almost constant yelling (belittlement, criticism, ridicule, etc.), moderate beatings, and just plain meanness, like forcing me to eat failed cooking attempts.

What Quang and Thuy saw as my leap from the frying pan into the fire was to me just a final step toward becoming the woman my mother would want me to be.

So, in April, I dropped out of my freshman year at Sidney High and prepared for the move to Glen Rose, where I finished out the last three weeks of my freshman year, and started my sophomore year in the fall of 1976. I still struggled somewhat with real proficiency in English, but most of the teachers were understanding and patient. Because of their dedication—to their profession and to me—my English improved dramatically, to the extent that I began to "think in English" before I spoke. This was a tremendous breakthrough that cascaded through all my other subjects. It allowed me to ask questions when they occurred to me (not after a United Nations translation) and make small talk in kitchens and cafeterias, in soda shops and on street corners, with friends and strangers alike. Americans are a gregarious people. I now shared that special gift.

Unfortunately, Al lasted only three months with B&R before he quit. To be fair, he had worked his way up from manual labor as a small-time contractor and house painter in Hollywood after World War II to supervisory jobs in Vietnam, not to mention several years as his own boss in the Philippines and at Fish Farm. As a "blue collar" worker, he felt his career had taken a step back just at an age when he couldn't compete for managerial positions against younger men with college degrees. His attitude and personality did not lend themselves to being cooperative, and the chip on his shoulder became a log. He began to quarrel with his co-workers and soon had a falling-out with his immediate foreman. The alternative after B&R was self-employment—again—this time as a freelance handyman painting houses and doing light carpentry, plumbing, and tile work for well-to-do Glen Rose citizens. My heart dropped to my stomach when he asked me one day, shortly after beginning this new career, if I would like to help him on a couple of jobs.

I myself had been looking for work to exploit my newfound English skills and allow Thu to remain a stay-at-home mom and look after little Bubba. The last thing I wanted was to replay those old scenes in the cabin kitchen, when Sissy-the-Apprentice couldn't do anything right, and the penalty this time would be eating real spackle instead of bad gravy.

But Al's attitude seemed different. This time he *asked* me for help, not demanded it. In fact, he went out of his way to mention that my skills in math and reading, all gained at schools he thought I had no business attending, would be an asset when checking blueprints, measuring tiles, setting and aligning tools like his well-used miter box, and installing carpets and baseboards. This was a side of him I'd never seen, and since I'd gone along with him this far, another roll of the dice didn't seem to make much difference. Fortunately, the gamble paid off. I became very skilled at measuring precisely floor tiles for cutting, especially for corners and up against baseboards. I did it so there was little waste, and I did it better than Al, which he actually came to appreciate. The jobs I participated in went faster and smoother. The customers were happy, so Al was happy. He got paid on time, and some of that money came to me, which I used to augment my job-hunting wardrobe. I cleaned houses and washed windows after school, which was a no-brainer, but I also finagled a part-time job at a nursing home. This didn't bring in a lot of money, but all of it was mine. The funds I kicked in to the household treasury were no more and no less than I felt I could afford, and even that simple act felt like a sea change in my life. High School in Glen Rose was part of that new picture.

Poor, quiet, and wearing mostly clothes that I made for myself or that had been obviously purchased second-hand, some might think this did not lend itself to "fitting in" with others in high school. Generally, however, that was not the case. I may not have been Homecoming Queen, but I made friends and found most everyone in the rural, moderately well-to-do community of Glen Rose to be accepting, considerate, and friendly.

One day, after finishing a house-cleaning job for a gracious neighbor, my employer took me for a late dinner at the local Dairy Queen. Flipping burgers was one of the best-looking young men I'd ever seen. I tried my best to make small talk with my benefactor while staring at the handsome boy, taking care not to get caught. The odd thing was, as soon as I started describing this hunky guy from DQ to my girlfriends at school it appeared that everyone, but me, seemed to know him. His beautiful blue eyes, infectious smile, the way he dressed, and his charm was enough to melt any young girl's heart. I learned his name was Ronnie Choat, a name that apparently originated from Native Americans. He drove a white pickup truck to part-time construction jobs and always wore Army boots, a sort-of trademark, the way other kids wore college sweatshirts or cool shades. My girlfriends said he was a senior at Glen Rose High, but if I'd ever seen him on campus, I would have remembered it, so I started looking for his white truck in the student parking lot. I found out later the white truck belonged to his father and Ronnie only used it for construction work. He usually drove a blue Pinto to get around town and to school, so I started to look for that, too.

Then, at school, something happened that could have come straight from one of my romance novels. I was late for class and hurrying. When

I rounded a hall corner, I ran into him—literally—I spilled my books at his feet. He bent to help me pick them up, and we bumped heads. He gave me his name, which I had already written in bubble letters (with a heart above the "i" in *Ronnie*, of course) a few dozen times on the back pages of my notebook, and I gave him mine. I ran to my history class and pretended to pay attention to my teachers for the rest of the day, but they could've been speaking Swedish for all I knew. I was too busy preparing some clever, spontaneous, witty remark to make in flawless English the next time I ran into Ronnie.

On the weekend and occasionally during the week, I held down my job at the nursing home, an easy walk from my house. I was making this commute a day or two later, eyes down, going over homework in my head, when I sensed a car slow down and pull alongside me. I looked up and saw Ronnie in his blue Pinto.

"Hey there, Van." He smiled. "Need a taxi?"

"Oh, no." I blushed. "I'm almost there."

"Almost where?"

"My job. The nursing home. Just the next block. I'm going to pick up my paycheck."

"Well, why don't I give you a lift?"

"No, really. It's so close."

"What if it's a big check? You'll need a ride to get it home!"

His smile was just gorgeous, but the stern voices inside my head—Grandma's, Aunt Thu's, Mo Nga's, even Mama's—were too loud to let me think. "No, thank you." I couldn't believe what I was saying. I had just turned him down three times!

"Okay, suit yourself. See ya at school." He gave me a friendly wave and drove off.

I continued to the home, mentally kicking myself. When I arrived, they were just starting evening meal service and were short-handed, so even though I was not on duty, I pitched in and helped take the trays around, assisting elderly residents who could no longer hold forks and spoons. I was in the middle of this when a nurse named Ann Daniel called me to the reception desk.

"Call for you, Van," she said, holding out the phone.

"For me?"

This had never happened before. I had given the number to Aunt Thu for emergencies, but she never used American phones, and Al wouldn't call me even if the house was on fire. The only thing it could be was that something happened to Bubba.

"Hello, this is Van," I said in a worried tone.

"Hi. I'm calling about your earlier offer of a ride to work with Ronnie." Ronnie's sweet Texas accent tickled my ear. "He just wanted to make sure you got to work safely."

I laughed with him. "Well, if you're his mom, you can tell that I did."

"Good. Then maybe you'll allow him to take you home today. What time shall he pick you up?"

This time I had the good sense to go along for the ride. His Pinto was out front a half-hour later, and we chatted and laughed for the short drive to my house. As we pulled up, he said, "You know, I already know all about you."

"You do?"

In Vietnam, that would've been very alarming. Anyone in my homeland could get in trouble if someone knew too much about them. Is your family from the North? Do you have relatives working for the South? Are you friends with the Americans? Dating a GI? Buy or sell on the black market? Just too much to know or hide!

"Yeah. I took a peek at your file in the principal's office. Found out where you came from, how long you been here, stuff like that. I bet you could tell a few stories!"

"I bet."

The car stopped. I got out and smiled back through the passenger window. "Thanks for the lift," I said, like a genuine American.

"Any time. Hey, you got a date for the Senior Prom?"

I thought a moment. "No. I'm not a senior."

"That doesn't matter. I am. Why don't you go with me? I'll throw in another car ride!"

This was too good to be true. "Well, I don't know. I'll have to ask Uncle Al."

"Sure thing. Let's do it right now." He shut off the engine and walked me to the door.

I walked in first and was about to announce our guest when Al got up from his chair by the TV as his face broke into a wide grin.

"Ronnie!" He held out his hand like a gentleman. "Good to see you again. It's been a while."

"Mr. Strauss," Ronnie said politely. "Still busting that tile?"

Al laughed. "Not if you'd come to work for me. Here, take a load off..." He pointed to a chair. I was shocked. Apparently Al and Ronnie knew each other from working on the same job site. Al turned to me and said, "This is the guy I wanted you to find. Hard worker and a positive attitude. I tried to hire him away from his last employer."

Al and Ronnie talked shop for half an hour (both of Ronnie's parents were B&R alumni like Al), then got down to business. Ronnie said he had asked me to go with him to the Senior Prom, and I'd accepted as long as it was all right with "Uncle Al." Al wasn't always a monster. He had performed a few fatherly functions for me over the years, most of them grudgingly, but this one he actually took to heart.

"Sure, Sissy can be your date," he said, wiping his nose with a handkerchief. "Just have her home by ten o'clock."

The deal was struck, and nobody was more pleased by it than me. The prom was two weeks away, and between two jobs, schoolwork, and my normal chores around the house, I had little time and much to do: find a pattern and fabric for a special dress, make it, fit it, then borrow some suitable jewelry from my friends. Luckily, I didn't have to invent a do-it-myself upswept hairdo—all the rage among the girls—because Ronnie said the first thing he'd admired about me was my silky waist-length hair. The big night went off as planned. We stopped first at Ronnie's home where his parents, Floyd and Imogene, wanted to take their family's "official" prom picture—and also, I was sure, check-out his exotic but timid Asian date. They were relatively quiet, and I was very shy and quiet as well. I was already very much taken by their son, and I hoped they would like me and approve of me. I was very aware of being Asian, and poor, and wearing a dress I'd made myself. I had not spent the afternoon in a beauty shop like most girls do on Prom Day. I wanted them to see beyond those things, to see only that I was thrilled and proud to be with their son that night. We posed for pictures, then went to the dance, which was magical for me. At the all-too-soon end of the evening, my hard work was rewarded by a soft, chaste kiss. My last big fear—that I would turn into a Cinderella-style "one-date pumpkin" after he dropped me off—failed to materialize when Ronnie immediately asked me out again. Home life had become tolerable and academic life was good, but none of that compared to having an honest-to-God American teen-aged boyfriend. My Guardian Angels were with me again.

§

After dating Ronnie steadily for a few months, I finally discovered what the Army boots were for. Because other members of his family had served in the military, Ronnie thought it was his duty to serve, too, and had signed on for the U.S. Army's "delayed entry" program, or DEP. This meant that in exchange for his promise to attend Basic Training on a certain date (in his case, after his graduation from high school), he would be given special consideration for a desired type of duty and receive advanced instruction from local recruiters on certain aspects of military life, such as code of conduct, military courtesy, chain of command, and all that. Meeting me, he said, had cooled his enthusiasm for leaving home, but his sense of duty was stronger than male hormones—at least for now. He'd made a commitment and felt bound to honor it. I had my own mixed feelings about men in uniform, but I had to admire his character. It was one of the things that made him Ronnie.

So Ronnie graduated and went off to Basic Training, and I began my junior year, heartsick with missing him. My girlfriends treated me as a "war widow," which was pretty much how I felt. No love is as wonderful and painful as young love, and if Cupid's bow shot poisoned arrows, I was a pin cushion. We wrote letters to each other almost daily, then after a month, his letters stopped. I was sure he had dumped me for another girl—big Army bases were surrounded by husband-hungry women, a lesson I'd learned in Vietnam—and I was depressed and inconsolable for weeks. I was never what Mrs. Gilchrest called "pleasingly plump," like some other Texas girls, and my inability to eat or hold food down eventually landed me in bed. Even Al knew I wasn't malingering, and since he, too, saw virtue in a guy like Ronnie, he actually commiserated with my situation. He put his gourmet cooking skills to use and made appetizing soups that he served to me himself. I don't know if it was the food or Al's unprecedented kindness that cured my lovesick soul, but I was up and around after a month. I even got a part-time job as a waitress at the Dairy Queen where I'd first seen Ronnie. Somehow, that helped me feel closer to him. Finally, Ronnie's letters resumed, but not until near the end of my Senior year. Having never been in the Army, I was unaware that a big part of becoming a soldier was learning how to stop being a civilian, and that meant spending a lot of time doing things the Army wants done instead of doing things you want to do, such as writing letters to a girlfriend. It was a month, in fact, before his training platoon was even allowed to leave its barracks to relax in the Post Exchange. While he was learning how to be a soldier, I was learning how to be a soldier's girl.

I later learned that there was another reason for his long period of silence. There really was "another woman," a hometown girl at his church, who, for a time, was probably favored by his family. Ronnie was confused, and conflicted. He knew who he loved, and that was me. But, because he was a loving and loyal son, pleasing his parents was also important. He prayed, and worried, and prayed some more. Finally, he followed his heart, and his letters to me began once again.

A big milestone of my senior year was saving enough money to buy my own car. Al was all in favor of this, since I had managed to sock away almost $5,000 while still contributing to household expenses. He was so enthusiastic, he went out on his own and bought a used Plymouth for $500, then offered to resell it immediately to me for $700, netting a tidy $200 profit. Maybe he was trying to teach me a lesson about free enterprise or felt I owed him something for his gourmet soups, but I didn't squawk and made the deal. I now commuted proudly to my DQ job and to school and parked each day in Ronnie's old spot.

§

In 1979, I graduated from Glen Rose High and was faced with an immediate decision. At eighteen, I was old enough to live on my own—open a bank account, rent an apartment, and do all kinds of things without parental permission. I had come a long way under Al's and Thu's hit-and-miss guardianship, and if I'd learned one thing from life, it was to get off the train when you reach the station. With me out of the picture, Aunt Thu would finally have the nuclear family—herself, Bubba, and (I hoped) a stable American husband—she'd wanted for more than a decade. It was time for me to go. But where?

I had been in periodic contact with Quang and Thuy. I knew my brother had moved to Oklahoma City after graduating from Beattie High. He had matured into a friendly, capable young man, but as the eldest in our family, he clung tightly to the old ways. He missed our homeland and was intrigued by the prospect of living in what had become a vibrant community of Vietnamese "boat people" who had escaped the communist regime and settled in the United States. Like several other big American cities that boasted open spaces and open hearts, "OKC" had established its own *Little Saigon*, and Quang wanted to join it. Besides, it was the closest Vietnamese enclave to what had become his American hometown, Beattie, where he had lots of high school pals, and the Gilchrests still considered us family.

While Quang set his sights on Asian neighbors and getting a

good-paying job, mine were aimed in another direction. Since I'd graduated from high school with honors, my teachers and counselors urged me to go on to college—as if I needed much prodding. Mama had always believed in education for women, and I thought I'd finally converted Aunt Thu as well. Dependence is natural for children, but it's something most of us try to outgrow. Independence in America meant acquiring skills beyond planting rice, having babies, and cleaning a house. In a nutshell, it meant making wise choices for yourself.

I decided to apply for a scholarship to Oklahoma State University and won a grant almost at once. I joined the wave of freshmen arriving at the Oklahoma City campus like an old hand (bureaucracies and timid newcomers are the same worldwide, and I was familiar with both) and settled into an apartment with Quang and Thuy in OKC's "Little Saigon." Like all freshmen, I looked forward to receiving my first mail from home, from friends in Texas, from anywhere! Among my first batch of envelopes was a letter from Ronnie. Its return address was an Infantry School in Georgia—education of a different sort. The first paragraph astounded me. He was wondering, he wrote, if, despite the tickly moustache he had grown in the Army, I would consent to be his wife. Since my first ride in his blue Pinto had worked out so well, I wrote back "YES!" on the first scrap of paper I could find.

We were married in December of 1979.

Chapter 13

Over the Rainbow 1979—1987

We did not have a big wedding, so there was plenty of room for my Guardian Angels to attend. Mama came to me on the first night of our honeymoon after Ronnie had gone to sleep. Her spirit was joyful, and she called my name so clearly that I awoke and sat up in bed. In a splash of soft moonlight from a slit in the curtains, she stood in front of me, as clear and defined as Ronnie was beside me. Radiantly beautiful, she spoke in a familiar voice. *My work is finished. Now I am at peace. It is time for me to rest. Ronnie*—a distinct movement of her eyes flicked to him—*will care for you as I have, and he will love you as I always have.* She smiled down at me as she had when I was a child, then left like a wisp through the window, fading with the moonlight. I went back to sleep, warmed by the certainty that I was no longer an orphan.

Ronnie proved to be a dedicated soldier. After a few years with the 82nd Airborne (appropriately called the "AA," or All-American division), he was promoted to squad leader—an NCO just like Papa. He knew the importance of his duties and mastered all aspects of his job, but his real joy came from his connection to his men, just as mine flowed from my connection to the family we had started: Eric born in 1982 was named after a Swedish saint with a nod to Erik Estrada, and Jon born in

1984 was named after Saint John and my other "CHiPs" hero, Officer Jon Baker from the popular TV show. They were spaced about as far apart as Thuy and I, so if that was good enough for Mama, it was good enough for me.

Ronnie and Van, The only soldier with a gun that didn't scare me

At the end of his first tour, Ronnie separated from the service to be closer to his family. He worked a few months for Brown & Root in Glen Rose, but his blood was red-white-and-blue. He missed the Army, rejoined with my blessing, and was reinstated to his old job as infantry squad leader. His first overseas deployment was to Asia, but farther north than I'd ever been—Camp Casey, a U.S. Army military base near the Demilitarized Zone in Dongducheon (also sometimes spelled Tongduchon or TDC), South Korea. Because of the harsh climate and perpetual tension between the North and South (old story!), the Army considered it a "hardship tour" and did not authorize dependents. This did not mean GIs stationed there could not be accompanied, only that the government would not pay for them. Still, Ronnie and I wanted to be together. I did not want his 2-year-old and 2-month-old sons to start life feeling like orphans or wondering, as I did, where their soldier-father was or if he was alive or dead. So Ronnie sold the gun collection he'd had since his teenage years, and between us, we scrounged up enough money for his family to join him in Korea. We rented a one-bedroom apartment (with indoor bathroom!) near the camp, and, being accustomed to living in small spaces with small kids, I set up house. I did the dishes and the laundry in a washtub and hung our perishable food out the window to keep it cold—no problem at all in winter. Ronnie had to live in the barracks with his men, although he was allowed one pass each month to stay with us. Being a young and healthy couple deeply in love, that was unsatisfactory, so, being my mother's daughter, I found a way to visit him with the boys, even sleeping a few nights in the open-bay Quonset hut. Just as Mama had done for Papa, I brought him homemade meals when I visited—a nice break for him from mess hall chow. In fact, such "food runs" were the official reason they let me through the main gate.

Although our conjugal visits were against regulations, the soldiers in his unit (and, I suspect, the officers, too) were sympathetic and quietly cooperative. They rearranged some office furniture to make a "nest" at the back of the hut, and we slept on the floor instead of an Army cot. The boys were generally cooperative—Eric the toddler was especially popular with men who'd left families back in the States—and on those few occasions when Jon woke up feeling fussy, baby formula soon quieted him down. All in all, it was an adventurous, memorable time, especially for me, because it ended with all of us going home together on a plane instead Eric and Jon riding away—alone—on some bus.

§

Ronnie's next assignment was as an Army Fitness Instructor at Fort Sill near the town of Lawton, Oklahoma, in the southwest corner of the state. This was good news all around. Quang and Thuy still lived in Oklahoma City. Bubba, who had moved with Al and Thu when they relocated to the Veteran's Colony in Wilburton, Oklahoma, was now out in the world, living in McAlester, Oklahoma, and working for UPS. Grandma and Grandpa Choat were just across the Texas border in Rainbow. It was here, too, that our life together took a different—and potentially sky-high—turn. Right after we were married, Ronnie had turned down two promotions to Warrant Officer (a potentially dead-end career move) because he did not want to be away from me. Now, as a reward for his exemplary leadership, the Army offered Ronnie a slot in OCS (Officer Candidate School), beginning in the fall of '86. This was doubly good news, since commissioned officers got more pay and better housing. The only condition was that he complete two years of college and earn an Associate's degree. His high scores on entrance exams excused him from many otherwise required courses, and for the remainder, he enrolled in night school at Cameron State University.

The fall of 1985 was a fabulous time for our young family, in many ways the time of my greatest happiness. I had a family that was *mine*, one that extended beyond my siblings, one that filled my heart and soul with the comfort and warmth that comes only from "belonging," from being with another who is truly a soul mate. We of course loved our sons, but we also enjoyed them. For this brief and beautiful period, we were a normal and happy American military family. The future looked hopeful and bright, and things were really good.

Still, we were making do on an E6's pay, and old habits die hard. Thanks to practical necessity and the frugality I learned from a childhood in Vietnam, I had developed penny-pinching to a fine art. We left Korea with almost $10,000 in savings—a decent nest egg, but still not enough to buy even a modest house in Lawton. And to tell the truth, even if we'd found the right fixer-upper, I would've blocked the door to the bank. Ronnie had plenty of common sense and was hardly a spendthrift. He trusted the purse strings to me—a role my mother had assumed in her marriage. Ronnie believed that life's goal was not necessarily to die rich, but to use whatever resources God gave you to live a happy and useful life. His optimism was admirable and was one of the reasons I loved him. To me, though, cash-in-the-hand was like an armored vest or steel helmet. I sometimes carried this defensive thinking to extremes, and Ronnie was very good at finding ways around it. We ended up spending all of our saving on the forty-plus acres of land that Al had pick out in Wilburton. Al convinced him that we should built our dream home next to theirs after his tour of duty with the Army.

When we were still living in Korea, I remember I was still wearing the same old sneakers I'd owned since high school, complete with frayed canvas toes and "fish lip" soles that slapped when I walked. Finally, when I wouldn't take his subtle hints to replace them, he took me on a "birthday shopping spree" to the retail district of Yongsan (Yongsan-gu) in downtown Seoul where most GIs bought their sundries. He stopped at a women's clothing store on the pretext of buying me some rubber flip-flops, then told the clerk once my shoes were off to "throw these damn things away!" Since I wasn't about to walk barefoot in the Korean winter, he got his way, and I got new shoes.

Ronnie was also sympathetic to workers struggling with low-paying jobs. Once in 1985, after our anniversary dinner at Red Lobster—my first meal at a restaurant specializing in something other than hamburgers and Cokes—we discussed the size of the tip we should leave our waitress. She was a friendly, hard-working young woman who was thrilled to serve us on our special night, so Ronnie thought she deserved something special, like five bucks. No, I said, three dollars was plenty, but it was Ronnie's night, too, so he left her a five-dollar bill. We had just reached our car in the parking lot when she caught up with us and gave each of us a hug. It was biggest tip she'd ever received, she said, and she hoped it wasn't a mistake. Ronnie had made her day, and maybe her week. It was a treat for her and a lesson for me, but it was "business as usual" for My Man.

He was sweet and gentle with beautiful blue eyes, and, to me, movie star good looks. But it was his generous heart that won over everyone he met. Sometimes he was late getting home and would apologize and explain that he was helping some stranger change a flat tire, or jump start a car, or assist someone otherwise stranded on the roadside. He told me he always did such things for me. He wanted to believe that his kindness to others would one day be returned to me should I ever need assistance or help.

I smiled and kissed him, and told him not to worry because strangers had often helped me. As I continued making dinner, for the first time in years I thought of the policeman in Hong Ngu who had taken Quang and me and Baby Sister to his home the morning after the firefight at Papa's post, and the taxi driver in Saigon the next day who had spent his whole afternoon and evening helping Quang and me find our grandmother in a city of millions of people, a seemingly impossible task. Generous strangers and Angels, each of them, and so was Ronnie.

Unfortunately, the pendulum of life swings both ways.

In 1986, as Ronnie was preparing to graduate from night school, he began to complain about persistent pain in his knees and back. At first, we assumed these aches and pains were the result of a soldier's life, which was anything but sedentary, and expected them to pass. When they didn't, Ronnie went to the clinic at Fort Sill, where the Physician's Assistant gave him a cursory exam and refused to pass him forward to a doctor. He actually accused Ronnie of "malingering" and "wanting to stay home with his wife and kids," and told him to "quit bitching and get back to work." In the PA's mind, his "diagnosis" was confirmed when Ronnie's X-ray came back and showed nothing out of the ordinary. Always the good soldier, Ronnie followed his orders. He lived with the pain, tight-lipped and stoic, for three more months until one afternoon in March while filling up at the gas station right outside Fort Sill, he collapsed.

An ambulance took him to the Post Hospital where the ER physician ordered extensive blood work and a CAT scan. A few days later the verdict was in. Ronnie, at age 27, was suffering from Stage IV bone cancer. Short of a miracle, the doctor said at Ronnie's bedside, he could count on living about six months.

A short time later, while Ronnie and I were still deep in shock, grief, and despair, the PA from the clinic came in and offered a tepid apology. "I'm sorry I didn't pass you on to my superior, Sergeant Choat," he said with a shrug. "Anyone can make a mistake."

Not like this one, buster! I was livid—white-hot with rage. "Your mistake cost my husband his life!"

Ronnie took my arm, which was probably cocked for a punch, and gently pulled me back. "Let it go, sweetheart," he said quietly. "He didn't mean to do it."

Maybe not, but a lot of tragedies had resulted from such well-intended mistakes. The fate of my homeland had been one of them.

That night, I curled up with the boys in the dark, thinking about all that had happened to Ronnie. I was numb with unspeakable pain. Separation by death from many of those who meant the most to me was going to happen to me once again. The "permanency" of death was a concept that always grabbed my heart. Never to have my mother comb my hair again. Never to have my father hold me once again. Never to have the comfort of my grandmother's touch. Never to have Ronnie's hand in mine again. That was my future. I could not bear it. I silently cried myself to sleep.

Within days Ronnie was transported to Brooks Army Medical Center (BAMC) at Fort Sam Houston, San Antonio for chemotherapy and radiation. Of course, the military looks after its own—eventually. I dropped the boys off with Grandma and Grandpa Choat at their home in Rainbow, where there was plenty of outdoor space for energetic and growing boys to play, and went to join him. When babysitting two rambunctious boys got to be too much and Ronnie's parents needed a break, Al and Thu volunteered to take them at the Veteran's Colony in Wilburton. Up to now I had seen them rarely, and their lives, like mine, had changed a lot. Al had always admired Ronnie and was pleased to look after his sons. Aunt Thu, I think, suffered from "empty nest" syndrome after her little prince, Bubba, moved out and so welcomed the chance to try her hand again at mothering. After all, if there was one thing she knew all about, it was orphans.

When it was clear that Ronnie's treatment would be difficult and (if we were lucky) take a long time, I looked for a place to live in San Antonio. I wanted to be near the hospital but also to have the boys with me so we all could visit their father. Amazingly, my search was in vain—and for reasons I had long forgotten. San Antonio was different from the rest of Texas, or even Oklahoma. It was surrounded by military installations filled with people who still remembered the war and blamed me either as a "welfare VC" in the U.S. fraudulently collecting benefits incognito or simply another "slope" who couldn't defend their own country. I was turned away from even the poorest neighborhoods and most squalid apartments simply because I was Vietnamese. Fortunately, the hospital staff—seeing me sleep night after night on a sofa in the lobby—produced a recliner from a nurses' break room so I could stay with Ronnie. When I just had to get away from the noise and smells of the hospital, I slept a few hours in the back seat of our car but always returned to the ward when I woke up. Not all the staff was so understanding. One administrator objected to my constant presence and complained to the colonel in charge. "It's against regulations for civilians to sleep in the ward," he said. Reportedly, the colonel stroked his chin, thought a moment, then replied with a solution: "Leave her alone."

Eventually, Grandpa Choat offered to bring his "fifth wheel" trailer to San Antonio so that the boys and I could be together while staying close to Ronnie. I immediately found a half-empty trailer park near the hospital and went to the office to make arrangements. The tough Texas woman running the place looked me up and down and said, "Sorry, we just filled up." I didn't bother to argue with her—there were plenty of vacant spots—but went to the nearest pay phone to call Grandpa Choat. He asked me for the number of the pay phone and told me to stick close. A few minutes later it rang.

"We're all set," Floyd said. "I'll be down with the trailer in the morning and pick you up at the hospital."

I wasn't sure what *all set* meant until he drove me back to the same trailer park, and we walked in the door together. He identified himself as Floyd Choat from Rainbow with a confirmed reservation for three months. The same woman manager who had thrown me out was on duty and, seeing me behind Floyd, knew exactly what had happened: my "being set" meant that she'd been had. She shoved a lot diagram and registration form across the counter to Floyd and said, "Take your pick."

Still, my victory was not complete—and my long-term stay was far from guaranteed—unless this woman understood "how the cows eat the cabbage," as Mrs. Gilchrest used to say, before we left the office.

"You remember me?" I asked.

She knew it was a trick question. "Sure. You was in here yesterday."

"You said you had no vacancies. Now you tell my father-in-law he can have his pick?"

"We had some cancellations."

"*Ten* cancellations in one day?"

She took a puff on her cigarette. "We had a bad day, sweetie."

Floyd completed the form but before he passed it back to her, I stepped forward and added my name to the blank marked *Authorized Residents*.

"I'm sorry to hear that," I said firmly. "I hope you don't have another."

My command of English had become a whole lot better.

§

Sadly, we didn't need all the time Grandpa Choat reserved. When it was obvious that Ronnie was not improving, he was transferred to the VA Hospital in Oklahoma City. At least his remaining time would be spent in familiar, friendly territory. A few weeks after arriving, they transferred him again to a smaller VA facility in Muskogee, Oklahoma. It seems the big VA hospital was reserved for patients with at least a fighting chance: they needed their bed space for the living. All anyone could do for Ronnie now was to manage his pain and keep him comfortable. Maybe finishing his life the way it began, in a small rural town, was the best way to end his story. Yet even that small bit of grace was denied him.

After a month of medical fumbles, the Muskogee VA decided they were ill-equipped to handle a terminal patient with his particular needs, so they bounced him like a basketball back to the Oklahoma City VA. Administrators there complained they still had no available beds, so he would either have to return to Muskogee or check into a local nursing home. This seemed to me the height of bureaucratic callousness until I realized that to the military, all soldiers were expendable, and death, in or out of uniform, eventually came for everyone. So instead of dragging what remained of My Man a hundred miles back to eastern Oklahoma, I rented an apartment in the suburb of Bethany and took care of him myself for as long as I could, which was not as long as I'd hoped. Ronnie himself never complained, although he said once that maybe fate was punishing him for not giving enough to his church, the Assembly of God. Maybe his stern Protestant Lord objected to the way he had attended Catholic Mass with me. I assured him that the God I knew wanted us only to love and care for each other, and Ronnie always scored 100% on that. Besides, like Papa, he was a good soldier. Self-pity just wasn't in his Manual.

It wasn't long before a visiting nurse told me Ronnie would need skilled attention 24/7. The VA subsequently arranged to place him in a nursing home, where he stayed until his condition deteriorated so badly that the ICU at their main hospital was again the only option. In this case, they made a bed available because they knew his "stay" would be short. It was Ronnie's last place to be.

Toward the end, an "ethical" struggle took place literally right in front of me, at Ronnie's bedside. The attending Head Physician decided to end all treatment with the exception of pain medication. There was no consult with Ronnie or with me, no request for permission from either of us, no explanation. A younger doctor objected, vehemently, and strong words passed between them, with me in the middle, almost as if I were not there. The younger man argued that the senior physician was essentially euthanizing my husband, that he wanted no part of this decision, and that he would leave the floor. The older doctor replied, "If you leave, you're fired!" but the young man left anyway. I never saw the young doctor again.

Ronnie hung on for a few more days. The boys and I stayed with him the entire time, and he seemed to take comfort in our presence. He loved to hold his boys, and we took turns lying with him on the bed, or simply holding his hand. The day before he died, Ronnie asked me to put Eric and Jon on the bed beside him.

Ronnie spoke to Eric. "Daddy has to go away soon, and you're going to be the man of the house now. It's your job to take care of your mother and brother." Eric seemed to be aware of the situation and accepted this responsibility with a solemn nod, though I wasn't sure he understood what it meant.

I thought back to myself at that age, watching my mother being lowered into a makeshift grave, refusing to believe what I'd seen. I realized now, as I had secretly admitted for years, that my father most likely had perished in the same battle, leaving only a few yellowed photos to show he had walked the Earth. From first-hand experience, I knew that swearing allegiance to the dead could far outweigh even the strongest person's ability to serve the living.

When I put Eric back on the floor, Jon reached for my arm and said, "Mama, when I grow up, I want to be a doctor so I can take care of you, too."

With my eyes full of tears, I rubbed Jon's head. I was so sorry that my little son was just too young to have any strong recollection of his father, of his father's love. Three years later, at the age of five, Jon asked me to get money out of the bank and buy him a Daddy, so he could have one with him at his baseball games, like the other boys did.

I leaned close to Ronnie and said, "I hope Eric won't carry that burden his whole life."

"Don't worry." Ronnie shared one of the last of his famous smiles. "He's a strong boy. So is his brother. Now he has a sense of purpose."

I believe Ronnie was right. I believe Eric was proud to have his father's trust in such a deep way, and he has not forgotten his father's words.

A sense of purpose. Until then, I had never thought of my life that way. To be an orphan, to be abused, to be threatened and afraid—those are burdens we are given, but we choose how to bear them. If we choose to live, to survive, to prevail, it is because we've made that our purpose.

Ronnie Floyd Choat

Those were pretty much the last words I ever heard from Ronnie. Both boys had picked up a cold from hanging around the hospital, so I was anxious to get them home, clean them up, and put them to bed. We started off in the car, and I thought about turning around and going back to the hospital—if not to reassure the boys one last time that their father was still alive, then to prove wrong my own premonition that he was not. Then I heard his voice. *Take our boys home. It's okay.* So I did, and it was. They were asleep as soon as their heads hit their pillows and so was I. At 5:30 a.m., I was awakened by a telephone call from the Charge Nurse at the hospital. Ronnie had just passed away. *It's okay,* he assured me. *It's okay.* When a Guardian Angel talks to you, I had learned it's best to listen.

I reflected on my mother's last visit with me on my wedding night, and I wondered why she had been so happy about the life I would have with Ronnie, when she perhaps knew it would be so short. After a while, I believe I found my own answer. Ronnie left me with two beautiful, healthy, and intelligent children, and he left me with an inner strength I might never have discovered but for the time I had with him. That was why Mama had been so happy for me. She did not promise me a long life with Ronnie, but what she did tell me was that his love would grow within me and gives me my own strength and perseverance...

By the grave, Rainbow Texas

We laid Ronnie to rest in a small cemetery in Rainbow, Texas, on the east side of Glen Rose. In a rural setting surrounded by a rolling, grassy field, the sighing breeze made the cemetery a soothing place, his grave marker a mere hundred yards from his parents' door. Before he was lowered into the ground, I tucked a small photo of our boys and a lock of my long silky black hair, now shorn to my shoulders, under the jacket of his dress uniform. I slipped Papa's wedding ring—the one Mama had given to Quang in Hong Ngu—on one of Ronnie's fingers in the hope that he could find his way to Papa, that Papa would recognize the ring and so recognize Ronnie. It was my dearest, most fervent wish that the spirits of the two men I had loved most in my life would now be together in someplace beautiful, connected by my love for them. His military funeral with an Honor Guard was provided by the Veteran's Administration, complete with a meticulously folded flag, a haunting rendition of "Taps" by a lone master bugler, and the startling, loud traditional 21-gun salute, but there were no officers, no non-coms, no "foxhole buddies" from his previous commands. No condolences to his family from the Army he loved almost as much as he loved us. It was as if he had just disappeared from the Army, another missing man, another *soldier* like Papa.

EPILOGUE

A Sense of Purpose

Life, of course, went on, and so did I. A good daughter, and a good mother, like a good soldier, never quits her post.

§

It was January, 1987, and I had two small children, four and two years old and already half-orphans. According to Grandma Mau, Papa had been orphaned when he was fourteen. I lost my parents when I was four. I was not a Buddhist, but at Ronnie's graveside, I swore that our sons would not repeat that karmic cycle.

With Ronnie's passing, all decisions that used to rest with him, Al, or Grandma—about what to do and where to go and how to live—were now mine. For the sake of my sons, I vowed to make them wisely.

Shortly after Ronnie died, Al presented me with a bill detailing the $3,100 he claimed he spent constructing a ramp for Ronnie's wheelchair, with costs itemized down to the last screw. The whole thing could not have amounted to more than a few hundred dollars, but he demanded full reimbursement. While this topic was being discussed, he further demanded that after his death, all us kids—me, Quang, and Thuy—would reimburse Aunt Thu with a monthly stipend, as compensation for raising us and bringing us to America. *Fine*, I thought, but right then I did not have that kind of money. I told Al I would settle his bill for the wheelchair ramp when the Army paid Ronnie's GI life insurance, which I wouldn't receive for a year. For some inexplicable reason, the Veteran's Administration did not initially believe I was Ronnie's wife, and it took months of back and forth paperwork, along with the assistance of a dedicated young Army JAG Officer, before they were convinced. I repaid Al for the ramp—down to the last penny. Like everything else in our troubled relationship, he could never make up his mind to be a devil or a saint.

Al died in 2002 at the Veteran's Colony in Wilburton, Oklahoma, where Aunt Thu still lives. He is being judged now by a power far higher than me, and I can only pray his soul finds peace.

In 1990, I applied for and got a job as a coding clerk with the Veterans Administration (a bureaucracy I at least knew something about) in Atlanta, Georgia. The boys and I left Durant, Oklahoma (where I was continuing undergraduate studies at Southeastern Oklahoma State University), for the South, where in 1991 I completed my undergraduate studies and earned a BA in business from Saint Leo University. I will always grateful to those professors (perhaps Angels themselves?) who permitted the boys to attend night classes with me when babysitters were unavailable. The boys' Guardian Angels must have kept them quiet in the back of the classroom, for they were very well behaved. They never asked for a bathroom interruption until class break time. I was blessed!

Thuy—my little sister who was so shy and afraid of school—received a BS degree from Southeastern Oklahoma State University. She and her daughters (Vi-Vi and Ngoc) joined us in Atlanta, where she also became employed with the VA in the IT Department. She met her husband Horace at the VA, and they remain in Duluth, Georgia, today.

Quang has enjoyed a long and successful career with General Motors. He lives and works today in Arlington, Texas. He has three grown children: Minh, Michael, and Tu Anh.

Bubba, a longtime and loyal employee of UPS, lives in McAlister, Oklahoma, with his wife Mary, only about 30 miles from his mother, Thu. They have three children: Tyler, Miranda, and April.

In 1995, I returned to Oklahoma City and a year later began a career as a civilian employee with the Department of the Air Force, working for the Air Logistics Center at Tinker AFB. While there, I obtained a Master of Science Degree in Management and successfully passed the oral exam required for appointment as a Contracting Officer, meaning that by signing my name—long-practiced in its various forms, in both Vietnamese and American schools during years of difficult circumstances—I could obligate contract purchases for the U.S. Government. Not bad for that skinny young teenager who so loved her pens and purple ink! My first position as a Contracting Officer was supporting the B-2 Stealth Bomber program, but later assignments would virdtually, if not literally, carry me into space via various satellite programs.

My Air Force career eventually took me to Southern California in 2005, and I live there still. I accepted a position with the USAF Space and Missile Systems Center at Los Angeles Air Force Base. Located in the beach city of El Segundo, it is literally the only "air base" in the country with no runway! I continue to serve as Deputy Chief in several acquisition divisions.

On the domestic front, as all single parents know, raising children alone is a hard job. The boys were a handful as teenagers—smart, but with their own ideas about things, often different from their mom's. We all survived and both sons graduated from college—one as an engineer, one in computer science—each obtaining a responsible position at Tinker AFB. Jon married a Vietnamese woman, Tam, and they have given me four grandchildren—Jaimee, Justin, Tyson, and Whitney—all blessed with their own sets of Guardian Angels. In 2014, Eric and Hong were married. Both of my sons continued their father's tradition of uniting through love two peoples whose uneasy past now points to a brighter future.

In 2017, Eric left the Air Force for the Department of the Navy and is now living in San Diego with his wife. Jon remains with his family in Oklahoma City and continues his work at the Oklahoma City Air Logistics Complex, Tinker AFB. We all visit several times each year, and including regular reunions with Aunt Thu and Grandma and Grandpa Choat, vigorous great-grandparents who in their own way help to keep our past alive.

§

In 1991, I made my first visit to post-war Vietnam with my brother, Quang. I was looking forward to seeing Grandma and Uncle Chieu, and maybe to learn something more definite about the fate of our Baby Sister. We visited with Uncle Thanh and Papa's oldest sister, Aunt Thoi. We reminded them of their promise to us when we were children, that they would reveal the truth about our Baby Sister when we became adults. Uncle Thanh gave us a sad and bewildered look. "I'm sorry. I can't tell you what happened, so please don't ask anymore."

My heart dropped, and I knew then, finally, that we would never know the truth. Quang and I looked at each other.

"We have waited for a long time, and this is not the answer we expected," Quang said.

Uncle Thanh and Aunt Thoi remained silent...

Grandma Mau smoking her favorite cigarette at Vung Tau Beach (1991)

I saw Grandma Mau for the last time during this visit in 1991. She was living with Uncle Chieu and his sons, Ngoc and Duc, still enjoying her evening pipe. She admitted to missing all the grandchildren she had helped raise but was content that Quang, Thuy, Bubba, and I were safe, secure, and living comfortable lives in the United States, and that we had given her great-grandchildren.

I remembered the stories she had told us of growing up in the North, from her pampered and affluent childhood and young adulthood to her happy marriage to Grandpa Phan and their happy life on Grandpa's plantation with their eleven children. After they lost everything—including six of their dear children—and had to flee the North, she lived the life of a very poor peasant woman. But grief for her lost children, her lost home, her lost country, and, all too soon after settling in the South, her husband, and another daughter and her son-in-law (who left behind four young orphans) did not make her immobile with self-pity. She was resourceful, clever, and determined, and demonstrated an instinct for survival under the most terrifying of circumstances. She alone was responsible for the lives and care of seven of her grandchildren—all under the age of eight in the beginning—throughout the worst part of the Vietnam War in the 1960s and early 1970s. Without her love, her courage, and her dedication to us all, none of us would have survived the war, nor would we have remained intact as a family. Somehow, even in the worst depths of poverty, she managed to feed, shelter, and clothe us while a brutal and vicious war swirled around, literally, at our door. And I never heard a word of complaint from her, never a wistful sigh, never a note of anger or harshness in her voice on the rare occasions when she spoke about the privileged life she had lost—only a soul-deep sadness for her lost children that stayed with her throughout her life.

I couldn't imagine what the world would be like without her but found out in 1995. Uncle Chieu fell while leaving a pub one evening and hit his head against a rock. He died a short time later. This was apparently too much for Grandma. Nine of her eleven natural-born children, except Thu and Hai, who had both immigrated to America, had preceded her in death. She had no wish to continue on any longer without them. Grandma simply stopped eating and passed away after a Biblical forty days and forty nights. Sadly, she died a week before I arrived back in Vietnam with my sons, a trip I had planned so they could meet their great-grandmother, and she, them. She had lived to be 106. When she died, a great Light left the world.

In December, 2011, Quang and I landed at Tan Son Nhut International Airport (SGN) after another long flight across the Pacific. For me, it was my fourth trip to Ho Chi Minh City, formerly known as Saigon, since my hasty departure in 1975. For Quang, it was only the most recent of many. For both of us, each return brought optimistic, if unfounded, expectations that things somehow might be different, that we would piece together old puzzles and rediscover lost faces. We hoped for the best while preparing ourselves for the worst, because even bad news can be welcome if it solves old and haunting mysteries.

Uncle Chieu (1991)

Unlike the shopworn, post-colonial complex we abandoned in 1975, Tan Son Nhut welcomed us with a gleaming, glass-and-steel structure representing the new Vietnam's aspirations more than its reality. I marvel on each visit at the growing number of school kids with American flags sewn to their trendy backpacks as a way of looking "cool"—the same way fast-food outlets in glittering malls post signs with similar flags proclaiming "100% American beef sold here!" And, it is not without a little pride that I think about the clothing I wear today, which often bears the label, "Made In Vietnam". As always, Vietnam remains a great place to visit—and even to enjoy a Starbuck's or pizza.

For Quang and me, our mission was to just find some answers. We wanted to return to Hong Ngu to see if Mama's grave was still where we buried her in 1964 on the Isle of the Dead in the Mekong River. I knew there would be little chance we would find a familiar landmark, but our hearts told us to try. We also hoped to find, just maybe, an old veteran still living in the area, one who might have known Papa and his fate, who might be willing to talk to us. And we hoped to find someone—anyone, on either side of the family—who remembered Baby Sister and had some inkling about what happened to her. Notwithstanding the certainty of "never knowing" after our previous discussion with Uncle Thanh and Aunt Thoi, there remained a deep desire to solve the riddle of her disappearance. We still prayed that she might somehow be alive and well, and surrounded by a loving family, even if it wasn't her own.

We were met outside the airport by a short, attractive, thirty-something woman in stylish Western clothes. She zig-zagged through the crowd waving a paper over her head, calling Quang in a friendly voice.

"That's Nhung," Quang said.

"Your guide?" I asked.

"Our Visitation Advisor. A lot of businessmen and foreign journalists use them here. Whatever you need—hotel or dinner reservations, transportation, access to buildings, an appointment with key people—she's your go-to person."

"A Fixer?" *Fixers* are an indispensable part of Asian life. They have access to just about anybody, anywhere, and anything—for a price. Think of a concierge who can get you an interview with the Minister of Agriculture or a mob boss, a gold Aston-Martin or a quart of 21-year old Glenlivet, all on an hour's notice and in the middle of a jungle. Some Fixers specialize in more dodgy items that can cause problems with the law, but officials tend to wink at them since information flows both ways.

"Fixer?" Quang shrugged. "More like 'arranger.' She works for a Dutch importer during the day. This is part-time work. Nhung just likes to help people."

They shook hands and Quang pressed a big wad of bills into her palm. This was not her salary: just an advance for the expenses she'd have to pay to get us in and out of places, good tables at restaurants, and honest cab drivers. He introduced us and Nhung greeted me like a sister. "*Chao chi!*" she said, which literally means, "Hi, Sister!" She put a cell phone to her ear, spoke quickly, and a late model Mercedes van immediately appeared at the head of the queue. The driver hopped out, opened the passenger doors, and stowed our luggage in the trunk.

"That was fast!" I said, impressed. This was a big change from my last couple of trips where I seemed to spend half the time hailing taxis and the rest explaining how to get to an address.

"Nothing but the best for VIPs," Nhung replied with a smile. "We'll take a private van and driver to Hong Ngu tomorrow. No busses for you this time!"

On the way to our hotel, I borrowed Quang's phone to call my old friend, Thom—the same "Skinny Thom" who had defended me from fifth grade bullies during my Fish Farm days. I made a point of visiting her every time I returned and this trip was no exception. From her, I'd learned a lot about life in post-war Vietnam. Da Minh, where she still lived, was just enough out of the way to escape much of the harsh treatment many Southerners had endured. She now had a husband, Bang, who reminded me of Ronnie, and two fine kids. "We get by," was all she'd say unless I asked specific questions. When the walls have ears, it pays not to talk too much. This time, Thom would be going with her "Big Sister" to Hong Ngu—not a pleasure trip, but necessary.

Modern Saigon—HCMC—is, as it always was, a curious blend of old and new. The post-war government spent lots of money to prettify the city, preserving the broad, tree-lined avenues that gave Saigon its nick-name, the "Paris of the Orient," while building glass-walled high-rise offices and apartments. Late model Mercedes and BMWs, Fords and Toyotas, all in good repair, jam the streets like they do in any major city. Even during the few years I'd been going back, new development had engulfed the airport and the drive to city center was increasingly cluttered with Western (and mostly American) fast food chains, corporate logos, billboards and small business signs, frequently in English—the universal language of business. On the sidewalks, Buddhist monks with orange robes and alms bowls sit cross-legged with cell phones held to their ears. Taking its model from Shanghai and Tokyo, the old capital now sprouts millions of lights, even while many villagers in the countryside still read by kerosene lamps. Catholic churches and Buddhist temples—Karl Marx's "opiate of the masses"—are not only tolerated, but encouraged since religious holidays put more cash in circulation. Every other house seems to have its little Buddha or Virgin Mary in a sconce on the upper floor.

The manager of the Ha Hien Hotel greeted us at curbside with his entire staff. The intimate "narrow rise" boutique hotel was Quang's usual accommodation and they greeted him and Nhung like royalty. The small rooms were thoroughly modern and decorated in American style, from electronic key-cards and flat-screen TVs to polished marble floors. No comfort was overlooked and any that were could be quickly wrangled by Nhung or the hotel's solicitous staff. I had certainly survived worse places in Vietnam and accepted these small nods to modernity as more signs of the government's grudging détente with the 21st Century.

At precisely 6:30 the next morning, the man at the front desk called and said a "Mrs. Thom" had arrived to see me. I told him to send her up.

"Skinny Thom" had changed little from our days together in Da Minh. She was pretty, petite, and full of energy, and giving her a big sisterly hug was like embracing my own past. When the country began to liberalize in the 1990s, she and I began to correspond. When long-distance telephones opened up for ordinary citizens, we once again heard each other's voice. Now her voice chattered at me nonstop as I finished dressing, brushed my teeth and hair, and prepared for an even deeper journey into the past.

We joined Quang and Nhung in the lobby and, after breakfast, met our driver and the Mercedes van Nhung had hired—with unlimited mileage and gas included—for five days. This may seem like a luxury to self-drive Americans but it's the rule for foreign visitors seeking private transportation. In a way, it's smart policy. Visitors come to gawk at new sights or recall old ones, neither of which promotes heads-up driving on Vietnam's narrow, crowded roads. And between a courteous native driver who knows the turf and a "concierge-fixer" like Nhung who knows everything else, we out-of-towners were free to concentrate on what mattered most: making sense of the past. By 11 a.m., we hit the road for the top of the Mekong delta and the provincial capital of Hong Ngu, some five or six hours away.

Even without my personal agenda, the drive northwest was like a journey back in time. The sprawling Saigon suburbs slowly gave way to a belt of farmer's markets and freelance fruit stands, uniformed school kids ambling in loose groups, kicking up dust and teasing each other on the way to afternoon classes, old ladies with baskets and buckets, and young men with shovels and hoes. Like a fading breeze, the rush and bustle of glass and steel gave way to country stillness where rice cultivation continued as it had for thousands of years, watered by makeshift irrigation, monsoon rains, and generations of human sweat.

Hong Ngu Market

We arrived in Hong Ngu about 5:30 p.m. Unlike cosmopolitan HCMC, most restaurants closed around sundown, so we had an early dinner. This left us time to visit a coffee kiosk next to our hotel. Quang's idea was to pick up some intelligence on local doings and, if we were lucky, get some leads about old-timers who might remember the Hong Ngu battle. As it turned out, the owner of the kiosk, a skinny, fiftyish man named Viet, was one of those old timers. Quang, always the jovial guest, struck up a friendly conversation and after a few minutes asked if Viet knew anything about the "old Army post" that had guarded the town in the early Sixties and the battle in 1964 that wiped it out.

Viet was quiet a moment, apparently pondering his answer. Trust is a two-way street, and this nice man had no way of knowing if Quang was the casual tourist he claimed to be or a government agent out looking for subversives. In the end, Quang's honest face and open manner won out.

"I got here about a year after that battle," Viet said solemnly. "People were still talking about the massacre. I'm not sure what they called the outpost. It was attacked and rebuilt three times. Some of the veterans who fought there are still alive and might be able to tell you something. Why do you ask?"

Quang said, "Our parents were killed there and we have questions."

Viet gave us a wistful shrug. "I lost my parents when I was fourteen. Half the young people in this country were raised by parents who were orphans."

"We want to visit our mother's grave and find out what happened to our father," I said.

"You and everyone else," Viet said sadly. "So many bodies were washed away from the shallow graves. The river, you know—keeps flowing. If they interred your mother on the isle, then her remains are probably long gone, washed down the Delta to the South China Sea or maybe excavated over the years, in the building and rebuilding of homes and businesses along the river's bank. Your father? Who knows? Maybe he was killed in the battle and put into a mass grave. Lots of bodies were unidentified, and not just here, but all over the country. If he was in charge of the outpost, the VC probably got him first. If they captured him, they probably questioned him, then killed him right away. In those days, Northern forces this far south didn't keep prisoners for long. If that's what happened, they probably dumped him in the river, and he floated out to sea like your mom. If he survived or got away, I think you'd know by now. He sounds like a man who wouldn't give up, especially on his family. Trust your heart. Trust the angels. They usually tell the truth."

Viet did introduce us to an old veteran who he believed to have been a participant in the battle at Papa's post. The man was a merchant, the owner of a nearby convenience store and, for obvious reasons, known as "the One-Legged Veteran." Viet offered him coffee and invited him to join our conversation that evening. The Veteran arrived and though somewhat reticent, he did tell us that he knew who our father was, but he could not confirm his fate. He also told us that he knew the policeman who found us the morning after the battle, and that he had just recently passed away. Quang and I were sad we had no chance to see him again.

As the Veteran was leaving, he spoke to us much like Viet had. He advised us to honor our parents, to keep their memories alive by visiting Hong Ngu when we could, and accept our purpose in life, which cannot be known except by God.

With these last words of advice from Viet and the old Veteran, we finally left Mama's resting place—and any further knowledge of Papa's fate—to lie within our Homeland's stoic history, and we watched the Mekong River flow quietly to the sea.

Looking across the Mekong River where Mother was buried, Hong Ngu

In December, 2013, I made my last visit to Vietnam before undertaking the writing of this story. Quang went with me again, and so did my now-grown-up son, Eric, and his fiancée, Hong, as well as an old friend and co-worker from my early days at Tinker AFB in Oklahoma, a kind and helpful man named John Gatlin. Our agenda this time was to show the next generation of Choats how one half of their family grew up, where Hien became Van and Van became "Sissy," and how Uncle Quang's good nature survived the unspeakable. But it was also something more. Quang and I had never closed the book on Baby Sister, and those who might write that last chapter were long gone—Uncle Thanh, who died in 2003, and Aunt Lan, who had passed on in 1985. Thus Baby Sister's ending or her rebirth remains a mystery that can't wash away like Mama's and Papa's bones. We might have thought we knew the truth with our heads, but with our hearts, we still clung to the hope that maybe, just maybe, that truth was still "out there" undiscovered: perhaps she was somewhere in a quiet village, in a bustling city, running a business or teaching school, making pottery or planting rice, surrounded by a loving family or watching sunsets all alone—we simply had no idea. This was our last chance to find out.

Again Nhung arranged for a private van and driver, and once more, Thom accompanied us. We revisited Phu Nhuan, Go Vap (where Baby Sister was born), Rach Gia (where Grandpa Phan and Grandma Mau settled after leaving the North, and where we were born), Thu Duc, Da Minh, Tan Mai, and Bien Hoa, and made one last pilgrimage to Hong Ngu to say good-bye to Mama and Papa on the riverbank of the Isle of the Dead (today, a little "suburb" of Hong Ngu in the middle of the Mekong River) and assure them that they would always be remembered by their descendants. We also wandered among the weedy ruins of Fish Farm with its crumbling buildings and dried out ponds. Only the main house and pig-stall apartments remained habitable, with the house used for evening classes and the stalls converted by the government to one-bedroom units provided free of charge to beginning teachers. The front gate Al had been so proud of was off its rusty hinges and seemed somehow forlorn. Small homes and businesses now lined the path that Thom and I used to take to school. I'm sure Eric and Hong rolled their eyes and sighed a lot as his mom and her old friend giggled and gasped over some half-forgotten sight or memory, but at least they'll know what to do when it's their turn to show the new generation the history and passages of the old.

Home at Fish Farm (2013)

Our most important stop was Bien Hoa, where Uncle Thanh's only son, Hieu—who had never left Vietnam—lived with his family. Hieu knew about our search for Baby Sister from earlier trips and had once called Quang in the United States. He told Quang he "had news" about Baby Sister but preferred not to discuss it on the phone, saving it instead for our next visit. Quang, of course, refused to leave it at that. He pressed Hieu for the whole story, offering to reverse the charges or call back if necessary. Hieu hemmed and hawed and finally dragged out the old "given to an orphanage" story that Quang and many others had discounted years ago. This time he told us the orphanage was at Phuong Lam, a small town northeast of Saigon. On the strength of this, Quang called Nhung and Thom and asked them to visit Hieu to get more details, and to check out the orphanage before our arrival. But this all led us nowhere.

When we met up with Hieu in Bien Hoa, he acknowledged that the information he got was from our cousin Nhiem's (Aunt Thoi's oldest daughter) husband. Hieu claimed that cousin Nhiem and her husband knew what happened to our Baby Sister. Unfortunately, Nhiem had vowed to carry the answers to her grave, so all we got was a deeper mystery. If any of the stories were true, what was so secretive or shameful about giving a child to an orphanage (it happened all the time) or placing her with a wealthy family, even for a fee? It didn't add up.

Quang and I left Hieu's house in a somber, reflective mood. As with Papa's disappearance, there were plenty of guesses about this last big question in our orphaned family, but very few facts to go on. Like so many others from that dark time and place, Baby Sister's life probably came to an untimely and violent end. All fingers pointed to Aunt Lan as the likely instrument of this tragedy, but nobody could—or would—say for sure. All we knew was that any war, whether waged in an ancient land or within a single human soul, can summon disaster in an instant. I would once again have to trust my heart and listen to the Angels.

§

Back in the U.S., in the dead of night, I had another visitation from my mother. She appeared in a dream and said benignly, "Lan. Her name was Lan."

Killer or victim? Both? I will never know. Oracles speak in riddles, but the words and wings of Angels are meant to lift us up. I awoke in a state of bliss. Baby Sister finally had a name, something to inscribe on the invisible marker we orphans will carry forever in our hearts and pass down to our children.

Acknowledgements

I want to express a very special thanks and appreciation to my Developmental Writer, Mr. Jay Wurts, whose experience and talent gave color and polish to my manuscript. Jay was a teacher and a mentor to a first time author, always patient and gracious. I also wish to thank my Copy Editor, Ms. Jessica Wulf, whose professional attention to detail and words of advice regarding the final text were invaluable and very much appreciated.

At the Da Lat Night Market during my visit in 2013, I met a skilled practitioner of the world's "second" oldest profession: telling a story in pictures, "cowboy" artist Phong Van. The sketches that appear in this book reflect poignantly what my child's eyes saw decades ago. Thank you Phong Van, for this work, and our new friendship!

I owe most sincere gratitude and thanks for the assistance of many in the preparation of my story: My brother Quang and my sister Thuy for their own memories and the validation of my recollections; my Uncle Hai and Aunt Thu for the information they provided regarding my mother and father, and my mother's parents and grandparents; my friends in Vietnam, Nhung, Loan, Viet, and Thom, for the research and work they provided to assure that my visits to Vietnam were successful, and enjoyable. Also, to my old friend and colleague from Tinker Air Force Base in Oklahoma City, thanks, Johnny.

My most humble and heartfelt respect rests with the American and Allied soldiers, sailors, and airmen who fought in Vietnam, and, especially, to the more than 55,000 who gave their lives there, and who we remember today, their names inscribed with honor on The Wall. I want to thank, with all my heart, two men, strangers—a policeman in Hong Ngu and a taxi driver in Saigon—who, within the space of twenty-four hours, interceded in my life and that of my brother Quang, acted as our Guardian Angels, and saved us both from life in an orphanage, or worse. I don't know their names, and I never will, but they together exemplified the best of the heart and soul of my Countrymen. May God bless them and keep them.

To the country people of rural Texas in Beattie and Glen Rose, my High School teachers and classmates, thank you for your exceptional kindness to and acceptance of the Asian refugees who landed in your midst. And my special thanks to Mrs. Charlene Gilchrest, who gave us all a roof over our heads, peanut fields for honest labor, flower-patterned flour sacks for my sewing and my clothes, good-natured understanding, and, most importantly, love.

About the Author

Although her birth records were lost in the flames of war, **Van Bich Choat** was born Nguyen Thi Hien in the village of Rach Gia on the Gulf of Thailand southwest of Saigon.

Her maternal grandparents—once wealthy landowners in North Vietnam—fled south after the French defeat in 1954 and the establishment of Ho Chi Minh's communist regime. Like her older brother Quang and younger sister Thuy, Van saw her father only a handful of times before he disappeared in a battle that also took their mother's life.

Orphaned by war, Van and her siblings were shuttled among a variety of custodians whose guardianship ranged from her grandmother's stoic love to open abuse by other relatives. Later, her Aunt Thu married an older American who adopted the orphaned children: beginning a decade-long flight from the war and a narrow escape from massacre during a brief stay in the Philippines. Back in Vietnam, Van's hopes for a new life were crushed by a near-fatal collision on the eve of Saigon's collapse.

Relocating with her adoptive parents to a small Texas town, Van worked two part-time jobs and graduated high school with honors, winning a Pell Grant to Oklahoma State University. Eventually she married her high-school sweetheart, Ronnie Choat—a U.S. Army paratrooper. Over the next few years, she gave him two sons before Ronnie died.

Left alone to raise two boys, Van moved to Atlanta in 1990 and took a job with the Department of Veterans Affairs, completing her undergraduate studies and earning a BA in business. Returning to Oklahoma, she began to work for the Air Force Material Command at Tinker AFB as Contract Specialist. Later, she obtained an MS in Management, and was credentialed as an Air Force Contracting Officer. In 2005, she transferred to the USAF Space and Missile Systems Center in Los Angeles [today, a component of The United States Space Force (USSF)] and continues to serve as Deputy Chief of several acquisition divisions.

For more information, visit her website:

VanChoat.com

www.ingramcontent.com/pod-product-compliance
Lightning Source LLC
Chambersburg PA
CBHW021401290426
44108CB00010B/342